SUPERNATURAL TEXAS

A FIELD GUIDE

Brian Righi

Schiffer Publishing Ltd

4880 Lower Valley Road · Atglen, Pennsylvania 19310

Schiffer Books are available at special discounts for bulk purchases for sales promotions or premiums. Special editions, including personalized covers, corporate imprints, and excerpts can be created in large quantities for special needs. For more information contact the publisher:

Published by Schiffer Publishing Ltd.
4880 Lower Valley Road
Atglen, PA 19310
Phone: (610) 593-1777; Fax: (610) 593-2002
E-mail: Info@schifferbooks.com

For the largest selection of fine reference books on this and related subjects, please visit our web site at **www.schifferbooks.com**
We are always looking for people to write books on new and related subjects. If you have an idea for a book please contact us at the above address.

—

This book may be purchased from the publisher.
Include $5.00 for shipping.
Please try your bookstore first.
You may write for a free catalog.

In Europe, Schiffer books are distributed by
Bushwood Books
6 Marksbury Ave.
Kew Gardens
Surrey TW9 4JF England
Phone: 44 (0) 20 8392-8585; Fax: 44 (0) 20 8392-9876
E-mail: info@bushwoodbooks.co.uk
Website: www.bushwoodbooks.co.uk

Copyright © 2009 by Brian Righi
Library of Congress Control Number: 2009925088

Designed by RoS
Type set in Demon Night/New Baskerville BT

ISBN: 978-0-7643-3309-5

Printed in China

Dedication

To the people of this great state for giving me a place to hang my hat and to all those captivated by tales of things that go bump in the night.

Acknowledgements

In the Congo, there is a saying among the tribesmen, *Omwana taku-lia nju emoi*, or when translated into English, "A child does not grow up only in one house." It's true that the Congo is a long way off from Texas, and whether or not this is the way tribesmen raise a child, I do not know. What I *do* know through hard experience is that it's exactly the way you raise a book—and it takes a lot of hardworking, dedicated people to get something like this onto the shelves of your local bookstore. Since my name is the only one that appears on the spine of this book, it's only fitting that I should take the time to thank some of the people that helped to "raise" this book to full maturity. To the wonderful people at Schiffer Publishing who believed in this project, including the indomitable Dinah Roseberry. To my beautiful and talented wife, Angela, an ever-present companion who provided invaluable advice concerning content, layout, and photography, as well as putting up with me in my worst moments. To Karli Burt for trudging around the countryside with us taking photographs and to Michael Shelton for the regional maps found within. Finally, a special thanks to the people of this great state for opening up their homes and places of business, for sharing their stories and experiences, and for making Texas the truly amazing place that it is today.

Contents

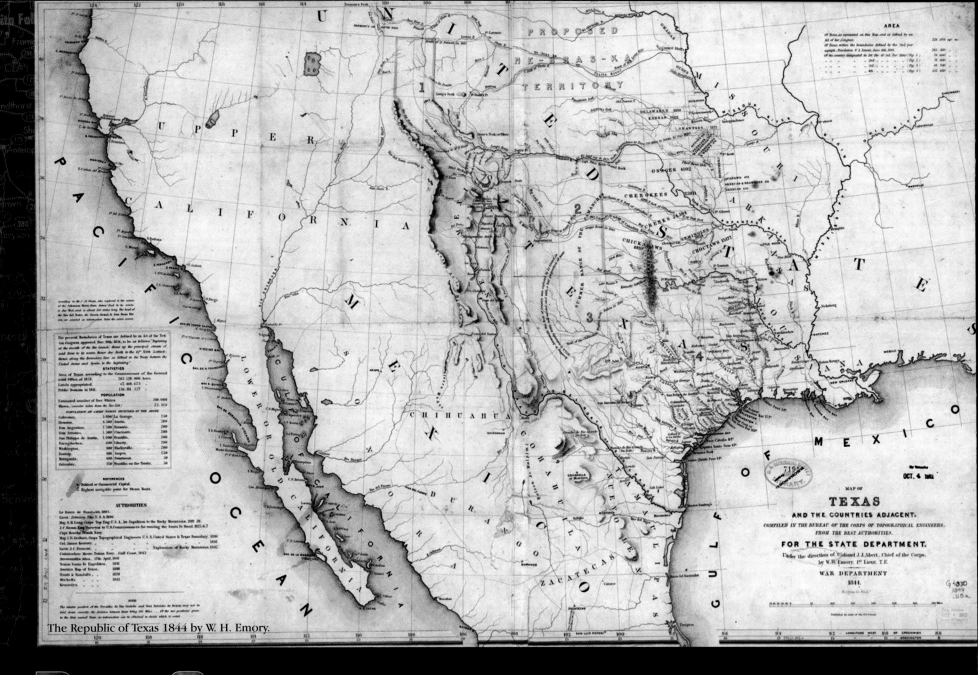

The Republic of Texas 1844 by W. H. Emory.

Part One: Getting Started

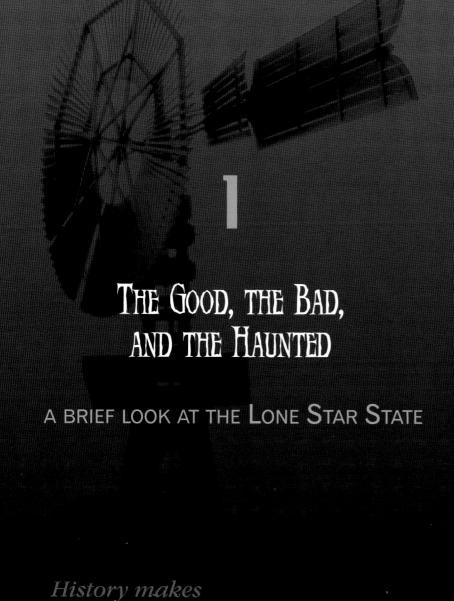

1

The Good, the Bad, and the Haunted

A BRIEF LOOK AT THE LONE STAR STATE

History makes

the best ghosts.

~An Anonymous Texan

Even as the cartographer Alonso de Pineda mapped the hazy coastline from the swaying deck of his waterlogged ship in 1519, he had no idea that the land he sketched would someday come to play an important part in building a future nation; a land one day known as Texas. Although Pineda drew one of the first maps of the Texas shoreline as he explored the Gulf of Mexico, there is no record that he ever left the safety of his ship. Yet as early as the Paleolithic period around 10,000 BC, groups of humans wandered across its expansive plains hunting herds of giant bison and mammoth with little more than stone implements. As the centuries passed, these early hunters were replaced by more complex and powerful cultures such as the Apache, Caddo, Comanche, and many more. The name "Texas" itself was derived from a term the Caddo used when first meeting Spanish conquistadors and means "those who are friends or allies."

The first Europeans granted the honor of actually setting their booted heels on Texas soil belonged to an ill-fated French expedition in 1685, who literally washed up on its shores by accident. Led by René-Robert Cavelier, Sieur de La Salle, the colonists originally intended on establishing a settlement at the mouth of the Mississippi River. After a rather serious navigational error, however, they beached their ships 400 miles to the west at Matagorda Bay, near present-day Houston. Resigning to make the best of their bad luck, the survivors built a small fort from the timbers of their wrecked ships and christened their new home Fort Saint Louis. Conditions in the new settlement were far from idyllic, with disease, malnutrition, and other hardships decimating their numbers. To make matters worse, La Salle's men foolishly attacked the first Indians they encountered when making landfall, creating a powerful enemy and setting the stage for later tragedy. Now stranded in Texas, La Salle tried unsuccessfully to relocate to the Mississippi River and follow its course to the safety of the French missions further north. The dream of rescue was short lived, however, when in the spring of 1687, La Salle's men reached their breaking point and murdered him in cold blood. Leaderless, the half-starved colony continued to struggle on until 1688 when an assault by Karankawa Indians reduced the fort to ashes. None of the colonists survived the brutal attack, with the exception of a few small children taken captive and assimilated into the local tribes, and Fort Saint Louis and its inhabitants were no more.

Soon after the bungled French attempt, the Spanish rushed to claim parts of eastern Texas by establishing a series of catholic missions in the piney woods region. Led by the adventurer Alonso de Leon, the move to beat the French to new territories fared little better for the Spanish. Epidemics of smallpox brought by Leon's men as well as their harsh treatment of the surrounding native population led to an uprising. The result of the upheaval led to the destruction of several missions and forced Spain's withdrawal from the area for almost twenty years. By 1711, however, the Spanish were at it again, this time establishing missions along the southern banks of the Rio Grande. The most notable of these new missions sprang up when Martin de Alarcon established a settlement and presidio near the San Antonio River. Named after the river that marked its location, the small mission would later play a key role in the struggle for Texas independence.

Although Spanish holdings in Texas continued to expand, a revolt by Mexican peasants under Augustin de Iturbide in 1821 eventually spelled disaster for the colonial rulers. When the cannon smoke finally cleared, the nation of Mexico was formed from the lands that once comprised New Spain (including Texas) and the Spanish crown forever lost control of its North American territories.

After a short-lived attempt by Iturbide to install himself as the head of a new Mexican Empire, he was forced into exile and a new constitution was ratified in 1824; making Mexico a Republic. That same year, Mexico enacted the General Colonization Law, giving all heads of household, regardless of race or immigrant status, a chance to claim land. One of the first to take advantage of the new land grab was Stephen F. Austin, the "Father of Texas," who led a group of settlers known as the "Old Three Hundred" to settle along the Brazos River and form the first of many official Anglo American settlements to come.

As the American immigrants settled into their new homes, regional tensions over cultural, political, and religious differences began to surface. Tensions escalated as the government, which was becoming increasingly more draconian under the regime of General Antonio Lopez de Santa Anna, moved to clamp down on the settlers. The government outlawed any further immigration from the United States and moved troops to the region to enforce its increasingly restrictive policies. Angered by these tactics, the upstart settlers proposed separating from Mexico and forming an independent state of their own in 1833. As events continued to build, Texas became a powder keg of dissent waiting to explode. On October 2, 1835, the match was finally lit when a troop of Mexican dragoons attempted to retrieve a smoothbore cannon from the Anglo settlement of Gonzales touching off the first battle for Texas independence.

Several skirmishes followed the Battle of Gonzales, and as the drums of war beat across the land, the Mexican army invaded. On February 23, 1836, as General Santa Anna's army of 6,000 crack troops forced their way further into Texas, they came upon a small, crumbling outpost at the Alamo mission in San Antonio. Defending the walls stood almost 200 rebel Texans and Tejanos, including famous personalities such as David Crockett, Jim Bowie, and William B. Travis. In the thirteen day siege that followed, the mission was captured and all its defenders killed. Despite the massacre, the battle for the Alamo effectively stalled the Mexican army just long enough for the rebels under Sam Houston to gather enough men and supplies for one more fight.

On March 2, 1836, the Texas Declaration of Independence was enacted and soon after the final showdown between the armies of General Santa Anna and Sam Houston began at the Battle of San Jacinto. For three days, Houston avoided Santa Anna's forces; ever drawing the Mexican army farther away from their supply lines. On April 19, 1836, believing Houston to be cornered, Santa Anna decided to rest his exhausted men and attack the next day. Instead, the Texans turned and surprised the over-confident Mexican forces in a lightening strike that lasted just eighteen minutes. With the battle cry "Remember the Alamo" upon their lips, 800 Texans charged at the Mexican encampment. During the battle that ensued, all of Santa Anna's 1,600 soldiers were killed or captured with the General himself becoming a prisoner. In exchange for his freedom, Santa Anna signed away any further Mexican claims to Texas, allowing for the creation of the fledgling Republic of Texas.

After almost a decade of independence, Texas was annexed to the United States on December 29, 1845, as the twenty-eighth state in the union. In the bloody struggle that soon after embroiled the country during the American Civil War, when the nation tore at itself and brother fought brother, Texas sided with the Confederate states. As history would come to prove, however, this would be a mistake and the new state of Texas found itself on the losing side of the war. At the close of the conflict, with its land occupied by federal troops and its economy in ruins, Texas, along with the rest of the south, suffered through a period of postwar reconstruction. On March 30, 1870, Texas was finally readmitted back into the union.

For much of its rebellious history, Texas has relied on ranching and farming to help fuel its economy giving rise to the stereotype of the Texas cowboy driving herds of long horn steer across the plains. Yet when oil or "Texas tea" was discovered at the turn of the nineteenth century, the resulting economic boom that followed changed its landscape forever. The state's first major oil well was drilled on the morning of January 10, 1901, at a place called Spindletop, a little hill south of Beaumont. Since that day, oil production has grown by leaps and bounds with some of the largest reservoirs in the Untied States being discovered deep under the hard Texas earth. Texas grew rapidly during the difficult period of the 1930s and suffered along with the rest of the nation through the Great Depression and subsequent dust bowl. In time, Texas grew to have the second largest population in the U.S. and develop a diversified economy with a growing base in the technology industry.

It's true that much has changed since the first Texans came to this land looking for a new life, and I doubt that today any of them would recognize the beloved state they lived and died for. The asphalt of superhighways have replaced the wagon tracks that once marched across its prairies and the frontier forts that stood guard over the land have crumbled into tourist attractions. What does remain, however, is the long-standing love affair most Texans have with the ghostly lore of their state. When the first hardy pioneers set foot in this new land, they brought more than just their hopes and dreams with them; they also brought the traditions and superstitions of their far-off native lands that in time helped to color the landscape of this great state. From the sun dappled waters of the Texas coast, to the endless reaches of the west Texas plains, to even the soaring towers of Dallas's concrete and steel skyscrapers, everywhere you look there are tales of the supernatural. In fact, about the only thing Texans love more than a cool glass of ice tea on a hot summer's night is the chance to enthrall listeners with tales of spirits rising from the grave to haunt the living.

When I first came to Texas many years ago, I began collecting every scrap of information I could on haunted places around the state. Initially, I was disappointed that a single source or guidebook did not exist listing the state's most well known haunted places in order to make my job easier. Although many wonderful books have been written on the topic by knowledgeable authors in the field, most seemed limited in scope or resigned to cover only a specific region or city. Now, after years of tromping through the state's ancient cemeteries, darkened buildings, and dusty library shelves, I not only developed a passion for the subject, but an office stuffed to the gills with case files that sorely needed to be

cleaned out. In order to remedy the problem (as well as clean out my office) I hatched a mad plan to create a comprehensive guide to the most haunted locations around the state of Texas. Of course, this book is by no means a complete listing of all the great places to investigate around the state, which would take more room that what this humble volume could provide, but it is a start.

In sorting through the mountain of locations to include in this book, I tried hard to steer away from those in which there was an obvious urban legend factor. No talk of hook-handed-killers prowling desolate back-road-make-out-spots or rumors of bloody dead girls appearing when you say their name three times to be found here. I also tried to avoid those locations in which the owner of the property wished not to be bothered by "meddling ghost hunters," and so you might notice a lack of private residences listed in this book. Instead, I settled on those locations that had the greatest accessibility to the public and therefore to you the reader. With each I have tried to provide as much information as to its whereabouts in the hopes that everyone will visit them and share in the adventure for themselves.

2

USING THIS GHOSTLY GUIDE

upernatural Texas: A Field Guide is something of a bizarre map to the dark side of Texas—a compass if you will, pointing out the supernatural landmarks along the way for anyone brave enough to travel its haunted roads. Among its pages you will find a wide assortment of places to visit, including haunted college dormitories, cemeteries filled with strange ghost lights, and houses where the dead still linger.

The information contained within can be used by anyone from modern ghost hunters looking for a few good places to investigate to those simply wanting to "spook up" their travel plans by staying the night in a haunted hotel. Either way, this book promises to have something for every ghost enthusiast.

In the first few chapters, we'll briefly discuss the nature of ghosts and hauntings in light of present day theories before turning to look at some of the tools used by modern researchers in the field today. After we have laid the groundwork on ghosts, we'll focus our attention on haunted locations around the state, which will be divided into geographic regions for quick and easy reference. Rounding out some of the final sections of the book will be a list of resources to assist the aspiring ghost hunter in learning more about the subject, including books, ghost hunting groups, and Halloween happenings around the state.

> **Before we grab our ghost hunting gear and rush out into the night, however, it is important to keep in mind that trespassing and vandalism are serious crimes that carry with them the threat of fines and even imprisonment. With this in mind, permission should always be sought from property owners before setting foot on a location. The goal after all is to have a safe and happy ghost hunting experience; something easily ruined with a night in jail.**

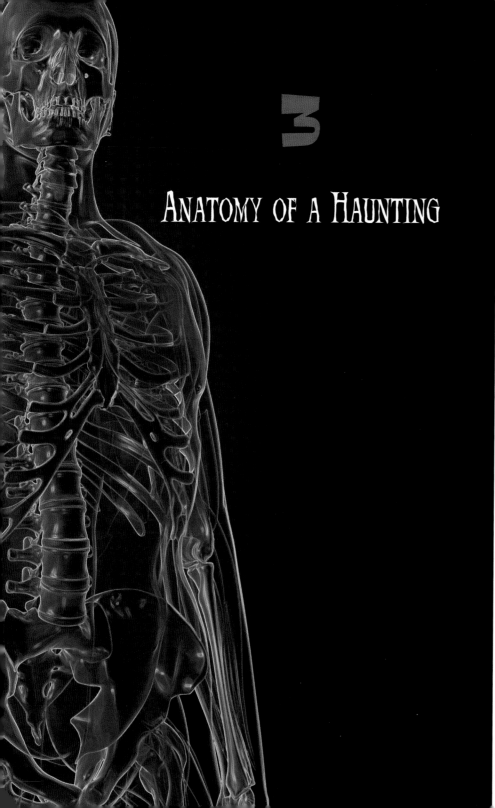

3

ANATOMY OF A HAUNTING

In order to prepare ourselves for what lies ahead, it is important that we understand just what ghosts are and how a location comes to be haunted in the first place. By most of today's definitions, a ghost is the spirit, personality, or energy of a person (or animal in some cases) that under certain conditions may remain earthbound after they have died. Also known as postmortem apparitions, these discarnate entities can remain at a locale for a period of time giving rise to what we traditionally call a haunting.

Hauntings differ from case to case in the frequency and duration they may last. The far more common type is known as a transient haunting because the haunting only continues for a brief period of time before ceasing altogether. Sometimes a ghost will manifest itself over a lengthier period of time, however, and is often referred to as a continual haunting. These hauntings may last for years or even centuries and fluctuate between times of great activity and quiet dormancy. As you will see later in this book, a haunting can occur just about anywhere imaginable. From old churches to modern apartment complexes, from deserted coastlines to elementary schools, and from moonlit cemeteries to retired battleships, ghosts can be found anywhere that people once lived and died.

Generally, there are two forms of hauntings that occur and although it can sometimes be difficult to tell which is actually transpiring at the time, both are very different from one another.

INTELLIGENT HAUNTINGS

The first is known as an intelligent haunting, because the manifestations involved display a strong sense of awareness and motivation. Ghosts in these hauntings have been known to play tricks, answer questions, move objects, or reveal unknown information. In short, they display intelligence and interact with the living.

This has led many researchers over the years to believe that when a person dies, the life force or spirit that remains is still subject to the same emotions, bonds, and fears that the person had when alive. If these are strong enough, they can become powerful anchors, trapping the ghost within a particular place until they are resolved. At other times, ghosts have expressed a fear of moving on to what awaits them in the next world and so linger on in the places they knew in life.

Finally, there are some ghosts that may not even know they have died. They may have passed too quickly or in a confused state and so continue under the illusion that they are still living in the same world they once inhabited. There are many reasons why a ghost may find itself sticking around after death and these vary in number and complexity from haunting to haunting.

Residual Hauntings

The second form of haunting is often termed a residual haunting. In these hauntings, the ghost in question seems content to wander over the years upon a stage that may no longer exist. Often they can be seen passing through solid walls that once held doors or floating up staircases that no longer exist.

The difference between a residual and an intelligent haunting is that in the former the ghost does not seem to be aware of the world around them nor do they recognize others or respond to attempts at communication. One theory about residual hauntings is that they are a playback of accumulated impressions from the past. A house or other structure is thought to absorb the emotions of its past occupants until it becomes a supercharged psychic storehouse of sorts. When conditions are ripe, a person with the proper psychic sensitivity can enter the affected area and feel the past emotions, shared desires, or experience a few phantoms. Think of it in much the same way you would a record player producing music. When the needle (the person or catalyst) touches the groves of the record (the impressions) music (the ghost) is produced. People, however, are not thought to be the only factors triggering the event, and any condition from the weather to specific times of the day may do so as well.

Manifestations

Regardless of which form a haunting takes, ghosts have been known to manifest themselves in a variety of ways. In some cases, a ghost may manifest itself with unexplained noises, including raps on walls, footsteps, phantom music, and disembodied voices. In the history of ghost hunting everything from in depth conversations to the sounds of long ago battles have been heard at haunted sites.

The manipulation of objects by an unseen entity is another form of manifestation and runs the gamut from doors opening and closing, to objects moving, disappearing or appearing on their own. The objects affected have been known to range from the smallest of children's toys to the heaviest of furniture. Witnesses report watching objects float across a room or even strike them when their back was turned, and in some cases, they have been known to drop from the ceiling as if from thin air.

Unusual smells have also been known to occur in connection with a haunting. These can range anywhere from pleasant odors, such as perfume, flowers, or coffee, to offensive smells such as cigarette smoke, sour liquor, or feces. How long the odor lasts or how strong it smells is different in each haunting, but in many cases, there is usually no natural explanation for its occurrence.

At times there may even be occasions where a person is touched by an unseen entity. The experience can be that of a comforting embrace, a tap on the shoulder, or even a slap or push that leaves physical marks afterwards.

Finally, in some of the rarest manifestations known to occur, a ghost can take a form that is either visible to the naked eye or able to be captured with photographic technology. This can include anything from mist-like clouds to glowing spheres or sometimes even full or partial human forms. At times, the apparition can be so convincing that they have even been known to be mistaken for everyday living people that cast shadows on the ground or reflections in a mirror.

On Encountering a Ghost

When encountering a ghost, one of the more common reactions that people have is one of fear; and why not? When something supernatural occurs it often strikes a primitive cord within us that harkens back to our days as cavemen building fires to chase away the terrors of the night. Yet, are ghosts evil—something within the darkness to be feared? Can they really hurt us or, as some long ago legends claim, kill?

To answer these questions, we simply only have to look at ourselves, after all, ghosts really are nothing more than people without bodies. That means that there may be good ghosts and even possibly what I prefer to call negative ghosts. Therefore, if a person lived a violent life filled with turmoil and anger, they may find themselves plagued by the same negative emotions after death.

There are really no verifiably recorded instances of a ghost causing someone's death other that what we find in the myths and legends of our ancestors. There are, however, reports of those who have been slapped, bitten, pushed, and even thrown to the ground by ghosts; but

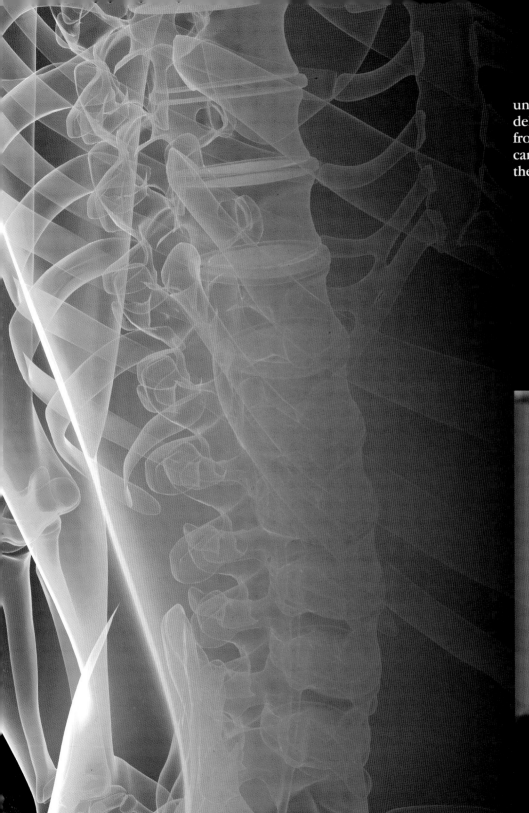

understand that these cases are the exception and not the rule. When delving into the supernatural, we have two reactions we can choose from. We can either play into our natural fears of the unknown or we can approach the subject of ghosts with the compassion and respect they deserve. After all, one day it may be us doing the haunting!

Final Advice

Just one final word of advice before we begin our strange journey through the unknown—ghost hunting is not like bird watching or stamp collecting. For man's entire history he has been running from or chasing ghosts and we have yet to obtain solid evidence beyond personal experience. Remember that one visit to a cemetery at night holds no promises of ghosts. Many in this field have gone for years without so much as a good photograph or audio recording. Instead, think of each of the following haunted locations as an opportunity to understand the stories of the past. If you do this, then somewhere along the way, you'll find the ghosts you're looking for.

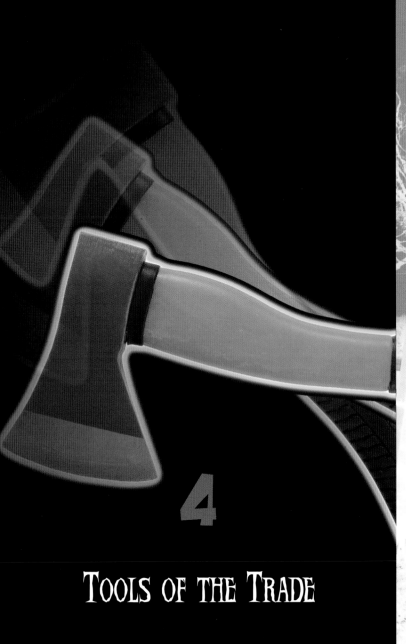

4

TOOLS OF THE TRADE

One of the first ghost hunts thought to have taken place was recorded by Pliny the Younger around 1000 AD. Although the tale was at least a hundred years old by the time Pliny put pen to paper, he nonetheless wrote the story as a matter of everyday fact. It seems that in the city of Athens, Greece, there was a house haunted by the ghost of a man in chains. No one dared approach the property during the light of day, much less try and spend the night there, because the specter that haunted its grounds was said to carry death and disease to anyone that laid eyes upon it. Then, one day, a stoic philosopher named Athenodorus came to town and bought the house—ghost and all. On his very first night in the old house the fabled ghost appeared and beckoned him to follow it into the garden where it disappeared into thin air. The next day Athenodorus called in the city officials, and after a search of the grounds, the skeleton of a man was found buried in the garden, wrapped in chains. After a proper burial and the necessary magic incantations, the ghost seemed at peace and Pliny tells us that the haunting ended. Although Athenodorus had little more that his own classically trained sense of reason to help him solve the mystery of the chain rattling ghost, later investigators have come to rely of a wide assortment of gadgets to help them chase spirits.

One of the first ghost hunters to use truly modern technology during his investigations was England's famous Harry Price in the 1940s. Many of the devices Price used were considered cutting edge for the time, including cameras with infrared filters and film, remote-control motion picture cameras, sensitive transmitting thermographs to measure variations in temperature, electric signaling instruments to reveal the movement of objects, and of course, a flask of brandy. After all, what self-respecting English gentleman would be caught without that last little item? (Price 1940, 6-7)

Since that time, theories on the nature of ghosts and hauntings, as well as advances in technology, have led to an ever increasing arsenal of tools for the modern ghost hunter to choose from.

THE TOOLS

The following is a brief list of some of the equipment used by ghost hunters today:

† A notebook and pens for recording field notes, diagrams, and sketching maps of the location.

† A tape measure for determining distances.

† Chalk to outline objects in order to determine if they have moved.

† A small first aid kit for emergencies.

† At least one cell phone in order to maintain contact with the outside world or to call for help.

† A pocket tool kit for repairing equipment that breaks down in the field.

† Lightweight, durable, and waterproof flashlights. Red lens caps work well because the light they produce is not as harsh as a clear lens.

† Glow sticks to serve as an alternative light source should flashlights malfunction. Candles, kerosene lamps, and other flammables are never a good idea and run the risk of starting fires.

† Two-way radios to keep team members in contact with one another as well as allow coordinating team functions and movements.

† Infrared motion detectors to secure an area or determine movement.

† Electromagnetic field (EMF) detectors are also very popular in ghost hunting today. Their use is based on the belief that spirits of the dead cause disturbances in the environment's magnetic field when present. EMF detectors measure variations in this field, alerting ghost hunters to a spirit's presence. A simple hiking compass works just as well, and if the needle suddenly swings erratically, a disturbance may be present.

† Infrared thermal scanners are another device used in tracking ghosts. Much like EMF detectors, thermal scanners measure temperature drops in the environment. These cold spots, are thought to occur when a ghost draws energy from its surroundings in order to manifest, creating a mass of cold air that can be felt by simply walking through it.

† Digital or standard cassette recorders are used for note taking, interviewing witnesses, and even recording the voices of ghosts. Electronic voice phenomena, EVP as the process is known, works on the principle that although spirit voices occur at a frequency too low for the human ear to register, they can still be captured on audio recorders.

† 35 mm, VHS, and digital cameras are also used to document the existence of ghosts. Everything from expensive point and shoot to cheap disposable cameras are used with success. Cameras are often used in conjunction with other verifiers such as EMF detectors or thermal scanners. This way, an innocent camera strap or water vapor isn't mistaken for wayward spirits when the film is developed.

† What type of film used can also make the difference and ghost hunters rely on everything from expensive infrared to common color film (some even swear by black and white). A Kodak 200 ASA to 400 ASA is normally used for inside jobs, while a higher speed 800 ASA is used outdoors. The camera's flash can also make a difference and the stronger the flash the better.

† Recently, a debate has arisen over the use of digital cameras. The majority of ghost hunters today find them convenient because the LCD screen allows them to see the pictures that they take and that can save money when developing the photos. There are some purists in the field, however, that claim that problems in the pixilation process can cause reflective images often mistaken for ghost orbs.

As you can see by this list, today's ghost hunters use everything from the simplest items, like flashlights and pencils, to the most advanced tools, such as EMF meters and thermo scanners. In response to the growing demand for new technology, numerous ghost hunting Web sites have sprung up selling the latest must-have devices (for a price, that is). In fact, the industry is booming right now as more and more ghost enthusiasts take to the field and try their hand at a little ghost wrangling.

However, you don't have to break the bank to be a well-equipped ghost hunter today and many stores from Radio Shack to your local camping outlet has the necessary tools for your next ghost hunting trip - at greatly reduced prices. Which items you choose to take along on your next adventure will be determined not only by your needs, but by your budget as well.

Just remember that no matter what you take along with you, you'll have to carry it all night long and tromping around graveyards all night with a ton of equipment can wear you out fast.

Part Two: Haunted Places by Region

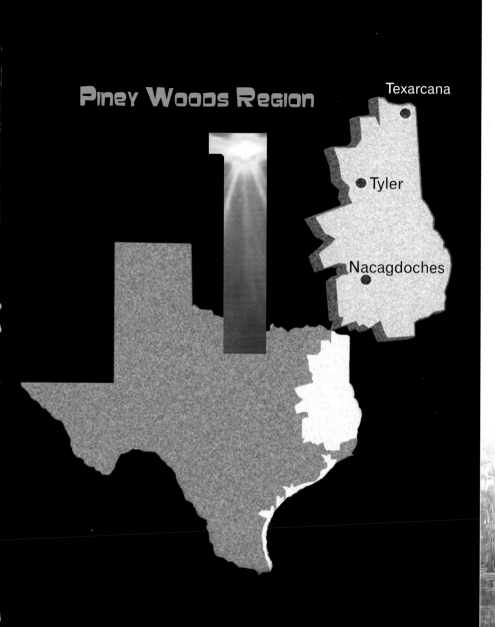

Piney Woods Region

Texarcana

Tyler

Nacagdoches

Comprising the easternmost section of the state, the land lies covered in dark forests of pine trees interspersed with hickory, oak, elm, and ash. Towards the southern reaches of the region, the spreading forests give way to lush bayous filled with alligators and cypress trees draped in Spanish moss. Often referred to as the "Cradle of Texas," the area contains some of the earliest attempts by Europeans to establish a foothold in Texas. The Spanish outpost of Nacogdoches, established in 1716, still remains one of the oldest towns in the state and a reminder of the region's colonial past. Yet before Spanish missionaries and soldiers ever penetrated the thick forests of East Texas, the land was home to the Caddo Indians, who left behind as evidence of their passing enormous mound dwellings and ceremonial sites.

For many years, the area remained sparsely populated until the Texas oil boom of 1902 created towns such as Kilgore, Marshall, and Longview. Today, the Piney Woods, which boasts four national forests and five state parks, has become a popular destination for hikers and campers looking to leave behind the hectic pace of city life for a few days.

For all of its natural beauty, however, these impenetrable forests and tangled swamps harbor dark secrets within them. Many creepy tales exist of haunted old plantation houses lost deep within the woods as well as what locals believe are ghost lights, which dance atop the swamp grass at night hoping to lure unwary travelers into the treacherous bog.

Big Sandy

Ambassador University

Built on land donated to the World Wide Church of God, the school first opened its doors in the Fall of 1964. Covering almost 2,500 acres, the campus struggled with financial problems over the years until it closed in May of 1997. Some of the more isolated portions of the campus, such as the former library and men's dormitory, have come to be known for a negative presence that haunts the grounds. Those spending the night in these areas report someone or something brushing against them or even grabbing at their throat.

To visit Ambassador University, travel two miles east of the town of Big Sandy on Highway 80, turning north onto Ambassador Way.

Burkeville

Country Road 2122

On a deserted section of country road near McGraw Creek, north of Burkeville, phantom lights are seen racing down the road in the dead of night. Witnesses encountering the glowing orbs say they pass right through the cars traveling this route.

Legend also tells of a house along the road in which the former owner's face appears on the fireplace.

To reach the haunted section of Country Road 2122, travel along it's course north of the town of Burkeville until you reach McGraw Creek.

Cason

Slaton Cemetery

Also known as Blue Light Cemetery, it's said to be home to a series of ghostly blue lights that appear at night, dancing among the tombstones. Cold spots are also reported, as well as disembodied voices that call out to those walking its grounds.

Legend tells of a couple that entered the cemetery one night looking for a quiet place to make out. Several days later, their cold bodies were found propped against a tombstone with a look of horror frozen on their faces.

Slaton Cemetery can be found at the end of CR 1117 just off of Highway 144.

Henderson

Henderson Civic Theatre

The building initially began as an opera house in 1885, but over the years has seen many businesses and professions come and go through its doors. The current theatre, which provides live theatrical performances for the city, purchased the building in 1988 and began renovations, which continue to this day.

The theatre troops stay here however, hasn't always been a quiet one and many believe the building is haunted by the spirit of a young woman they've named Daphne. The ghost is said to have first appeared during the stage production of the *Blithe Spirit* and has since made her presence well known. She is said to turn spotlights on and off during performances, whisper loudly from the wings during rehearsals, and follow people up the staircase. Her ghost has even been seen pacing the catwalk above the stage. Many believe that she is the spirit of a young woman who died giving birth on the second floor when it was a doctor's office in the 1930s.

The Henderson Civic Theatre is located at 122 East Main Street, Henderson, Texas 75652. For more information, visit them online at www.hendersoncivictheatre.com or call 903.657.2968.

HOWARD-DICKINSON HOUSE

The building was originally built by two brothers, David and Logan Howard, who were brick masons from Virginia. The two-story, one basement, Italian architectural style home that resulted was occupied from 1855 to 1950. In 1964, it was donated to the Rusk County Heritage Association and fully restored. During its earlier occupancy, one of the Howard sons was allegedly cleaning a gun in the basement when it discharged. Mortally wounded, the young man crawled through the house looking for help before he died.

Today, staff at the home report lights that turn on and off, cold spots, and items that appear and disappear on their own. On one occasion, a passing patrolman spotted a woman on the upper floor balcony waving for help. Rushing inside, he found the house empty and the alarms still set. Recent paranormal investigators recorded a voice saying, "Get Out," in the basement.

The Howard Dickinson House can be visited at 501 South Main Street, Henderson, Texas 75654. For more information call 903.657.6925.

Huntsville

BOWDEN ROAD

Those who have traveled it, call this five-mile stretch of lonely roadway Demon's Road, because of the bizarre figures seen along it at night, including one creature with no face. Some report that their vehicles are covered in strange handprints after traveling down the road.

Bowden Road lies approximately six miles southwest of Huntsville off FM 1374.

HUNTSVILLE PRISON

Also known as the Walls Unit because of its large brick walls, Huntsville is the oldest working prison in the state. Opening its heavy iron doors on March 13, 1848, the prison houses the state's infamous death chamber. Over the years, apparitions and unexplained noises have haunted the first floor of the South Building, which housed the prison's death row cells in the 1950s, as well as the East Building, and the catwalk adjoining the two. On Halloween night, in 1999, a guard told a reporter from the *Austin-American Statesman* that he left a voice-activated recorder in the former death row. The next day, while playing it back for his fellow guards, it revealed the sounds of cell doors clanging and a voice saying, "Hey Captain, hey Captain." Another story told among the prisoners and guards alike is of a ghost that they call the "Axe Man." Many claim to see this ghostly figure strolling down the halls with a head in his hands.

Huntsville Prison is located at 815 12th Street, Huntsville, Texas 77340.

SAM HOUSTON MEMORIAL MUSEUM

The museum sits on fifteen acres of park-like grounds containing eight buildings associated with Sam Houston and Texas history, including Houston's Woodland Home, the Steamboat House, and his former law office. In the loft of the Woodland Home, disembodied voices are heard by visitors, and on the gravel footpath leading to the building, footprints appear as if made by an invisible presence. The law office too is said to be haunted and objects from Houston's desk are seen moving by themselves.

The museum can be visited at 1402 19th Street, Huntsville, Texas 77340. For more information, visit them online at www.samhouston.org or call 936.294.1832.

Jacksonville

KILLOUGH MONUMENT

The monument's strange history began on October 5, 1838, when a band of renegade Cherokees, angry over white incursions on their land, killed eighteen unarmed members of the Killough party. The massacre is thought to be the largest Indian depravation in East Texas history. In the 1930s, the W.P.A. erected an obelisk of stone to mark the site with the graves of the victims around its base.

Visitors to the location tell of witnessing the apparition of a Cherokee Indian in full battle dress sitting on a white horse. In addition, a mysterious fog rises from the ground and many feel an overwhelming sense of fear as they near the monument. Investigators on the scene have recorded strange temperature and electrical fields during investigations.

Killough Monument can be found by traveling west on F.M. 855 from Mount Selman until reaching F.M. 3405. From here turn south on F.M. 3405, then west on F.M. 3411, and then south again on F.M. 3431 until reaching the end of the road where the monument sits waiting.

Killough Monument.

LON MORRIS COLLEGE

Founded in 1854 as the New Danville Masonic Female Academy before changing its name, it bears the distinction of being the oldest existing two-year college in the state of Texas. One of its student housing buildings, the Craven-Wilson Dormitory, is reported to be haunted by the ghost of a previous resident. Sources at the school claim the ghost belongs to a former dorm director named Ms. Brown, who died of cancer during her term there.

Residents of the dorm notice a host of unexplainable activity, including objects moving around, dresser drawers opening, electronics turning on and off, radio stations changing on their own, noises from unoccupied rooms, and a shower curtain that pushes inward when someone is showering.

Lon Morris College is located at 800 College Avenue, Jacksonville, Texas 75766. For more information, visit them online at www.lonmorris.edu.

Jefferson

EXCELSIOR HOTEL

Built in the 1950s, the structure has played host to historical personalities such as Ulysses S. Grant, Oscar Wilde, Rutherford B. Hayes, Jay Gould, and Lady Bird Johnson. Furnished in period antiques, the hotel front also sports ironwork that gives it a definite New Orleans flavor.

A number of specters are known to haunt the place, including a headless man who appears in the courtyard and wanders up to the second floor and a woman in black holding a baby. Strong odors of perfume manifest in some areas and the rocking chair in the Jay Gould Room has been seen swaying back and forth by itself. One story associated with the hotel involves Director Steven Spielberg, who became so frightened after an experience in the Jay Gould Room one night, that he packed up his entire staff at 2 am and moved twenty miles away to a Holiday Inn. The experience is thought to have inspired his later hit movie *Poltergeist*.

The Excelsior Hotel is located at 211 West Austin, Jefferson, Texas 75657. For more information or to book your next stay, visit them online at www.theexcelsiorhouse.com or call 800.490.7270.

FALLING LEAVES BED AND BREAKFAST

Originally built as a home in 1855 for John Sabine and his new wife, Victoria, it was later named Magnolia Hill, after the couple planted a magnolia tree in the front yard. Constructed in the antebellum Greek revival style popular at the time, the place went on to house a number of families over the years, until it was converted into a bed and breakfast in 1993 and renamed Falling Leaves.

The paranormal activity here is well known by locals and consists of doors opening and closing by themselves, objects moving or disappearing, and the sound of children running and playing through the house. Two apparitions have also been spotted, including the ghost of a fiddle player in the central hall during the early morning hours and the ghost of a woman in Victorian dress in the Magnolia Room. The latter is thought to be Eloise, one of the past ladies of the house.

The Falling Leaves Bed and Breakfast is located at 304 East Jefferson Street, Jefferson, Texas 75657. For more information or to book your next stay, visit them online at www.fallingleavesinn.com or call 903.665.8803.

Falling Leaves Bed and Breakfast.
Courtesy of Mitchel Whitington.

The Grove. *Courtesy of Mitchel Whitington.*

THE GROVE

The historic home that now sits on Moseley Street was built in 1861 by cotton broker Washington Stilley, as a home for his new bride Minerva Fox. Constructed in the Greek Revival style, it also incorporated many Creole influences from Louisiana and was considered by all accounts a most modern home for its time. Owners came and went over the years and as time went on, stories of supernatural happenings began to surface from it. One of the first involved a previous owner, who claimed to have been awakened one night to find a dark swirling cloud over her bed. Other occurrences include cold spots in the attic, items disappearing and reappearing later in a different location, and the sound of footsteps in the parlor. One of the most persistent manifestations is that of a man in a dark suit who wanders the garden with a big smile on his face.

The Grove is located at 405 Moseley Street, Jefferson, Texas 75657 and is currently owner by noted paranormal author Mitchel Whitington. For more information, visit them online at www.thegrove-jefferson.com.

HAYWOOD HOUSE

The historic home was first built at the end of the American Civil War in 1865 by a former Confederate general named Hinch P. Mabry as a hotel. After Union Troops occupied the city (and his hotel), Mabry fled to Canada. The building changed names many times, but was eventually inherited by a colorful character named Clarence Braden. Clarence was known during his life as an eccentric and a miserly man, who exhibited an intense obsession for coins. Upon his death in 1962, it was discovered that he had accumulated a fortune in coins, which he stuffed in every nook and cranny of the place. After his death the building became the Texas History Museum for a time, during which a secret tunnel was discovered running from the house to the town.

Those taking historical tours along the street that includes the Haywood House report seeing the apparition of a woman in white standing on the front balcony as well as sensations of being touched on the neck and shoulder. When the building housed the museum, a camera that was left recording over night captured the image of a ghostly figure walking in front of it.

The historic Haywood House can be found at 202 South Market Street, Jefferson, Texas 75657.

Jefferson Hotel.

JEFFERSON HOTEL

The building which now houses the hotel has had many names in its over 150 years of service, including such colorful titles as the Crystal Palace when it boasted its own bordello. Once a cotton warehouse in the 1850s when steamboats plied their trade along the bayou waterways, the building was transformed into a hotel in the 1870s when the city's port finally closed.

Today, the hotel proudly boasts of both its wild past and the spirits they say still roam it. Some of the phenomena they lay claim to includes knocking on walls, orchestral music from the closed dining hall, and the sounds of phantom children playing in the halls. Two of the more frequently seen apparitions are that of a man in a long coat and high boots in one of the rooms, and a thin blonde in white on the staircase.

The Jefferson Hotel is located at 124 West Austin Street, Jefferson, Texas 75657. For more information or to book your next stay, visit them online at www.historicjeffersonhotel.com or call 903.665.2631.

One of the rooms rumored to be haunted by an apparition. from the hotel's past

McKay House Bed and Breakfast Inn

First constructed in 1851 as a private residence for one of Jefferson's city founders, Daniel Alley, it was fashioned in the classic Greek revival style before being sold to a Captain Hector McKay in 1884 and has since carried his name. In the 1990s, the structure underwent an overhaul, which included a Victorian addition that gave it a second story. Since 2002, the house has played host as a bed and breakfast, lodging such distinguished guests as Lady Bird Johnson, Alex Haley, author of *Roots,* and the staff of former President George Bush Sr.

For years, both employees and guests reported cold spots, lamps that turned on and off by themselves, and an unplugged telephone that rings in the dead of the night. In the Lady Bird Johnson Room, a picture of one former owner, Bess McKay, mysteriously and frequently, changes locations, and on the second floor, the apparition of a woman seated on a settee briefly appears before vanishing. One of the more unusual tales involves a couple that was awakened one night to find the apparition of an elderly woman standing next to their bed trying to serve them pie.

The McKay House Bed and Breakfast Inn is located at 306 East Delta Street, Jefferson, Texas 75657. For more information or to book your next stay, visit them online at www.mckayhouse.com or call 903.665.7322.

McKay House Bed and Breakfast.
Courtesy of Alley-McKay House

Kilgore

Kilgore College

The college was originally established in 1935 at the height of the East Texas oil boom through the efforts of Kilgore's own citizens. Students here have long held that the spirit of a young girl who committed suicide when the building was an all girls dormitory haunts the eighth floor of Cruce Stark Hall. Immediately following the tragic incident, students began complaining of strange noises, footprints on their beds, cold spots, and the feeling that someone was watching them.

To stifle the reports, the school closed the floor for a number of years, only to reopen it after the building was remodeled. Since the reopening, students have once again started to report unusual activity on the eighth floor and accounts of the ghostly antics have appeared in the October 25, 2002 edition of the school's newspaper *The Flare*.

Kilgore College is located at 1100 Broadway, Kilgore, Texas 75662. For more information, visit them online at www.kilgore.edu.

Pirtle Cemetery

This quiet country cemetery lays claim to a most unusual ghost story. Legend has it that one day a young boy was buried in the cemetery grounds, who when alive, was terribly afraid of the dark. Distraught over the loss of her child, the boy's mother returned each night with a lantern and sat by the side of his grave until the sun came up. This continued every night for a year, after which the mother died from her grief and was buried next to her little boy.

Those traveling past the cemetery at night now say you can still see a light glowing above the boy's grave as the spirit of his mother returns with her phantom lantern to chase away the dark.

Pirtle Cemetery can be reached by traveling north on U.S. 259 from Nacogdoches, west on TX 204, and then north again on F.M. 2783. After a little over three miles, turn north-west onto a local road that runs in front of the Happy Valley Pentecostal Church and follow it to the cemetery.

Longview

Caddo Museum

Although the old museum no longer stands, residents of Longview still talk about the ghost that walks the site. Stories continue to circulate that the ghost of a little Indian girl with a head injury is seen standing on the road at night where the museum once existed. Among the many artifacts that once filled the museum were items taken from Indian burial sites across East Texas. One of these was thought to be the remains of the ghostly girl, which were kept in a glass display case.

The site of the former Indian museum rests on the corner of Hardy Street north of Loop 281. The artifacts it once held are currently being stored at the Gregg County Historical Museum.

Marshall

Marshall Pottery Company

In 1895, W.F. Rocker came to Marshall from Kentucky and established the Marshall Pottery Company. Competition with glass jar manufacturers almost spelled its doom in the 1920s, but when prohibition led to the moonshine business, the company stayed afloat by providing inexpensive jugs for the illegal liquor trade. In 1974, a 100,000 square-foot retail store was added, making it one of the main tourist attractions in East Texas. Each year, an estimated 100,000 people visit the facility, and to this day, it remains the largest manufacturer of red clay pots in the United States.

Some shoppers, however, claim to have walked away with more than just a few of the famous clay pots, but also the glimpse of a ghost. Shoppers are said to see the head of an apparition with long curly black hair and a pale, emotionless face, raised as if it were intently looking up to the ceiling. The vision normally lasts but a few seconds and is often accompanied by an intense coldness.

You can tour the Marshall Pottery Company at 4901 Elysian Fields, Marshall, Texas 75672. For more information, visit them online at www.marshallpotterystore.com.

Stagecoach Road

This site consists of a beautifully kept, one lane, sunken dirt road that travels for four miles and is maintained just as it was when stagecoaches used it to come from Shreveport to Marshall and points west.

Today, it is popular with horse riders and joggers, in addition to the ghosts said to haunt it. A spectral stagecoach is seen flying along the course as well as a group of apparitions carrying a coffin.

The old Stagecoach Road begins at the end of Harris Lake Road just off Highway 59 in Marshall.

Mount Pleasant

Pizza Hut Restaurant

During the 1980s, a grisly set of murders took place at the restaurant in this small community, in which four employees were brutally killed after closing one night. The perpetrator of the crime was arrested soon after and later died in jail, but the spirits of his victims are still seen at the eatery form time to time.

Patrons report seeing the apparition of one of the murder victims gliding past the windows. Employees also report ghostly happenings and say that the intercom phone sometimes rings, which it's not supposed to, and when they pick it up they can hear someone whispering on the other end; although they can never make out what is being said. The jukebox also turns on and off by itself and workers setting the tables with silverware often return a few moments later to find them rearranged.

The Pizza Hut Restaurant is located at 1902 South Jefferson Avenue, Mount Pleasant, Texas 75455.

Nacogdoches

Stephen F. Austin State University

The University was originally founded as a teacher's college in 1923 and named after one of Texas' founding fathers, Stephen F. Austin.

On the third floor of Griffith Hall, an all girls' dormitory, the spirit of a young girl who committed suicide by jumping out a window is said to still haunt the place. Legend claims that she became obsessed with playing with a Ouija board, which drove her to the act. Since then, at the exact time of her death each night, the community shower lights flicker on and off without explanation. Some even report seeing her ghost at the end of the hall in tattered clothing before quickly disappearing. Finally, around 2 am every morning, residents of the south wing report hearing the sounds of footsteps running down the hall and even feel a gust of air as the noise rushes by.

Another ghost believed to roam the campus can be found in the Turner Fine Arts Auditorium. Chester, as he's affectionately called, is thought to be the ghost of the theatre's former architect who died before the building was finished. Numerous stories surround his death, but most claim that when his architectural plans were misinterpreted and the building constructed backwards, poor Chester took his own life in disgrace. Today, both instructors and students alike report his presence in the form of cold spots, rustling stage curtains, and the feel of cold fingers on their necks. Chester is even supposed to have made a stage appearance during a 1987 production of *Macbeth*. In one scene where eight ghosts were supposed to be projected on a stage screen, the face of a ninth mysteriously appeared also.

In another popular tale, one of the actors playing Hamlet fell sick just before the production was set to begin. Suddenly another, unknown actor stepped forward and performed the line perfectly. When a picture of the cast was taken that night, all that appeared of the actor in question was a faint glowing light. Psychics brought into investigate the theatre have described a strong male presence attached to the building.

The Turner Fine Arts Auditorium is located at 1936 North Street, Nacogdoches, Texas 75961. For more information, visit them online www. sfasu.edu.

STERNE-HOYA HOUSE

Adolphus Sterne constructed the house in 1830 for his new bride before Texas was even a republic. Always a bit of a rebel rouser, Sterne was active in both the failed Fredonia Rebellion of 1826 and the later Texas Revolution. Given his status and wealth, the Sterne-Hoya House became an important gathering place for many significant figures in Texas history, including Sam Houston, Thomas Rusk, Davy Crockett, and Cherokee Chief Bowles.

One previous caretaker of the house reports that, while cleaning the upstairs room one day, she felt a benevolent presence touch her, followed by a feeling of vertigo that lasted until she descended the stairs. Also, the attic is said to be filled with a happy presence attributed to the spirits of children, which diminishes in the lower portions of the house. The cellar, however, is the opposite and has a dark, negative feeling about it.

The Sterne-Hoya House is now a museum open to the public and is located at 211 South Lanana Street, Nacogdoches, Texas 75961. For more information, call 936.560.4443.

Scottsville

SCOTTSVILLE CEMETERY

This cemetery is considered by many to be one of the most picturesque burial sites in all of East Texas. The stone Gothic revival chapel, which was erected in 1904, and the statue of the weeping angel that marks the grave of William Scott Youree, have become popular photographic attractions. Many stories are told of balls of light weaving through the headstones at night or the sound of the chapel's bell ringing when the building is closed.

What most are not aware of, is that the area bordering the cemetery to the northwest of the chapel is thought to be haunted as well. Just beyond the cemetery's fence line is a house with a staircase leading to the top of a hill. A two-story home once occupied the crown of the hill, and before burning down in the 1950s, it had a rather sinister reputation. Old timers still remember standing outside the structure as kids and listening to the odd sounds of voices and furniture moving about in the empty house. Although the building no longer exists, it is said that if a person stands at the top of the staircase, they can hear the disembodied sounds of a woman weeping.

Scottsville Cemetery.

Scottsville Cemetery can be reached by traveling east of Marshall for approximately five miles along F.M. 1998 before turning north just past the F.M. 1998 – CR 2213 intersection.

Sulphur Springs

Dead Man's Run

There is a rather sinister story in connection with this site known well to the residents of Sulphur Springs. It's said that on November 12, 1890, a railroad worker lured his estranged wife to a section of tracks with the intent of murdering her. Once there, he attacked her, and after knocking her unconscious, tied her to the rails. Exhausted from the struggle, he lay down next to her and was soon asleep.

Once he was slumbering soundly, however, his wife came to, and slipping her bonds, she quietly tied his shoelaces to the track. Just as she finished, the sound of the train's whistle filled the air and the engine came barreling down on them. As she fled, the husband awoke and cried out in surprise as he found himself unable to escape the oncoming train.

Each year, on the anniversary of the event, the incident is supposed to replay itself for onlookers, complete with the sounds of the husband's screams and the wife's laughter.

Dead Man's Run can be found by taking Highway 19 south through Sulphur Springs. Turn west on Highway 11 and then north onto a blacktop road until it crosses the tracks. The section can be found to the right of the road.

Texarkana

Spring Lake Park

On April 14, 1946, the bodies of Paul Martin, 17, and Betty Jo Booker, 15, were found in the heavily wooded park. Both were riddled with bullets from a .32 revolver belonging to a notorious serial killer terrorizing the area, who the press had dubbed the Phantom Killer of Texasarkana. The Phantom would continue his murderous reign for another month, striking twice in the park, killing three more and attacking several others before disappearing altogether, and to this day, the case remains open.

At the time, the community was so terrified by the phantom that houses remained dark after sundown and nightly patrols of shotgun-armed citizens marched through the streets. The killings so captivated the country that in 1977 a movie was made based on the events entitled *The Town that Dreaded Sundown*.

Visitors to the thick-forested, seventy-five-acre park claim that residual impressions from the 1946 killings still linger on the grounds. Standing next to the tree to which the two were tied and murdered, it is said that you can feel the sensation of a rope tightening around you.

Spring Lake Park is located at 4303 North Park Road, Texarkana, Texas 75503

TYLER

TYLER JUNIOR COLLEGE

The college was originally established in 1926 as part of the Tyler public school system and is considered the largest single-campus community college in the state.

One of the buildings that occupy it, the Wise Auditorium, is said to be haunted by the ghost of a little boy who can be heard screaming at night by students as they leave the building.

Tyler Junior College is located at 1400 East Fifth Street, Tyler, Texas 75798. For more information, visit them online at www.tjc.edu.com.

WHITE HOUSE

BASCOM CEMETERY

In 1860, William R. Griffen, a member of the Bascom community, donated seven acres for a cemetery and church, which became the Bascom Cemetery East. A short time after that, he donated more land on the road opposite the cemetery, which became the Bascom Cemetery West.

Some local residents say that on dark nights the figure of a woman dressed in white can be seen crossing the road between the two cemeteries. Often she is said to carry a knife in her hand and a story has developed that she is the ghost of a woman who tried to kill her husband when alive. Since she failed, her ghost is said to search for him still, hoping to complete the deed.

The East and West portions of Bascom Cemetery can be found north of White House along Bascom Road.

WHITE OAK

SHILOH SCHOOL

At the close of the American Civil War, newly freed slaves established the community of Shiloh, which included the Shiloh Baptist Church and a one-room schoolhouse. By the 1930s the small schoolhouse was replaced by a larger brick building, which in turn closed in 1966 with the end of segregation. For a time the vacant building was used to store chemicals and plastic until it burned to the ground in 1993.

Local legends, however, tell a different tale; claiming that the school was burned down by angry members of the Ku Klux Klan resulting in the death of a number of children. The legend continues to state that at night the sounds of children's' voices and screams can be heard, along with unexplained cold spots. The area is highly sought out by both local teenagers and investigators looking for evidence of ghosts.

The ruins of the Shiloh schoolhouse can be found on Shiloh Road just north of White Oak, Texas and is marked with a historical plaque.

GULF COAST REGION

Houston

Corpus Christi

Brownsville

Running along a strip of land from the Sabine Pass near Louisiana to the mighty Rio Grande River in the south, are 624 miles of stunning Texas coastline. Divided between rich, tidal marshlands in the north near Beaumont and the tropical waters of Padre Island to the south, the region has become a Mecca for environmentalists and sunbathers alike.

In the 1700s, the barrier islands and coastal inlets that make up the shoreline were home to another kind of visitor as well and pirates found its isolated shores an excellent place to hide after raiding rich Spanish galleons in the Caribbean. One of the more notorious buccaneers to ply his trade in these waters was a French rogue named Jean Lafitte, who is rumored to have left a vast fortune of gold doubloons buried somewhere among the Texas sand dunes. Not long after the era of the pirate, the coastal region was witness to the birth of a new nation when forces under Sam Houston defeated the Mexican army at the Battle of San Jacinto in 1836, granting Texas its independence.

Far deadlier than a pirate's cutlass or soldier's musket, however, is the wrath of Mother Nature. In 1900, a hurricane touched down in the coastal city of Galveston with destructive winds reaching as high as 135 mph. In the blink of an eye, almost 12,000 people died and an entire city was reduced to rubble in what became the second deadliest natural disaster in U.S. history. Two years after the hurricane, oil was discovered at Spindletop near Beaumont, touching off the Texas oil boom and lending an economic boost to the region. Today, the Gulf Coast thrives with economic prosperity, making the city of Houston one of the busiest ports in the world.

Given the colorful and often violent history of the coastal region, it's of little surprise that when the sun goes down, the wave-swept shores are said to fill with the phantoms of its past. Like bits of sea-washed flotsam, tales of haunted old sea taverns, phantom ghost ships, and buried treasured still guarded by the ghosts of long dead pirates, wash up everywhere.

Alice

Alice High School

Established in 1970, the school has for years been known as a place haunted by spirits of the dead. In the school library, books are thrown off the shelves and the sounds of someone walking and talking among the shelves can be heard. In the school theater, students also hear strange noises as well as see the apparition of a man on the catwalk above the stage and in the upstairs costume room. In one incident, red and yellow feathers inexplicably rained down from the ceiling during a rehearsal. It is said that much of the ghostly activity is the result of a worker being killed during the construction of the school.

Alice High School is located at #1 Coyote Trail, Alice, Texas 78332, or visit them online at www.ahs.aliceisd.net.

Alice Terminal Reservoir

Also known as Alice Lake, the reservoir was created in 1965 by damning the Chitipin Creek and acts as the municipal water supply for the city of Alice. Many of the residents of Alice believe that if you go out to the marina at night, and stand on the pier, you can hear the sound of oars rowing in the water, although there is no boat in sight. Fishermen late at night have also heard a little girl crying out for help followed by the sound of someone falling into the water. After a careful search, however, no one can be found.

The Alice Terminal Reservoir is located three miles north of Alice at the end of North Texas Boulevard.

Rialto Theater

Opening in 1948, the old theatre was originally designed to seat 712 people. It got the name Rialto during a later remodeling but has been largely neglected since its closing in the 1980s.

Former employees of the theatre claim that on many occasions they've witnessed shadowy dark figures in the upper hallways of the building. At times, a feeling of dread would overwhelm those working there at night followed by the sensation of being watched.

The Old Rialto Theater is located at 319 East Main Street, Alice, Texas 78323.

Sutherlands Lumber and Home Improvement Center

Formerly a Walmart before being converted into a Home Improvement Center, it is now said to be haunted by a number of ghosts who like to roam the aisles, playing jokes on the workers. Merchandise and equipment are often unexplainably damaged and minor accidents blamed on the spirits are frequent. The staff has named one of the ghosts Matilda, but prefer to avoid her whenever possible because they believe she is a malicious entity. Some claim that the building was constructed atop one of the first homesteads in Alice and that the nearby Collins Cemetery may be the source of the haunting.

The Sutherlands Lumber and Home Improvement Center is located at 1250 East Houston Street, Alice, Texas 78332.

Alvin

Harby Jr. High School

Constructed in 1980, the school is believed to rest above a hasty burial site for victims from the Galveston Hurricane of 1900.

Faculty at the school report seeing the faces of people in the school's windows and that the showers in the locker rooms have the disturbing habit of turning on by themselves.

The Harby Jr. High School is located 1500 Heights Road, Alvin, Texas 77511.

Baytown

Baytown Premiere Cinema 11

Reports persist that during the night shift, from 10 pm and on, employees get the eerie sensation that they are being watched. In the projection room, many feel as if someone is walking directly behind them; a sensation which is generally followed by the disembodied sounds of muffled conversation. In the ticket box as well the computers sometimes go crazy and start printing out tickets without explanation. Movies start or stop by themselves even after the breakers have been turned off and the sound fluctuates without reason.

The Baytown Premiere Cinema 11 is located at 1518 San Jacinto Mall, Baytown, Texas 77521.

Beaumont

Ghost Road Scenic Drive

Also known as Bragg Lights Road, the isolated dirt track that runs through a section of the Big Thicket Forest was once the path of a railline, installed by the Gulf, Colorado and Santa Fe Railway (GCSF) in the early 1900s.

Around the 1940s, strange tales of ghost lights began to surface from the locale. Even today, drivers along this lonely stretch witness glowing vaporous lights that appear to hover over the road, even coming to rest on the hood of cars before zooming off again.

Many tales exist to explain the presence of these strange lights; from the spirit of a hunter who became lost in the woods and died, to the decapitated victim of a railroad accident.

One of the earliest tales, however, stems from the American Civil War. In 1865, Confederate Captain, Charlie Bullock, set fire to a section of the Big Thicket Forest to flush out union sympathizers hiding in the woods. Those who escaped the blaze were shot as they ran, in an incident known as the Kaiser Burnout. Over 3,000 acres were destroyed and some think the ghost lights are victims of that fire still looking for a way to escape.

The Ghost Road Scenic Drive begins at a bend in FM 787, two miles north of the intersection of FM 787 and FM 770 near Saratoga. For more information, contact the Big Thicket Association, P.O. Box 198, Saratoga, Texas 77585.

Lamar University

The university initially started in 1923 as the South Park Junior College and achieved its dream of university status in 1949.

One location on the campus grounds known for being haunted is the Sigma Phi Epsilon House. Legend says a farmer originally built the house in the early 1900s. After the owner died, the house was sold and turned into a whorehouse. At some point, the cathouse closed, and after sitting empty for a number of years, it was bought by the fraternity in the 1980s. The ghost that is believed to haunt the old house has been named Chester by the fraternity brothers who stay there. He is said to make his rounds late at night, knocking on doors, as well as opening and shutting them. His phantom footsteps have also been heard walking on the staircase.

Lamar University is located at 4400 Martin Luther King Boulevard, Beaumont, Texas 77703. For more information, visit them online at www.lamar.edu.

Brownsville

Farm Road 511

As a well traveled route on the southeast tip of the state near the Mexican border, the last thing you'd expect to hear are reports of late night travelers running into ghost cows. Many driving along this stretch, however, claim a cow will suddenly appear in the middle of the road. As they swerve to avoid the bovine blockade, they often look back to find the road empty. Stopping the car and inspecting the area, witnesses' report that no signs of the phantom cow can be found anywhere. Because some serious accidents have occurred as a result of the phenomenon, local newspapers and media report on it with some frequency.

The haunted section of the road runs along the northeast portion of the city from Highway 77 to Indiana Avenue.

OLD CITY CEMETERY

Although the burial ground wasn't deeded to the city until 1868, a number of the tombstones bare inscriptions from the 1850s and contain some of the earliest settlers of the city. During the 1849 epidemic of cholera that swept through the area, mass graves were dug throughout the cemetery to accommodate the hundreds that fell victim to the disease. This section of the graveyard became known as *el pasto de las almas* or the "pasture of lost souls."

Since the mass interments, glowing lights have been seen moving through the cemetery at night. Many Brownsville citizens believe these are the souls of *desconocidos* or "unknown people." Sightings of these eerie ghost lights are believed to be more numerous around the time of All-Souls-Day than any other time.

The entrance to the Old City Cemetery is located at East Madison and East 5th Streets in Brownsville, Texas.

STANOLIND AVENUE

Running through a residential subdivision in Brownsville, legend has it that at a section where the road bends to intersect with Southmost Road, a man lost his life while driving too fast. In the aftermath, friends and mourners placed a small white cross at the corner in remembrance.

Not long after, however, some began to see his phantom standing next to the cross waving to passing cars. If someone stops, it is said, he approaches the car and vanishes.

Stanolind Avenue can be found on the city's south side just off Southmost Road.

UNIVERSITY OF TEXAS AT BROWNSVILLE

Established in 1926 under the name, Junior College of the Lower Rio Grande Valley, the University of Texas at Brownsville sits on the former site of a military post known as Fort Brown. In 1845, the U.S. Army began construction of a new fort on the northern side of the Rio Grande River. The fort was besieged for a time by Mexican forces during the Mexican-American War of 1864. During the American Civil War, Confederates held it until 1863 when it was wrestled back by Union Troops landing at Port Isabel and marching on Brownsville. Later, the fort was reoccupied by the Confederates and held until the end of the war.

Since becoming a university, the faculty, staff, and students have come to encounter bizarre activity that can only be associated with the spirits of the fort's bloody past. On some nights, usually after 10 pm, explosions have been heard, followed by the sounds of men screaming. One witness even claimed to have seen a line of soldiers standing at attention in the parking lot near her car as if they were unaware of what was going on around them.

One of the oldest stories known to exist centers on the university's library. A janitor working late at night stepped out to have a cigarette when he was startled by a phantom regiment of cavalry soldiers on horseback followed by infantry soldiers marching on what was the fort's former parade ground. In addition, other soldiers stood nearby saluting a flag. The scene lasted only a few moments before vanishing into the darkness of the night. Others also claim to see a young girl about nine years old on the second floor of the building wearing an antiquated dress.

Another paranormal hotspot on the university's campus is the old morgue building. Now used by the university for storage and to house the accounting offices, the building acted as the fort's morgue in the 1880s. Strange noises are heard in this building late at night, books fall from shelves, chairs move, voices are heard, and doors open and close by themselves. Also, electrical devices stop working in the building, only to begin again sometime later, and electrical plugs have been ripped right out of the walls.

Numerous apparitions have been spotted wandering through the rooms as well, including that of a woman in period clothing and a small child. The apparition of a woman dressed in black has also been seen sitting on the wall in front of the old morgue. In May of 2001, a picture was taken by visitors that revealed what appears to be the appriton of a body hanging from the ceiling.

The University of Texas at Brownsville is located at 80 Fort Brown, Brownsville, Texas 78520. For more information, visit them online at www.utb.edu.

CONROE HIGH SCHOOL

On August 23, 1980, Cheryl Lee Ferguson, a sixteen year old, was found in the loft above the school auditorium raped and killed. A janitor at the school, Clarence Brandley, was convicted of the crime and sentenced to death. In 1990, the United States Supreme Court overturned the conviction and found Brandley innocent. In 1991, a book about the incident was written entitled *White Lies,* followed later by the motion picture, *Whitewash: The Clarence Brandley Story.*

Although many are familiar with the infamous crime, very few are aware that in the area where the girl's body was found, cold spots are felt, and at times, the sounds of a young girl crying can be heard.

Conroe High School is located 3200 West Davis Road, Conroe, Texas 77304.

HUNTSMAN CHEMICAL PLANT

Employees at the sprawling industrial facility report doors slamming and opening, footsteps, voices, and the unknown apparition of a tall pale man. Many further claim that they get a strong feeling as though they're being followed or watched while in the company's training building. Tales linking the haunting to an explosion several years ago resulting in the death of two men, however, are untrue. There was an explosion at the nearby Port Arthur plant, but no one was killed.

The Huntsman Chemical Plant is located on Jefferson Chemical Road, Conroe, Texas 77301.

CORPUS CHRISTI

BILL WITT PARK AIRPLANE HANGAR

Built in 1932, the airplane hanger was originally part of an air force base used during WWII. For many years after its closing, the hanger was rumored to be haunted by the ghost of an airman who hung himself from the rafters. Numerous witnesses encountered his ghost over the years as both an apparition seen looking out through the broken windows, and as a strong presence following people around the hangar and stairwells. In May of 2007, the hangar was demolished, but many believe the ghost of the airman haunts the grounds still.

The Bill Witt Park Airplane Hangar was located at 6869 Yorktown Boulevard, Corpus Christi, Texas 78414.

BLACK BEARD'S ON THE BEACH

It's said that one night, in 1955, when the building housed a popular bar, two men got into a fight over a pretty redhead. One of the men drew a pistol and killed the other. The redhead and the man then fled the bar and headed north on the causeway, never to be heard from again. In 1962, a business man and amateur magician named Colonel Larry Platt, purchased the property and demolished the bar, rebuilding a bigger structure he named the Spanish Kitchen. Today the popular bar and grill is called Black Beard's On the Beach, and many that have come here walk away with paranormal tales of their own.

The kitchen staff reports that the sound of pots and pans can be heard moving around when no one is in the kitchen; yet upon investigation, it appears as if nothing has been moved. Other workers have seen the ghost of a woman they claim is a former employee of the bar, who died when she tried to retrieve a piece of jewelry she lost during a fire. Two other ghosts are said to haunt the bar and grill also. One is said to have died in the infamous 1955 fight over the redhead and the other is of a man who committed suicide at the Stewart Courts Motel next door in the 1960s, after his wife left him. To this day, phenomenon continues, including moving chairs, cold spots, and salt shakers that jump off of tables.

Black Beard's On the Beach is located at 3117 East Surfside Boulevard, Corpus Christi, Texas 78402.

BLACK HOPE CURSE

In 1982, a couple purchased a home in this neighborhood and were in the process of building a swimming pool in their back yard when they discovered human bodies buried in crude wooden coffins under the soil. A long-time resident and former grave digger later informed them that the area their house sat on was once the Black Hope Cemetery and mostly contained the bodies of dead slaves from the old McKenny plantation. The couple respectfully reburied the bodies, but soon after, houses in the surrounding neighborhood began to experience paranormal activity. Dark phantom shapes, strange noises, cold spots, and ill health became common occuances; including one young girl who died of a heart attack, which the family blamed on malevolent spirits. Garage doors open by themselves and televisions turned on in the middle of the night. People began to leave their homes after a short time. A book chronicling these bizarre events was written by John Shoemaker in 1993, entitled *The Black Hope Horror: The True Story of a Haunting,* as well as a made-for-television movie titled *Grave Secrets,* staring Patty Duke in 1992.

The events reported here are said to have taken place in the Newport subdivision of Crosby, Texas along the eastern section of Poppets Way.

CENTRE THEATRE

Built around 1942, stories persist that a couple had a fight one night during a show, and in a fit of rage, the husband murdered the wife upstairs near the women's restroom. Since then, many of the theatre's patrons report the feeling of being watched while upstairs followed by an intense sensation of coldness. Theatergoers are even said to feel a push or slap if they are making too much noise during a show and disturbing the ghost.

The Centre Theatre is located at 510 North Chaparral Street, Corpus Christi, Texas 78715.

CORPUS CHRISTI CATHEDRAL

Built in 1940, the grand cathedral over-looks downtown Corpus Christi from the bluffs forty feet above. Designed in the Spanish Revival style, it features asymmetrical bell towers with painted terra cotta domes, art glass windows, and a low-pitched gable tile roof. In February of 1965, Bishop Garriga died and was entombed in the crypt chapel of the Cathedral along with the remains of his earlier predecessors. Yet since his burial, parishioners have come to believe that his ghost haunts the cathedral's basement and many visitors to the crypt claim that there is a sensation as if something is not right.

The Corpus Christi Cathedral is located at 505 North Upper Broadway Street, Corpus Christi, Texas 7840. For more information, visit them online at www.cccathedral.com.

DAYS INN HOTEL

It is said the spirit of murdered Tejano singer Selena still wanders the doorway of the hotel room where she was shot the morning of March 31, 1995, by Yolanda Saldívar, the president of her fan club and the manager of her boutiques. Yolanda committed the murder after Selena confronted her for stealing money. Now guests and workers report the faint sounds of singing from that doorway as well as the smell of roses and an overpowering sense of sorrow.

The Days Inn Hotel is located at 901 Navigation Boulevard, Corpus Christi, Texas 78408. For more information or to book your stay, please visit them online at www.daysinn.com.

DEL MAR COLLEGE EAST CAMPUS

Founded in 1935 as a community college, one of the classrooms in the Memorial Classroom Building is said to be haunted by an unknown presence. Often late at night in room 222, the custodial staff encounters the sounds of howling and laughter as well as furniture moving around.

The Del Mar College is located at 101 Baldwin Boulevard, Corpus Christi, Texas 78404. For more information, visit them online at www.delmar.edu.

HERITAGE MUSEUM PARK

The park-like museum includes nine historical Corpus Christi homes, the oldest dating back to 1851. Many of the homes are recorded Texas Historical Landmarks and each is beautifully restored and displayed as a tribute to the ethnic diversity and culture of the region. Of the nine buildings, at least four of them are said to be haunted by some type of activity.

In the Sidbury House, the ghost of a child haunts the children's room by playing with dolls, moving objects, and throwing things from the shelves. In the Galvan House a ghost is said to tap people on the shoulder, and on the second floor, footsteps are heard on the stairs leading to the attic. Also, in the Christian House Bistro, a woman in a long, old-fashioned dress and big hat is seen at night walking to the front door and disappearing. Finally, in the MacCambell House, a ghost the staff calls Mary, who was supposed to have died of pneumonia, is known to lock the tour guides out of the house at times.

The Heritage Museum Park is located at 1581 North Chaparral Street, Corpus Christi, Texas 78401. For more information, visit them online at www.cctexas.com.

Galvan House. *Courtesy of the City of Corpus Christi, Parks and Recreation. Department.*

OLD NUECES COUNTY COURTHOUSE

Originally built in 1914 in the Classical Revival style, additions were made to the buildings in the 1930s and 1960s. Courtrooms and offices were on the first four floors, while the top two floors, which were separated from the rest of the building by an air space to eliminate noise, served as the jail. In addition to government offices, apartments were provided until the 1950s for the jailer and other county officials.

During the 1900 hurricane, which almost leveled the city, hundreds of refugees sought shelter here. In 1977, county offices moved to a new courthouse building and the old courthouse was abandoned to vandals and the elements. Former courthouse staff, however, testifies that even while in operation, the building was known to be haunted. Those working the graveyard shift often encountered sounds of people talking, knocking, and footsteps in what used to be the gallows chamber. On nights that the moon shined into the cells in the South wing, they could even see the figure of an older woman in old-fashioned clothes sitting on one of the bunks in an unused cell. Recent investigations buy ghost hunters have yielded numerous EVPs and ectoplasmic mist in photographs.

The Old Nueces County Courthouse is located at 901 Leopard Street, Corpus Christi, Texas 78401.

SMITH BUILDING

During a recent remodeling of the building, workers complained of the sounds of objects moving or falling, as well as doors that closed by themselves. One worker even claimed to see the apparition of a little girl in a white dress. When no one believed him, he returned one day with a video recorder and captured her image several times before running out screaming. The video can be found online at www.youtube.com/watch?v=DUA4z2vwBJk.

The Smith Building is located at 425 Schatzel Street, Corpus Christi, Texas 78401.

USS Lexington Museum on the Bay

Known as the "Blue Ghost," because the Japanese mistakenly reported the ship sunk four times during Word War Two, it was commissioned in 1943 and served longer and set more records than any aircraft carrier in U.S. Naval history. During its service, the *USS Lexington* witnessed a great deal of violence and bloodshed. On December 4, 1943, a Japanese torpedo stuck the *Lexington,* killing nine crewmen and wounding thirty-five others; one year later, in December of 1944, forty-nine men died in a kamikaze attack. Decommissioned in 1991, the 910-foot, 16-deck, 33,000-ton aircraft carrier, which once carried a crew of 2,500 men and 250 officers, now serves as a floating museum.

Visitors to the museum have long reported ghostly happenings throughout the ship that may be tied to its violent history. Some have spotted the apparition of a young man in a white sailor's uniform in the boiler room and describe him as having blonde hair, blue eyes, and walking with a limp. Heavy footsteps have also been known to follow employees around at night and the apparition of a medical corpsman is sometimes spotted in the sick bay. Faucets are known to turn on by themselves in rooms that have been locked and closed off to the public, and in the cafeteria, a worker was pushed aside by an invisible presence. Finally, visitors have photographed in the Pilot's Ready Room, the apparition of a pilot with a skull-like face.

The *USS Lexington* Museum on the Bay is located at 2914 North Shoreline Boulevard, Corpus Christi, Texas 78403. For more information, visit them online at www.usslexington.com or call 361-888-4873.

USS Lexington. *Courtesy of Bryan Tumlinson and the USS Lexington Museum.*

Wilson Tower

In 1951, Mr. Wilson built a seventeen-story office tower with a four-story penthouse and a 400-car, six-story, parking garage. The penthouse atop the tower was Wilson's pride and joy. The twentieth floor was finished out as a game room with a private bar constructed on a grand scale, with mahogany and trimmed in tufted leather and brass. Over the years, it was the scene of many exclusive parties and the location from which Mr. Wilson conducted his most important business deals.

After his death, many of the tenants became witness to strange sounds and shadows in their offices. In the elevators, too, passengers get the creepy feeling that they are not alone, which seems more common in the early morning hours.

The Wilson Tower is located at 606 North Carancahua Street, Corpus Christi, Texas 78476.

EDINBURG

MUSEUM OF SOUTH TEXAS HISTORY

The museum was originally a jail built in 1910 along with the Hidalgo County Courthouse, which stood in the County Square nearby. The jailer's office and living quarters were located on the ground floor, while the prisoners' cells were located on the second floor along with a hanging room in the tower. According to records, the hanging apparatus was used only once in 1913 to take the life of a man named Abram Ortiz, who was convicted of rape and murder. In the 1930s, the jail saw use as a community center, firehouse, and then a city hall. In 1967, it became the Hidalgo County Historical Museum and then later the Museum of South Texas History, which features exhibits on the history of the Rio Grande Valley, as well as the rest of South Texas.

Visitors to the museum claim that the hanging tower holds an eerie feeling as well as unexplained cold spots. The noose that still hangs as part of the exhibit is said to swing back and forth and the apparition of a man hanging from the rope has been seen on several occasions. Others have heard disembodied voices, wailing, and other unexplained sounds.

The Museum of South Texas History is located at 121 East McIntyre, Edinburg, Texas 78541. For more information, visit them online at www.mosthistory.org or call (956) 383-6911.

Ashton Villa. *Courtesy of David Canright and the Galveston Historical Foundation.*

GALVESTON

ASHTON VILLA

Built in 1859 by James Moreau Brown, a wholesale hardware merchant, railroad corporation president, and banker, the Ashton was one of the first of Galveston's Broadway "palaces," as well as the first brick house to be built in Texas.

Today, the Ashton is said to be haunted by several ghosts in 1800s period dress. Even Miss Bettie, the daughter of James Moreau Brown, is seen from time to time on the second floor landing in a long turquoise gown. Other reports include hand-shaped impressions left on bedspreads when no one is looking, as well as beds found unmade even though they are off limits to the public. Some have also heard the piano in the Gold Room playing at night and one caretaker witnessed a white filmy apparition at the piano before it faded away. Finally, the security alarm system occasionally trips with no explanation as to why.

The Aston Villa is located at 2328 Broadway, Galveston, Texas 77550. For more information, visit them online at www.galvestonhistory.org/1859_Ashton_Villa.asp. Haunted tours during the month of October are available also.

Fire Station No. 6

Once one of the city's oldest fire stations, it became the home of the Alford Air Conditioning Company when the building became too small to house the more modern fire engines.

Even in the early days of the station's history there were tales of a haunting. Firemen complained of having the sheets and blankets ripped off them during the middle of the night by an unseen force, as well as the phantom sounds of someone walking up the stairs in full fire fighting gear. When it became a business, the unusual reports continued, including the overpowering smell of men's cologne and the sounds of scratchy music, as if it were played on an old Victrola. Employees believe the haunting is caused by a fireman who died in the 1920s named Captain Jack O'Mara, who worked out of station number six.

The building that once housed Fire Station No. 6 can be found at 3712 Broadway, Galveston, Texas 77550.

Hotel Galvez

Constructed in 1911 on the city's seawall overlooking the Gulf of Mexico, the hotel flourished as a hot spot during the Jazz Age and the Big Band Era, becoming known up and down the coast as "Queen of the Gulf." Some of its guests included General Douglas MacArthur, Presidents Franklin Roosevelt, Dwight Eisenhower, and Lyndon Johnson. During World War II, the hotel operated as a U.S. Coast Guard training facility and today stands as the oldest hotel in Galveston. Room 505 is reputed to be haunted and many guests check out before their stay is over; reporting an extremely uncomfortable feeling in the room as well as the smell of gardenias and a speaker phone next to the bed that comes on by itself late at night.

The Hotel Galvez is located at 2024 Seawall Boulevard, Galveston Island, Texas 77550. For more information or to book your next stay, visit them online at www.galveston.com/galvez or call 409.765.7721.

Luigi's Italian Restaurant

Located in the historic 1895 Sealy-Hutchings building in the Strand Historic District, Luigi's has been serving Tucson style cuisine since 1997.

Workers at the restaurant report seeing the apparition of a woman walking down a set of stairs whimpering aloud to herself. Others claim to hear her voice calling out their name late at night. Those familiar with the spirit have named her Sara and claim that during the 1900 hurricane that battered the city, she helped pull victims from the tidal surge into the building to safety. She is thought to have died from disease following the hurricane a short time later.

Luigi's Italian Restaurant is located at 2328 Strand Street, Galveston, Texas 77550. For more information, visit them online at www.luigisrestaurantgalveston.com.

Mediterranean Chef Restaurant

The newly renovated restaurant in the heart of Galveston's Historic Strand District features an array of Mediterranean-Style Greek Cuisine. The building is also rumored to be one of the many used on Strand Street as a temporary morgue following the hurricane of 1900. In 1920, it was being used as a bank when a Galveston police officer, Daniel Brister, was killed during a foiled bank robbery on October 2, 1920.

To this day, employees of the restaurant report the apparition of a police officer in a 1920s uniform. Some even hear his footsteps on the vacant second floor above, which seem to mimic the movements of the listener. Others say he has a mischievous side and likes to turn off the freezer and play with the lights. One psychic that visited the second floor ran out after only a few moments claiming that there were too many spirits there screaming at her.

The Mediterranean Chef is located at 2402 Strand Street, Galveston, Texas 77550.

Queen Ann Bed and Breakfast

Built in 1905, the bed and breakfast features original stained glass windows, twelve-foot ceilings, exquisite inlaid wood floors, pocket doors, and has many fine antiques from the Victorian era.

The apparition of a tall, thin man has been seen standing over the shoulder of the employees while they are using the computer in the office. There are also reports of phantom footsteps, a rocking chair that moves on its own, and a dark shadowy figure that moves through walls. Finally, employees sometimes hear the sounds of someone rummaging around in the butler's pantry when there is no one there late at night, but upon further investigation they find it empty.

The Queen Ann Bed and Breakfast is located at 1915 Sealy Street, Galveston, Texas 77550. For more information or to book your next stay, visit them online at www.galvestonqueenanne.com or call 409.763.7088.

Samuel May Williams House

Built in 1838 for Samuel May Williams, secretary to Stephen F. Austin and founder of the Texas Navy, the historic home is a rare combination of Creole-plantation and New England architectural styles. The house is also the second oldest residential building still standing on the island Galveston. In 1859, the house was purchased by Phillip Tucker and occupied by the Tucker family until 1953. The house was then purchased by the Galveston Historical Foundation in 1954 to save it from demolition and has since been restored and open to the public for tours.

Williams died in 1858, but within weeks of his demise, his former slaves reported seeing him sitting in his rocking chair on the L-shaped front porch. Tourists and employees also sense his dark spirit in his upstairs bedroom and neighbors report seeing a light in the window late at night or a mysterious figure walking on the narrow balcony that surrounds the third floor observation room.

The Samuel May Williams House is located at 3601 Avenue P, Galveston, Texas 77550. For more information, visit them online at www.galvestonhistory.org/1839_Samuel_May_Williams_House.

Stewart's Mansion

Built in 1926 for George Sealy, Jr. and his family, the Spanish Colonial Revival style mansion overlooking Lake Como eventually came under the ownership of the powerful Stewart family for which it is now named. Long before the mansion existed, however, the infamous pirate Jean Laffite ousted Galveston's original residents, the friendly Karankawa Indians, in a battle on the ridge overlooking Oak Bayou, which later became the Stewart Mansion property.

The current tenants report the phantom sounds of a piano playing late at night, although no such musical instrument exists in the mansion, as well as the voice of a child crying out for help. To this day treasure hunters believe that Laffite buried a vast treasure to the west of the property, which has yet to be found.

The Stewart's Mansion is located on the southwestern shores of Lake Como, at 14520 Stewart Road, Galveston, Texas 77554.

University of Texas Medical Branch

Noted for being the oldest medical school west of the Mississippi, the campus covers eighty-five acres of land with seven hospitals, an assortment of clinics, centers, institutes, and a medical school.

One of the buildings that occupy the grounds, Maurice Ewing Hall, is well known for a rather peculiar phenomenon. It's said the image of a face appears on one of the concrete walls of this fairly modern structure, which cannot be removed despite many attempts. The face is rumored to be that of the original owner of the land that the university now sits upon. He supposedly told his family not to sell the land after he died and to keep it in the family, but upon his death, the family quickly sold it anyway. According to legend, the face first appeared on the top panel of the building. Despite being sand blasted and painted over, the face then appeared on the panel directly beneath it. This panel was subsequently sand blasted as well, causing the face to move to the panel that it resides on today. The university eventually gave up trying to remove the face and it has become a permanent addition to Ewing Hall.

The University of Texas Medical Branch is located at 301 University Boulevard, Galveston, Texas 77555. For more information, visit them online at www.utmb.edu.

WITWER-MOTT HOUSE

This Victorian home, built in 1884, was constructed for Marcus Mott, a Colonel with the Confederate forces who was often referred to as Captain Mott. In 1906, the well-known captain died of natural causes and the Witwer family later purchased the home in 1946. Still owned by the Witwer family today, the first floor of the home has been converted in suites for businesses, while the second floor remains a family residence.

Recent generations of Witwers report the sounds of voices and footsteps in the attic, as well as objects moving or disappearing. On one occasion, a mattress (complete with occupant) was thrown across the room. Most often, however, the ghost likes to appear to young children, who claim to have spoken to a man they call "the Captain." During a series of séances held over time, a spirit communicated that three women had been murdered by the Captain's son, Abey, and thrown into a covered well on the property.

The Witwer-Mott house is located at 1121 Tremont Street, Galveston, Texas 77550.

Goliad

MISSION ESPÍRITU SANTO STATE HISTORIC SITE

Mission Nuestro Señora del Espíritu Santo de Zúñiga, as it was originally known, was established in 1722 near Matagorda Bay among the Karankawa Indians. In 1749, it moved one-half mile south of Goliad on the San Antonio River where it continued for 110 years. The mission chapel, granary, and school, all within a walled compound, were restored between 1935 and 1939 by the Civilian Conservation Corps and the Works Progress Administration under National Park Service direction.

The apparition of an Indian on horseback has been spotted at the site as well as the sound of drums as night and the smell of pipe smoke in some of the buildings. There are also reports of a phantom wolf seen running into the woods and disappearing, as well as a spectral nun wandering through a section where more than twenty unmarked graves are said to exist around the old stone church and compound.

The Mission Espíritu Santo State Historic Site is located at 108 Park Rd 6, Goliad, Texas 77963. For more information, visit them online at www. tpwd.state.tx.us./park/goliad.com.

PRESIDIO LA BAHIA

Presidio La Bahia (Fort of the bay) was originally built near Lavaca Bay in 1721, but the site proved unsuitable, and after being moved several times, it was finally relocated to its present location in 1749. On October 9, 1835, a group of Texians attacked the presidio, defeated the Mexican garrison, and took control of the fort. The first declaration of independence of the Republic of Texas was signed here on December 20, 1835. On Palm Sunday, March 27, 1836, during the Texas Revolution, the Goliad massacre occurred here when General Antonio López de Santa Anna ordered the Mexican army to execute Colonel James Fannin and 341 of his men, who had surrendered after the Battle of Coleto.

Visitors to the fort today have experinced a wide range of unexplained activity, including cold spots in the living quarters, the phantom sounds of babies crying, sounds of a woman's choir singing in the chapel, as well as strange mumbling voices as if in prayer. In addition, some have even witnessed apparitions from the fort's past, including a short friar in a black habit, a woman in white, who appears to be searching the unmarked graves, and a woman in a black veil by the candle offerings inside the chapel weeping. Some, simply passing by the site late at night, as they cross the San Antonio River, have gotten a fright when a ghostly form materializes in their vehicle. Recent investigations by ghost hunters reveal strange mists and orbs as well as ghostly voices caught on audio tape.

Presidio La Bahia is located at 217 Loop 71, Goliad, Texas 77963. For more information, visit them online at www.presidiolabahia.org.

Houston

Battleship Texas State Historic Site

Launched in 1912, the *USS Texas* (BB-35) carried fourteen-inch guns that were the largest in the world at the time. It served with the British Grand Fleet in World War I and was the flagship of the entire U.S. Navy between the two World Wars. During the Second World War, the *USS Texas* supported amphibious invasions in North Africa, Normandy, Southern France, Iwo Jima, and Okinawa. In 1948, it became the nation's first historic ship museum. The 27,000-ton ship is 573 feet long, with massive guns and armor a foot thick.

The ship is reportedly haunted by a redheaded sailor who appears on one of its decks dressed in a white sailor's suit and standing near a ladder, smiling. Also, a caretaker in the trophy room (located on the same deck) claims she entered a space/time slip that sent her to a cemetery at Normandy.

The Battleship Texas State Historic Site is located at 3523 Highway 134, LaPorte, Texas 77571. For more information, visit them online at www.tpwd.state.tx.us/spdest/findadest/parks/battleship_texas.

Cinemark Tinseltown 17

Before the theater first opened in the Woodlands Mall, the area was said to be the site of a trailer park. During this time, several deaths occurred on the property, including a young boy who was murdered and a man who died in a trailer fire. Since the theater was built, the apparitions of a boy and a man have been seen throughout the building, as well as doors that open and close by themselves, phantom voices, and lights that turn on and off.

The Cinemark Tineltown 17 can be found at 1600 Lake Robbins Drive, The Woodlands, Texas 77380. For more information, visit them online at www.cinemark.com.

Federal Court Building

The tenth floor of this building is said to be haunted by the spirit of U.S. District Judge Woodrow Seals, who died after surgery in October 1990. The former judge's chambers are always colder than the rest of the floor and the smell of phantom cigar smoke lingers in the air at night. Janitors and security guards report being touched, hearing voices, and doors rattling when no one is around.

The Federal Court Building is located at 515 Rusk Street, Houston, Texas 77002.

Griffin Memorial House Museum

The Griffin house is one of ten historical buildings that have come to comprise the Tomball Museum Center. Built in 1860 by Eugene Pilot, an early Texas lumberman, the house was moved to the park in 1969.

Both the attic and the parlor are said to be haunted by the ghost of a young woman who died in the home when the Faris family occupied it. On a number of occasions, her apparition is seen about the house, but most frequently in an old rocking chair in the parlor. So often does staff spot her that some refuse to work in the building alone.

The Griffin Memorial House Museum is located at 510 North Pine Street, Tomball, Texas 77375. For more information, visit them online at www.tomballmuseumcenter.org.

Jefferson Davis Hospital

In 1924, the Jefferson Davis Hospital was dedicated and became the first city-owned permanent hospital accepting indigent patients. In time, it would come to be praised as one of the most modern medical facilities in the United States. The four story neo-classical structure had everything from modern operating rooms to separate floors for male and female patients, as well as a rooftop garden and playground.

Long before the hospital came to rest here, a municipal cemetery was established on the site in the 1840s, donated to the city by two of Houston's founders, Augustus and John Allen, and over the next few decades, thousands of people were buried there. The cemetery was not maintained, however, and by the early 1920s, there was almost no trace of its former use. Archeological digs in the 1980s also uncovered evidence in the form of more primitive graves suggesting that the area was once an English settlement in the 1600s.

In the fall of 2005, the building was renovated into the Elder Street Artist Lofts after sitting vacant for more than twenty years. Some residents, however, report that the specters of the hospital's past have returned once again. Strong feelings of being watched, shadows, and the overwhelming scent of sterilization chemicals are reported. Some even claim to see the apparitions of doctors and nurses wandering the halls or passing through solid walls.

The old Jefferson Davis Hospital is located at 1101 Elder Street, Houston, Texas 77007.

Julia Ideson Building

The Julia Ideson Building, which is part of the Houston Central Library System, first opened in 1904 as the Carnegie Library. Later, the library was renamed in honor of Julia Ideson, one of the early founders of the Houston Library System. Completed in the Spanish Renaissance style, the building looms overhead with an exterior of carved limestone, red tile roofs, and decorative wrought-iron gratings. In 1926, an old jack-of-all-trades named Julius Frank Cramer took a job at the library as the janitor, living with his dog in the basement until he died there on November 22, 1936, of sudden heart failure. "Cra," as everyone knew him, was said to wander through the library shelves after closing each night playing his violin while his German shepherd tagged along behind. Now librarians and other staff report hearing the faint strings of violin music playing throughout the library on days that are overcast. They also claim to find sheet music scattered around the library floor when opening the building on some mornings. Others get the uncanny feeling that they are being watched or hear the phantom sounds of a dog's nails clicking on the marble floors and staircase as it runs by.

The Julia Ideson Building is located at 500 McKinney Street, Houston, Texas 77002. For more information, visit them online at www.ideson.org.

La Carafe Wine Bar

Listed on the National Register for Historic Places, La Carafe Wine Bar is believed to be the oldest bar in Houston. Built by developer Nathaniel Kellum in 1847, it was home to the Kennedy Bakery. Later, it served as a Pony Express station before becoming the La Carafe in the 1950s.

Workers and guests alike report a number of strange happenings, most of which seem centered on the building's second floor. These include the sounds of footsteps and heavy furniture being moved across the floor, wine bottles and glasses that explode, out of place shadows, and cold spots. On more than one occasion, workers were opening up in the morning when they saw the apparition of a "strange looking" woman on the second floor looking out the window.

La Carafe Wine Bar is located at 813 Congress Street, Houston, Texas 77002. For more information, visit them online at www.owlnet.rice.edu/~hans320/projects/lacarafe/index.html.

Old Greenhouse Road

At a spot where the road makes its only turn near a bridge, it's said that a woman lost her life in a car accident. Legend holds that now, on nights just after a rain, if you drive slowly along the road with your headlights off, a mist will form over the bridge as you approach. In time, the mist will form into the figure of a woman, and if you stop on the bridge, she will approach the vehicle before vanishing.

Old Greenhouse Road is a mile and a half section of blacktop in Northwest Houston connecting Keith Harrow Boulevard with Greenhouse Road.

OLD TOWN SPRING

Spring, Texas, started in the 1800s as a railroad boomtown and has changed over the years from a farming community to a saloon town, to finally a shopping village. The town also bears the distinction of being the victim of one of the Bonnie and Clyde robberies in 1932, when they made off with $7,380. The gunshots that were fired during the robbery are still present in the old bank building walls. Today, the town is a historic village filled with cobblestone streets, restored homes from the turn of the century, and Victorian-style souvenir shops. Many of the buildings are also known to be haunted and paranormal tours are offered to the public.

Doering Court

One of the homes to see a lot of activity is Doering Court. In 1881, a woman named Mary Kelly bought the land that is now Doering Court from Charles Wunsche and later sold it to M.E. Hamilton, who built a large house on the property in 1917. Henry C. Doering later purchased the home and property with his wife, Ella Klein, and their four children. Records indicate a twelve-year-old girl known only as Sarah, died from a fall in the barn while playing hide and go seek on the property; leading many to believe that it's her ghost haunting the place. Tenants of the building today report hearing noises of children's laughter and hearing the name "Sarah... Sarah," being called out. In addition, they also report noises that sound like someone running across the roof and the eerie feeling of being watched.

Wunsche Bros. Cafe & Saloon

Another building rumored to be haunted is that of the Wunsche Bros. Cafe & Saloon. In 1902, the Wunsche Brothers constructed a two-story Saloon and hotel to meet the needs of travelers along the rail line. One of the brothers, Charlie Wunsche or "Uncle Charlie," as he was called, died in one of the upstairs rooms in 1915. Since then, there have been instances of doors being locked for no reason, tables and chairs overturned, items lost or misplaced, only to turn up in unexplained places, and footsteps. These usually coincide with changes to the building or when the furniture is rearranged. On other occasions, former guests report dreaming of Uncle Charlie and describing him in perfect detail the next morning with no previous knowledge of what he looked like. One recent owner even claims to have seen his apparition staring out the window of his old room.

Puffabelly's Depot Café

The next stop on any haunted tour of Spring Town is that of Puffabelly's Depot Café. This 1900s era train station was moved to Spring in 1985, and later became a restaurant in 1994. Since it was brought to Spring, strange lights have been seen in and around it, as well as the apparition of a headless man in overalls, who is waving a lantern and rumored to wander through it on dark nights. The story is that before the station was moved, a railroad yard switchman was involved in a tragic accident as he was attempting to flag down an engineer whose train was headed down the wrong tracks. As the switchman ran toward the oncoming train, waving his lantern and yelling frantically, he suddenly tripped on the rails and fell underneath the locomotive. The accident decapitated the poor railroad worker, whose mangled and bloodied body was taken inside the train station by his co-workers.

Whitehall House

One of the final homes on the haunted tour is the Whitehall house. Built in 1895 by the Mintz family, the beautiful two-story, twenty-five-room structure is one of the finest examples of Victorian architecture in the area. Since it's beginning, the structure has come to house everything from a funeral parlor to a hippie commune. Recently, the residence was restored and refurbished with original Hudson family heirlooms and has opened for tours.

In 1933, a young couple out late one evening became distracted on the darkened Riley Fussel Road that crosses Spring Creek. The young man driving the auto inexplicably ran off the bridge, plunging the car into the ravine and killing the two occupants. Early the next morning, the bodies of the young couple were found by local hikers and taken to Whitehall, which at the time was the local funeral parlor. Since then, their apparitions have been seen together in a swing on the second-story porch and in a secret room within the house.

Another story tells of three boys who attempted to build a tree house in a huge pecan tree growing on the property. Obviously, the spirits didn't like the idea and began shaking the tree and making noises. The boys became so frightened, they abandoned the project and never returned.

The Old Town Spring Historical Village is located at 405 Main Street, Spring, Texas 77380. For more information or to book your haunted tour, visit them online at www.oldtownspringtx.com.

Rose's Patio Café

This sandwich shop-type restaurant has long been known for its ghostly behavior. Many workers experience objects in the kitchen, such as a frying pans and water cans, being hurled across the room by an unseen entity. Workers have also been locked out of the building on a number of occasions and the front door sometimes opens and closes by itself. A rocking chair in the dining area is also said to be haunted by the ghost of a man named Luther. Luther was a long-time friend of the owner's family and died of natural causes in the chair. Often the chair rocks back and forth on its own.

The Rose's Patio Café is located at 219 Main Street, Houston, Texas 77002.

Spaghetti Warehouse

One in a chain of Italian eateries that stretch across nine states, the first opened in Dallas in 1972. The Houston location is more than a hundred years old and was once a cotton and then a pharmaceutical warehouse. In the 1930s, an employee was known to have fallen down the elevator shaft and died.

Today, wait staff sometimes hear their names being called even though no one is nearby. They also report chairs, place mats, and utensils being moved. Also, even when they are sure they have turned off all the lights in the building, the lights are mysteriously back on when they return to work the next day. Sandra McMasters, the Spaghetti Warehouse's manager, reports that when she was closing the restaurant one night, she saw four translucent spirits float by in front her. Since then no one has ever worked alone in the building, especially at night.

During remodeling after Tropical Storm Allison in 2001, a worker was so frightened when he saw a ghost that he rushed off, leaving his tools behind him. He refused to come back to the restaurant to get them. The apparition of a woman in white is also seen wandering the second floor.

The Spaghetti Warehouse is located at 901 Commerce Street, Houston, Texas 77002. For more information or to take the haunted tour of the building, visit them online at www.meatballs.com.

Treebeards

Built around the 1870s, the Baker Travis building is the second oldest building in Houston. Treebeards came to occupy a space here in 1980 when it outgrew its former location on Preston Street and specializes in spicy southern Cajun dishes. Many tenants have occupied the building over the years, including a seed store, a tailor shop, a toy store, and several lounges, including The Super Market, a popular psychedelic night club in the late sixties. Employees report hearing footsteps upstairs and soft murmuring when no one is there. The apparition of an elderly man has been seen, which matches the description of Mr. Danowitz, an elderly tailor who shared the building with Treebeards when it first opened.

Treebeards is located at 315 Travis Street, Houston, Texas 77002. For more information, visit them online at www.treebeards.com.

Walgreen's

In 1996, John Cedars, the store manager, was murdered execution style during a robbery. Since that time his spirit is believed to return to the store playing pranks on the employees just as he did when alive. Store workers have heard his heavy tread walking down the aisles at night and they say he loves to push stacks of diapers off the shelf onto the heads of startled workers. Toys are also known to turn themselves on and off or fly off the shelves and break. Although the activity continues to this day, it's said to have diminished since his killers were convicted in 1998.

Walgreen's is at 485 Sawdust Road, Spring, Texas 77380.

Kingsville

Texas A & M University

Texas A & M University was founded in 1925 as South Texas State Teachers College. The university's name changed in 1929 to the Texas College of Arts and Industries signaling the broadening of its mission and became a member of the Texas A&M University System in 1989.

For years, several buildings on this 1,600-acre campus have claimed to be the home of earthbound spirits, including the haunted bell tower of College Hall. Located at the center of the campus, the building was completed in 1951, and mirrored the Spanish mission revival style with its dominant bell tower replicated from the one found at the Mission San Jose in San Antonio. Students walking past the building at night claim that the figure of a man hanging by a noose can be seen from all four corners of the tower. Campus legend claims it's the ghost of a suicide victim from many years ago.

Another haunted campus hangout seems to be the student housing building known as the Turner-Bishop Hall. During the decade between 1960 and 1975, twenty-two new buildings were added to the campus for classrooms, laboratories, offices, and dormitories. One of these additions, the Turner-Bishop Complex, is a three-story dormitory housing both men and women. For many years, the second and third floors of the building have been rumored to be haunted by a protective female presence. Late at night, it is said her passing can be heard in the hallways, followed by cold spots. In some rooms, girls have awakened to the sensation of someone playing with their hair and breathing next to their ear. At times, doors lock by themselves and the showers turn on and off on their own. Finally, the noise of heavy furniture being dragged about can be heard from unoccupied rooms.

Texas A&M University-Kingsville is located at 700 University Boulevard, Kingsville, Texas 78363. For more information, visit them online at www.tamuk.edu.

Lake Jackson

Lake Jackson Plantation

Around 1840, Virginia planter Abner Jackson brought his family and slaves to the area to begin work on their first plantation, which they named Retrieve. Soon after, they began building a second plantation home in the bend of an oxbow lake between the Brazos River and Oyster Creek. First called the Lake Place, it later came to be known as the Lake Jackson Plantation. The new home was a sprawling complex with a columned, colonial-style main house, outbuildings, gardens, and sugar mill. In 1860, census takers listed Jackson as owning 285 slaves, making him the second largest slave owner in the state. After Abner's death in 1861, the estate fell to his two sons John and George. The two soon quarreled, resulting in George killing his brother in a fight in 1867. George went on to die of tuberculosis sometime later and was never prosecuted for his brother's death. In 1900, a hurricane destroyed most of the plantation's buildings leaving only a few scattered ruins.

Today, guided tours of the site are offered by the Lake Jackson Historical Museum, but the specters of the two feuding brothers may have returned to haunt the place. Tour guides and visitors alike report the apparition of a man in older period clothing within the ruins, as well as cold spots and an occasional touch on the shoulder. Some of the homeowners that now occupy portions of the lake to the north and west of the ruins also report the same apparition within their homes, in addition to strange noises.

The Lake Jackson Plantation can be reached from Lake Jackson, by traveling northeast one mile on F.M. 2004 from Texas 332. For more information, contact the Lake Jackson Museum at 979-297-1570 or visit them online at www.lakejacksonmuseum.org.

Early rendering of the Lake Jackson Plantation. *Courtesy of the Lake Jackson Historical Association.*

Lasara

Highway 186

Along an eight mile stretch of Highway 186, running from Raymondville to Lasara, is the story of a phantom hitchhiker. The traveler appears as a normal man walking along the side of the road at night towards the town of Lasara. Those that have stopped to give him a ride say that their car immediately fills with a sense of sorrow, and once he gets in, the air becomes cold. Although he doesn't say much, the directions he gives takes the car south along Cemetery Road to the Lasara Cemetery, where he asks the driver to stop and immediately disappears. No one knows the origin of the ghost, nor that he is even a spirit until he vanishes into thin air.

The phantom can be seen on Highway 186, running from Raymondville to Lasara.

McAllen

Casa de Palmas Hotel

The site was originally a city park with antelope, javelina, and deer, before the town of McAllen decided it needed a hotel to serve as a business and social center. The Casa de Palmas, a three-story structure with a red tile roof built around a central patio and twin towers, was erected here in 1918. One year later, it served as a shelter for many area residents during a severe hurricane, and in 1973, after a destructive fire, it had to be rebuilt.

The third floor is supposed to be particularly active with cold spots in the rooms, water faucets in the bathroom that turn on and off, the sounds of footsteps in the halls, and on more than one occasion, the night staff reports a white wispy figure.

The Casa de Palmas Hotel is located at 101 North Main Street, McAllen, Texas 78501. To book your stay or for more information, visit them online at www.marriott.com/hotels/travel/mfebr-renaissance-casa-de-palmas-hotel.

First Line Apartments

Located just off Highway 225, residents of this apartment complex report unusual activity both day and night. One of the more frequent occurrences is the sound of footsteps coming up the stairs and then the sound of keys in the door, but when the tenant answers the door to see who has arrived, there is no one there. In one apartment, the apparition of a woman is seen walking from the bedroom, through the hallway, and into another room. All the while she peeks into other rooms as if she is looking for someone.

The First Line Apartments is located at 1120 Red Bluff Road, Pasadena, Texas 77506.

La Lomita Mission

La Lomita originated with a grant of land from the King of Spain in 1767 and means "little hill" in Spanish. In 1861, the land came under the stewardship of the Oblates of Mary Immaculate and served as both a mission and a ranch. The mission continued until 1907, when it was parceled out for farmland and sold.

One legend associated with the site tells of three priests who broke their vows of chastity with the nuns. The children born from these trysts were suffocated and buried on the grounds in order to hide their secret. When the people from nearby towns and ranches discovered the truth, an angry mob stormed the mission and murdered two of the priests. The third escaped only to die soon after while searching for help.

The old mission chapel still stands today and is a shrine to Our Lady of Guadalupe. It is here that many pilgrims and tourists encounter a woman suspended in air while praying, she is believed to be the spirit of a nun and frequently shows up in photographs taken during the day.

La Lomita Mission is open to the public during daylight hours and can be found on FM 1016, three miles south of U.S. 83, near Mission, Texas 78572.

Toys "R" Us

The story is that, a number of years ago, a careless employee left a ladder standing in one of the aisles. A young boy who wanted a toy located at the top of a shelf decided to use the ladder to reach it, but once high above the isles, he fell and broke his neck.

Now, stockers who work overnight report the sounds of a child running and laughing through the aisles. Lights turn on and off by themselves, doors that were locked open and close, and toys have been seen to move on their own.

The Toys "R" Us is located at 1101 West U.S. 83, McAllen, Texas 78501.

Mission

Shary-Shivers Mansion

In 1917, John Shary, the "Father of the Texas Citrus Industry" moved to Mission with his family and built an extravagant mansion, complete with its own bowling alley, lake, bathhouse, and citrus orchard. Being the showpiece of the valley, many important events took place here, including a stay by President Dwight D. Eisenhower and other important figures. From 1949 to 1957, the home was the residence of Texas Governor Allen Shivers, who married John Shary's daughter, Marialice, in 1937. The home has recently been donated to the University of Texas Pan-American Foundation and is open to the pubic for tours by appointment. Some claim to have seen the apparition of John Shary walking from the nearby chapel where he is buried with his wife to the house where his figure disappears as soon as it touches the front steps. Others have seen him on the front porch in his favorite rocking chair.

The Shary-Shivers Mansion is located at 4915 North Shary Road, Mission, Texas 78573.

Port Aransas

Tarpon Inn

Built by Frank Stephenson, a boat pilot and lighthouse keeper in 1886, with lumber salvaged from a civil war barracks, the two-story structure with long galleried porches was first used to house men working on the Mansfield Jetty. When the Jetty was finished, the Tarpon became a hotel and has remained one ever since. After a fire in 1900 and a tidal wave in 1919, the main structure was rebuilt and reinforced to withstand the worst the elements could hurl against it. The inn is currently named for the tarpon, a huge game fish with large silver scales found in the waters around Port Aransas.

Guests report strange glowing lights in the bathroom at night, the sounds of footsteps from the ceiling, mumbled voices in the shower, and cold spots.

The Tarpon Inn is located at 200 East Cotter Avenue, Port Aransas, Texas 78373. For more information or to book your stay, visit them online at www.thetarponinn.com.

The Tarpon Inn. *Courtesy of the Tarpon Inn Port A, Lee Roy Hoskins, Owner; Dana Spinks, Innkeeper.*

Port Isabel

Ghost Ship of Jean Lafitte

Between Port Isabel and South Padre Island's Isla Blanca Park, a three-mast French Corsair at full sail has been spotted gliding across the moonlit waters from the south. It is said that the decks are empty, and that after only a few moments, it vanishes. Legend tells that the ghost ship belongs to the infamous gentleman pirate Jean LaFitte of New Orleans, who raided British and Spanish ships along the Texas coast in the early 1800s. Some say he still sails these waters looking for treasure he buried long ago.

Richmond Jailhouse

First built in 1897, the imposing Romanesque revival style structure with its massive arches was the Fort Bend County Jail until 1955. The entry to the jail was on the first level through a heavy iron door. Persons going to the second floor passed through an iron gate before ascending the stairway. Instead of bars, iron latticework covered the inside of windows and formed cells. Two large rooms on either side of the second floor housed double-decker cellblocks with the gallows located in the center section. In 1996, the building was renovated to become the new home of the Richmond Police Department.

Law enforcement officers working the graveyard shift often report the sounds of metal doors clanging, mumbling conversations, items disappearing off of desks, and shadowy figures on the second floor.

The Old Richmond Jailhouse is located at 600 Preston Street, Richmond, Texas 77469.

Sabine Pass Lighthouse

One of three such lighthouses built in the United States, Sabine Pass began operations in 1857. For almost 100 years it lit the way for passing ships and was finally extinguished in 1957 when newer technology replaced it. Although the docks, keeper's house, and outbuildings were all destroyed by marsh fire years ago, the main tower continues to rise above the eastern shores of Sabine Pass to this day.

Several apparitions have been spotted in the old tower. The first is described as a man in black with bold brass buttons and a light keeper's cap. Those who have seen the ghost, claim he resembles a former lighthouse keeper named Stephen Hill, who died in 1913. The second apparition is that of a Union soldier who is thought to have lost his life in the Battle of Sabine Pass.

Accessing the lighthouse is difficult today, but can be achieved by traveling south on Lighthouse Road one mile after crossing the causeway bridge into Louisiana. After traveling down a dirt road for about four miles, the track ends at a bayou that must be crossed on foot before reaching the lighthouse. For more detailed information, visit the lighthouse online at www.sabinepasslighthouse.org.

HISTORIC SAN PATRICIO COUNTY COURT HOUSE

Built in 1871, the original simple two-story wooden structure burned down in 1889, but during its time it became infamous for legally hanging one of the first women in the state of Texas. Josefa Rodríguez made her living furnishing travelers with meals and a cot on the porch of her shack on the Aransas River. When a traveler named John Savage was murdered with an ax nearby, Rodríguez was arrested for the murder. Her trial was a farce, and although the jury recommended leniency, the judge ordered her execution. While awaiting the passing of her sentence, she was kept chained in leg irons to the wall of the courthouse. When her day came, she was hung by the neck and then dumped into a coffin. One witness to the event claimed that he heard a soft moaning from the coffin as they carted her away to be buried in an unmarked grave.

A replica of the old courthouse was constructed in 1985 by the San Patricio Restoration Society on the original site. Visitors to the building now claim that the ghost of Josefa haunts the grounds, crying out in the night. She is said to appear as the specter of a woman with a noose around her neck. Recent investigations by ghost hunters reveal uncertain footage of what may be the ghost of Josefa.

The Historic San Patricio County Court House can be found on FM 666 just as you enter San Patricio from the south.

CINEMA FOUR THEATER

Located on the north side of town, this theater is said to be haunted by two very active ghosts. The first is of a woman who likes to call out the names of the workers while they are cleaning up at night. The second is of a little boy who runs up to the concession stand, but when the worker looks down to take his order, there's no one there. Finally, some employees experience cold spots and have even witnessed a trashcan rolling up a ramp.

The Cinema Four Theater is located at 5912 North Navarro Street, Victoria, Texas 77904.

Tomball

SPRING CREEK PARK

Spring Creek Park is a 114-acre, heavily forested area of trails and campgrounds bordering the banks of Spring Creek. In 1861, it was the site of a Confederate powder mill that produced cannon powder for the southern army until 1863, when the mill mysteriously exploded, killing three men. The result of the explosion left a massive crater, which filled with water and provided a swimming hole to local boys over the years. After several drowning accidents, the swimming hole was fenced off and now acts as a water retention pond for a nearby subdivision. A marker to the old powder mill can be found in the northwest section of the park near the creek.

Visitors who dare to brave the park at night claim to see apparitions peeking from around trees at them in the vicinity of the old powder mill as well as footsteps through the leaves and cold spots even on the hottest nights.

Spring Creek Park is located at 15012 Brown Road, Tomball, Texas 77377. For more information, visit them online at www.civilwaralbum.com/misc4/tomball1.htm.

PRAIRIES AND LAKES REGION

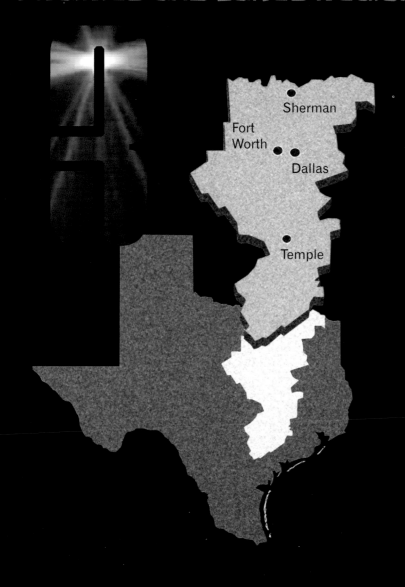

Bordered on the north by the Red River, the undulating prairie with its twisting riverbeds and fresh water lakes extends almost 350 miles to the south before meeting the more desolate southern plains. Rich farmland spreads across the landscape as well as big cities, small towns, and everything in between. One of the first settlers to stake a claim in the region without loosing his scalp, was an Indian trader from Arkansas named John Neely Bryan, who, in 1841, built his cabin at an important crossing along the Trinity River. Soon after, more settlers began to arrive and a tiny hamlet grew up around Neely's cabin, which in time became the city of Dallas.

Not far to the west of Dallas, another settlement was springing up from a military post known as Fort Worth. Strategically positioned on the Chislom Trail, weary cowboys driving herds to northern markets found its bars and bathhouses a welcome sight and often referred to it as the "Oasis of the Prairie." When a massive complex of stockyards was later constructed, Fort Worth became the center for the cattle and ranching industry for the state, earning it another nickname—"Cowtown."

In the 1870s, the Texas and Pacific Rail Road roared onto the scene with whistles blaring. The introduction of the steam engine to the region literally opened the floodgates to the west as more and more settlers began pouring in. Although the railroad granted an economic boon to the Dallas/Fort Worth area, it also brought with it a host of eclectic characters determined to make their mark in this new land. Cowboys, buffalo hunters, gunmen, and gamblers arrived to sample the saloons and gambling houses that quickly developed. As a consequence, robberies, shootouts, and prostitution became so rampant that some sections of the two towns became known by names such as "Hell's Half Acre," or the "Bloody Third Ward." When the citizens became alarmed at the growing crime wave sweeping through their towns, quick-draw lawmen such as "Longhaired" Jim Courtright were brought in to clean up the streets.

Today, the lawless past of the region is far behind it; unfortunately, so too are the vast stretches of tall prairie grass and stands of oak that once filled the region. By the 1900s, most of the prairie had been plowed under for the dark rich soil beneath it and converted into farmland or pasture. The earlier frontier settlements of Dallas and Fort Worth changed as well, growing into one sprawling metroplex of modern highways and lofty skyscrapers, making it the fifth largest metropolitan area in the U.S. Also some of the biggest and best museums, restaurants, shopping, and other attractions are found here for the urban explorer to enjoy lending credence to Dallas's nickname—"The Big D."

Despite the urbanized nature of the Prairies and Lakes Region, when the big city lights go dim, the streets take on a more sinister quality. No longer is it a place of bustling traffic and blaring car horns, but one where hundred year old gunfights between phantom gunmen replay themselves, where spooky old manors wait on dark city streets, and where the guests of some hotels can even stay the night in a haunted room, if they're brave enough.

Alexander

McDow's Watering Hole

In the 1870s, the Papworth family built a cabin near Green's Creek about two miles south of Harbin, Texas. While the husband was away on business one day, the wife, Jenny Papworth, vanished. A man named W.P. Brownlow initially blamed a local tribe of Comanche Indians, but when they proved innocent of the disappearance, the attention shifted back to Brownlow himself. In order to save himself, Brownlow redirected the attention back onto the grieving husband, Charlie Papworth, claiming he was a cattle rustler. After a hooded vigilantly party attempted to hang Charlie, he fled with his remaining son to parts unknown. On his deathbed Brownlow confessed to murdering Jenny Papworth because she witnessed some of Brownlow's own cattle rustling activities.

As early as the 1880s, families living near the old Papworth cabin were reporting that the apparition of Jenny Papworth, holding a baby, was seen wandering about the property at night. Today, those brave enough to venture out to McDow's Hole, claim to have seen a glowing figure in white walking along the creek bed as if searching for something. In 1979, author Mary Joe Clendenin wrote a book about the haunting entitled *The Ghost of the McDow Hole.*

The water hole is located three miles north of the ghost town of Alexander, in a deep part of a creek bed lined with a natural bedrock bottom and may take some tramping around to find.

Allen

Eagle Stadium

Legend holds that during the 1940s, a football player collapsed on the field and died of a heart attack. Although there is no evidence to substantiate this claim, spectators believe that on Friday nights after a big game, the shadow of the deceased player can be seen running down the field at midnight.

The field is home to the Allen Eagles and is located at 601 East Main Street, Allen, Texas 75002.

Arlington

Bird's Fort

Established in 1841 by Major Jonathon Bird, the wooden stockade and blockhouses were an attempt to attract settlers from the Red River area with the promise of military protection from the hostile tribes that occupied the land. Due to constant skirmishes with local tribes, failed farming, and dwindling supplies, the fort was abandoned in 1842. What remained of the compound later served as the site where Jacob Snively disbanded his forces after raiding Mexican gold shipments along the Santa Fe Trail. No trace of the plundered gold was ever recovered and its whereabouts remain a mystery to this day.

Although nothing remains of the fort today, but a weathered historical marker, some believe the ghosts of those who lived and died there have returned once again. One of the more common apparitions to haunt the place is a man dressed in simple older fashioned clothing seen out of the corner of the eye. When the witness turns to look directly at him, however, he disappears without a trace. Another apparition known to haunt the place is that of an Indian brave in full battle dress and covered in blood, who some think was a casualty of one of the many battles between the local tribes and soldiers from the fort.

Today, investigators have logged numerous photographic anomalies such as orbs, mists, and strange figures at the site.

The location of Bird's Fort can be reached by traveling one mile north of the Trinity River along FM 157, turn east on Trinity Boulevard and then south on Euless Main until it becomes a dirt track, which dead ends at the historical marker.

Cinemark Tinsel Town 9

Some say that during the construction of the building a worker died on the job. Patrons now report witnessing the theater chairs lowering on their own as if someone were sitting in them. Others claim that during movies a man appears to be seated next to them, but at some point he gets up, and as he is walking away, he vanishes into thin air. Employees also claim to have had their own run ins with the phantom and say that objects move when their backs are turned and the door to the projection room slams shut when no one is around.

The Cinemark Tinsel Town 9 is located at 2815 East Division Street, Arlington, Texas 76011. For more information, visit them on the web at www.cinemark.com.

CRYSTAL CANYON

In 1843, Colonel Jacob Snively and his band of men, who styled themselves the "Invincibles," raided a Mexican gold shipment along the Santa Fe Trail. The United States army, however, viewed the incident as an act of piracy against the nation of Mexico and pursued Snively and his raiders into a canyon just south of Bird's Fort. Finding themselves with their back against the wall, Snively knew the game was up, but before surrendering it's said they buried both their dead and the plundered gold somewhere in the canyon.

Today, those treasure hunters brave enough to search for the treasure have heard the disembodied voices of the dead that were buried with the gold and protect it still. Phantom footsteps are also heard within the canyon walls as well as crashing sounds through the foliage that chases intruders out of the canyon.

Crystal Canyon is located at 1000 Brown Boulevard, Arlington, Texas 76011.

DEATH'S CROSSING

Known by an assortment of names, including Screaming Bridge (although the bridge no longer exists), this railroad crossing in Mosier Valley has been the scene of a number of tragic motor vehicle accidents over the years resulting in a numerous deaths. One of the first occurred in February of 1961, when a group of high school girls were returning home late one night after a movie. Unknown to them at the time, the bridge that spanned the crossing was out and their car crashed into the ravine killing three of the six girls.

Time passed and with more accidents, the crossing became something of an urban legend, complete with glowing tombstones, phantom cars, and screaming ghosts. What numerous ghost hunters have found at the site are cold spots, disembodied voices, and pulsing orbs of light. During a 2005 Halloween special, a local news team captured the disembodied voice of a woman. Psychics working on the case often feel as if there is a strong female presence at the crossing.

Death's Crossing is located along an old road in the vicinity of Trinity Boulevard and Greenbelt Road.

LOST INFANT CEMETERY

Created with its first burial in 1904, the small cemetery was part of the Berachah Home for Unwed Mothers, founded by Reverend J.T. Upchurch in 1894. After epidemics of influenza and small pox struck the area in 1914, the cemetery quickly filled with the bodies of many small children and babies. In most cases, there were no headstones, but tiny plaques listing the infants by number rather than name. In 1935, the home closed with the death of Reverend Upchurch, and when the land was sold to the University of Texas at Arlington, the cemetery was forgotten. That is until local newscasters began reporting stories that the sounds of infants crying out in the night could be heard coming from the lost cemetery.

Others also claim to have seen shadowy figures darting between the trees that shade the cemetery, as well as the feeling of something caressing their hair. In some of the university's buildings that now occupy the grounds of the former Berachah home, including the student publications building and the theatre, the ghost of a woman dubbed Mary is reported. Many of those who have seen her claim that she is a woman with long blonde hair and a light summer dress that disappears the moment she knows she is being watched.

The Lost Infant Cemetery can be found in the northeast corner of Doug Russell Park at 801 West Mitchell Street, Arlington, Texas 76013.

Grave marker at the Lost Infant Cemetery.

Texas Candy Store

Located in the Texas theme section of Six Flags Over Texas Park, this building was one of the original structures that opened with the park in 1961.

Over the years, many employees have come to believe the building is haunted by the ghost of a little blonde girl they've named Annie. Legend holds that the little girl drowned in a creek located in the area before the park was constructed. The Texas Candy Store is thought to be built right atop the place of her death. Phantom footsteps are often heard in the store's storage attic and the apparition of a little girl has been seen on the faux balcony or peering out of the upstairs window. In her more mischievous moods she is said to turn lights off or move objects around.

Six Flags over Texas is located at 2201 Road to Six Flags, Arlington, Texas 76010. For more information, visit them online at www.sixflags.com/overtexas.

Aurora

Aurora Cemetery

According to page 5, of the April 18, 1897 edition of the *Dallas Morning News*, an exotic airship collided with Judge Proctors windmill in Aurora, Texas, and exploded. The startled townsfolk quickly recovered the pilot's body, and in doing so learned that "he was not an inhabitant of this world." The tale doesn't end there, however, but continues with the extraterrestrial's body being laid to rest in the Aurora Cemetery in a grave marked by a stone with several small circles drawn inside the Greek letter Delta. The story was later made into a movie in 1986 entitled *The Aurora Encounter* and although the fabled grave marker has yet to be found, the cemetery is well known for its paranormal activity.

Ghost hunters have measured unusual EMF spikes and cold spots in the burial grounds and one group has captured the EVP of an angry male voice cursing at them. This they claim was a recording taken from the grave of Ricky Lee Green, a serial killer, who, along with his wife, murdered four people. On October 8, 1997, he was executed for capital murder and buried in the cemetery.

Aurora Cemetery can be found by turning south on Cemetery Road from Highway 114 at the eastern edge of Aurora. Travel one half mile down the old road and the cemetery will be on the left.

Bedias

Bedias Baptist Cemetery

First used as a burial site for the congregation of the First Baptist church in 1859, the nearby town suffered a devastating fire that swept through its business district in 1927. Although little remains of the once thriving community, the old white washed Baptist church still stands next to the burial grounds.

Those who know the town and its cemetery claim that the ghostly figures of children can be seen in the cemetery at night playing among the tombstones. It's said they were victims of the great fire that once engulfed the town.

Bedias Cemetery can be found by traveling southeast from the intersection of FM 1696 and 2620 about a fourth of a mile where it sits to the right of the road.

Belton

University of Mary Hardin-Baylor

The University of Mary Hardin-Baylor began in 1845 in Independence, as the Female Department of Baylor University. By 1886, the university moved to Belton, in central Texas, and in 1971 it became coeducational.

Today, one building that occupies the campus, Presser Hall, has come to develop a reputation for a series of unexplained events. Most of the manifestations seem to occur on the third floor and include unexplained music, elevator doors that open and close unexpectedly, and the sounds of footsteps. So frequent and disturbing were the occurrences that the university converted the third floor into storage space and campus security are careful to keep it locked. Some students still report, however, that when passing the tall red brick building on their way to classes they see the apparition of a girl looking down at them from one of the building's third floor windows. Tales persist that she is a former student who was murdered in the building by her boyfriend.

The University of Mary Hardin-Baylor is located at 900 College Street, Belton, Texas 76513. For more information, visit them online at www.umhb.edu.

Walmart Supercenter

There have been several sightings of apparitions over the years by employees working the night shift. The first occurred when a night manger walked by one of the toy aisles and noticed a woman in a Walmart smock. No one was supposed to be working in this section so he stopped and went back to the aisle, but it was empty. After checking the time cards that night, he could not account for the woman's presence in the store. On another occasion, an employee working in the receiving section late at night, turned to find a little boy staring up at her. She turned her head for a moment and when she looked back the boy was gone. A search of the building by employees turned up nothing.

The Walmart Supercenter is located at 2604 North Main Street, Belton, Texas 76513.

Caldwell

Caldwell High School

Although Caldwell High School is a relatively new structure and there are no known tragedies on record, both staff and students claim that the school auditorium is haunted by a spirit they affectionately refer to as George. Most of the activity seems centered on the sound booth and projection room, where dials on the soundboard move by themselves and the lights flicker and dim unexpectedly. Cold spots and strange noises are also reported from these areas, and although the electrical wiring has been checked time and again, there is no explanation for the odd occurrences.

Caldwell High School is located at 550 CR. 307, Caldwell, Texas 77836.

Cedar Hill

Pleasant Valley Cemetery

Locally known as Ghost Mountain, the burial grounds have also been called Old Cemetery Hill, and Witch Mountain. Founded in the 1850s as the town of Cedar Hill sprang up along the Chisholm Trail, the area is now a suburb of Dallas. Legend claims that the cemetery is home to both cultists and a disfigured beast known as the Goatman. In one version, a group of teenagers came upon the cultists one night during their dark rituals. As the teenagers fled, a curse was placed on them resulting in their car colliding with another vehicle on the way home, killing four of the teenagers. Now their spirits are rumored to wander the cemetery at night as punishment for stumbling upon the evil cultists.

More frightening than these bizarre tales, however, are the occurrences of vandalism and grave robbing that has taken place over the years, leaving numerous graves desecrated.

Ghost hunters exploring the grounds have recorded cold spots, EMF disturbances, disembodied voices calling out in the night, and an assortment of photographic anomalies.

Pleasant Valley Cemetery is located by exiting Beltline Road to the west off of Highway 67. Next, turn left on Lake Ridge Road and look for a small road called Bonnet Street, which terminates at the cemetery gates.

Cleburne

Wright Place

First built as a hotel called the Hamilton House in 1874, the southern section of the building was ravaged by a fire in 1916. After the blaze, A.J. Wright bought the structure and converted it into a mercantile store.

Today, the first floor houses a café and other shops, yet it's the unoccupied second floor where the unusual activity is reported. For those that have ventured up to the second level, there are reports of being touched by an unseen presence, the sound of children laughing, cold spots, and the smell of cigar smoke. One legend tells of a redheaded woman who was thrown from the second story window and killed in 1882 when the building was still a hotel. Some surmise she was a prostitute working out of one of the rooms when she was murdered by one of her customers. Now her apparition is said to appear in one of the second story windows from time to time and her presence is often marked by a heavy citrus scented perfume.

The Wright Place is located at 1 East James Street, Cleburne, Texas 76031.

Adolphus Hotel

Once referred to as "The most beautiful building west of Venice," the hotel was opened on October 5, 1912, by beer baron Adolphus Busch. Designed in the style of the French Renaissance beaux art, the brick and granite building, crowned in slate and bronze, was the tallest in Texas until 1922.

Most of the hauntings seem centered on the nineteenth floor, which once functioned as a grand ballroom. Guests on this floor often call down to the lobby complaining of people talking, stomping, and playing big band music in the halls. When guest services investigates the disturbances, they find the halls empty and quiet. One of the more frequently seen spirits is that of a bride from the 1930s, who was supposed to have hung herself after being left at the alter. She is often heard crying at night through the halls and is known to manifest as a hot wind. Encounters with her are said to leave the witness with an overwhelming sense of sadness.

The Adolphus Hotel is located at 1321 Commerce Street, Dallas, Texas 75202. For more information or to book your next stay, visit them online at www.hotel-adolphus.com.

Adolphus Hotel.

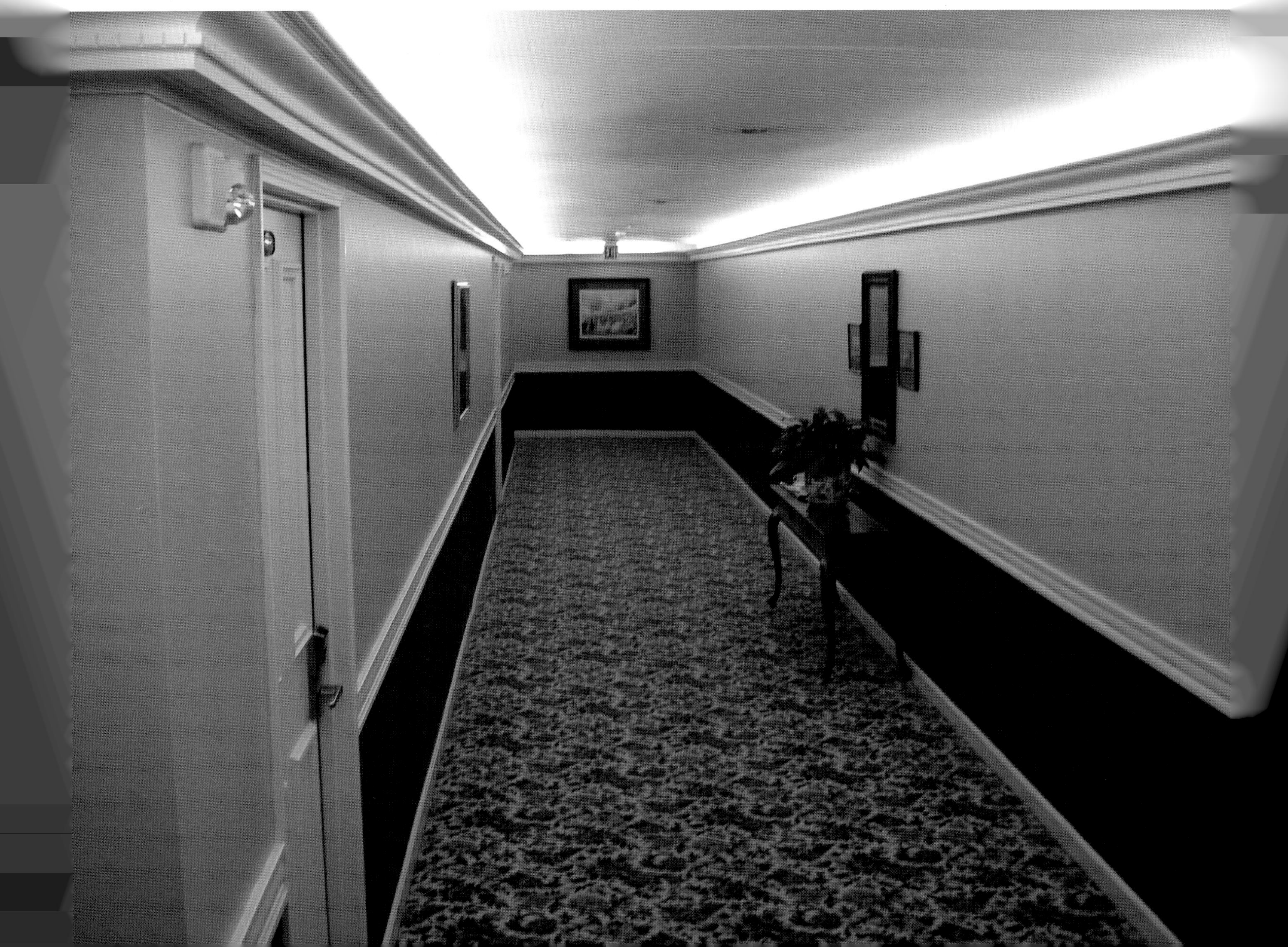

BACCUS CEMETERY

Initially known as Cook Cemetery, it saw its first internment in 1847. Rachel Cook Baccus later donated the land for the construction of the Baccus Christian Church Sanctuary, which was renamed Baccus Cemetery in her honor in 1915. By the 1930s, the congregation disbanded and today all that remains is the cemetery. Many traveling down Bishop Road, which runs along the cemetery's border, have witnessed shadowy apparitions crossing the road between the burial ground and a nearby field. Ghost hunters conducting investigations of the cemetery often encounter cold spots, photographic anomalies such as orbs, and the sound of footsteps following them around.

Baccus Cemetery can be located at Legacy Drive and Bishop Road just east of the North Dallas Tollway.

CVS PHARMACY

Located in East Dallas at the corner of Ferguson and Gus Thomasson Roads, the building is thought to be haunted by a former employee. When the building was still an Eckerd's an employee named Wayne was robbed and killed late one night after returning home from work. His assailants were never apprehended, but since his murder, employees report mysterious happenings in the building's upstairs storage area. The radio turns on by itself, footsteps can be heard on the staircase, cold spots appear, and boxes fall or are thrown from the shelves.

The CVS Pharmacy is located at 10306 Ferguson Road, Dallas, Texas 75228.

DALLAS HERITAGE VILLAGE AT OLD CITY PARK

The city's oldest public park, it is now home to a number of authentic buildings taken from locations all over North Texas and lovingly restored to their former glory. One of the very first structures to be added to the park was an old antebellum home known as the Millermore Mansion, and right along with it, some believe, a few ghosts.

Constructed in 1855 by William Brown Miller for his wife Minerva, it was fashioned in the Greek Revival style popular with the affluent at the time. Today the old home is thought to be haunted by the apparition of a woman spotted nervously pacing back and forth between the upstairs nursery and the master bedroom. Although she seems not to notice the presence of others, witnesses to the manifestation are often struck with overwhelming sensations of fear and nausea. Objects are also known to move around by themselves and rooms on the second floor suffer form dramatic temperature shifts for no apparent reason.

The Dallas Heritage Village at Old City Park is located at 1515 South Harwood Street, Dallas, Texas 75215. For more information, visit them online at www.oldcitypark.org.

DALLAS WHITE HOUSE

Finished in 1947, the house was built by R.B. Evans for his wife, Susannah, and is considered one of the truest examples of Greek Revival Colonial mansions in the south. Now in the possession of the Unity Church of Dallas, the building has for years been used as a reception hall for weddings and other gatherings. During this time, employees of the church have encountered what sounds like piano keys being struck randomly, even though no piano exists in the house. At other times, bits of muffled conversation can be heard in empty rooms and the toilets occasionally flush by themselves. One group of women witnessed what they believe to be the headless torso of a woman in white staring down at them from a second-story window late one night.

For most, however, there seems to be a strong presence about the house as if they are being watched. One psychic recently brought in during an investigation was able to observe two separate spirits. The first was a woman with a slight build and pointy nose who fit the description of Susannah Evans. The second was the image of a man just outside the house near the rear entrance dressed in shabby work clothes, with a stern, weathered look, who gave off an air of discomfort.

The Dallas White House is located at 6525 Forrest Lane, Dallas, Texas 75230. For more information, visit them online at www.unitydallas.org.

DeGolyer Estate

Built in 1940 by Texas oilman, geologist, and philanthropist Everette DeGolyer, the 21,000 square foot, Spanish Mission style mansion was part of a forty-four-acre estate named *Rancho Encinal*, which sat on the shores of White Rock Lake. In 1976, the DeGolyer estate became the largest portion of the Dallas Arboretum and Botanical Gardens, and with a later addition of the adjoining Camp Estate, the gardens increased to sixty-six acres.

Some of the docents that work the mansion after hours report a very uncomfortable feeling as if they are being watched by someone. At other times, piano music is heard coming from the mansion after it has been locked for the night and small objects, such as pictures, are moved to different places about the building when no one is looking.

The DeGolyer Estate is located at 8525 Garland Road, Dallas, Texas 75218. For more information, visit them online at www.dallasarboretum.org.

Flagpole Hill Park

Overlooking the northern section of White Rock Lake, Flagpole Hill has become a popular place for parties, picnics, and other large gatherings. Originally called Doran's Point, the Civilian Conservation Corps built a scenic overlook atop the hill in 1936, and raised a large flagpole at its highest point.

Since as early as the 1930s, a number of curious events have occurred on the hill. Cars traveling along the road that leads to the top of the hill have encountered showers of rocks falling from odd angles. Law enforcement officials investigating the claims are still at a loss to explain the phenomenon or suggest a possible culprit. Often, residents living close to the hill see strange lights at its summit dancing around as if the hill were on fire. In one incident on November 21, 2005, a woman driving along Northwest Highway noticed the strange lights, but claimed they came from a large circular object above the hill that hovered until military jets appeared, at which time it shot into the sky and vanished.

Flagpole Hill Park is located at 8700 East Northwest Highway, Dallas, Texas 75238.

Hotel Lawrence

Opening in 1925, the ten-story, cream-colored structure was initially intended to serve rail customers and other visitors to the city of Dallas. In the 20s and 30s, the hotel gained the colorful reputation of having an illegal gambling casino on the second floor, attracting everyone from bootleggers to card sharks. Over the years, the old place changed hands and names many times. First known as the Scott Hotel, it was renamed Hotel Lawrence in the 1930s, and later it became the Paramount Hotel until 2000 when it was rechristened the Hotel Lawrence once more.

Many have come to believe that the ghosts of former guests who may have died during their stay here haunt the hotel. Visitors and staff alike experience a wide range of activity, from the sound of invisible footsteps echoing through the lobby late at night to a spirit that resists anyone opening the door to Room 807 unless they first say, "Move over Smiley." In the basement, doors open and close by themselves, cold spots, disembodied voices, and strange feelings of being watched are common. On more than one occasion staff members report that heavy laundry carts move toward them as if being pushed by an invisible force. In addition, the figure of a man dressed in black has been seen roaming the underground corridors of the place, appearing and disappearing at free will. In a recent investigation, ghost hunters captured the sounds of a phantom cat and video footage of an EMF meter moving across a bed by itself.

The Hotel Lawrence is located at 302 South Houston Street, Dallas, Texas 75202. For more information or to book your stay, visit them online at www.hotellawrencedallas.com or call 214.761.9090.

LIZARD LOUNGE

Located in what is the Deep Ellum section of the city, the building started as a warehouse until hard times caused it to close. After that, a theater company moved in and opened the Grand Crystal Palace. Known for its 100-year-old Steinway piano and Baccarat chandelier, this is also when the first ghost stories started to arise. Actors taking the stage became well acquainted with the sight of the apparition of a man in a black suit and cape that haunted the audience. Most were frightened of the specter because it was said to give off a terrible dark aura and overwhelming feelings of sadness.

When the Palace eventually closed, also, a host of short-lived entertainment venues occupied the space. Today, the building houses a popular dance club known as the Lizard Lounge, and although the building has changed hands many times, the dark man that haunts it is still reported. Dancers and staff have seen the image of a dark man roaming around the building who disappears in the blink of the eye. Although the shadow figure is without discernable features, it definitely appears to have a masculine build. Some of the staff cleaning up after hours have even heard a voice whispering in their ear, but when they turn to face it, there is no one there.

The Lizard Lounge is located at 2424 Swiss at Good Latimer, Dallas, Texas 75204. For more information, visit them online at www.thelizardlounge.com.

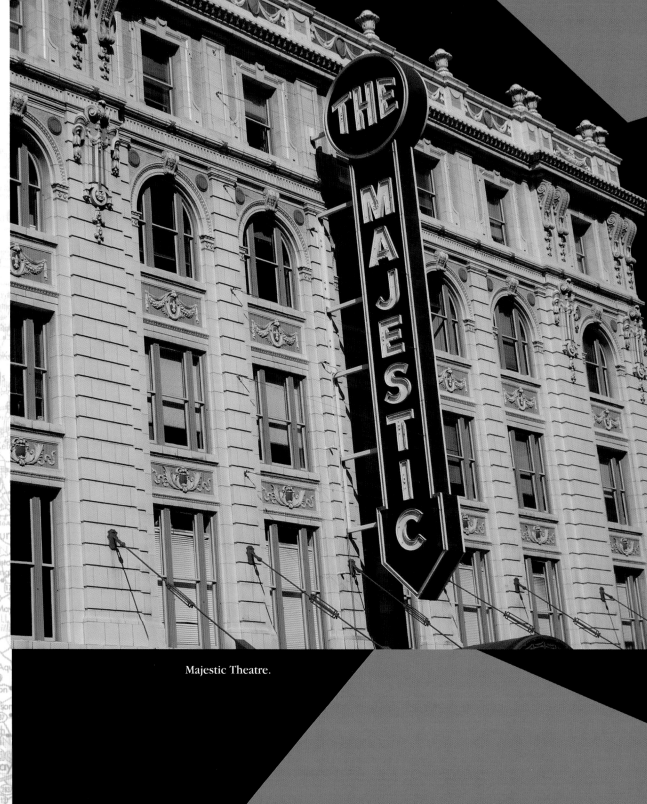

Majestic Theatre.

MAJESTIC THEATRE

Built at a cost of two million dollars by famed Chicago architect John Eberson in 1921, the five-story building catered to everything from vaudeville acts and jazz bands, to the block-buster hits of big screen during its life time. When the theatre finally "went dark" on July 16, 1973, after the last showing of the smash hit James Bond film *Live and Let Die*, it had entertained the city for five decades. It then sat dormant for ten years, until it was placed on the National Register of Historic Places on January 28, 1983, and reopened. Today, it continues to serve as a venue for Broadway plays and musicals. Everyone from comedians to musicians and movie stars to magicians have graced its stage, but some also believe the theatre plays host to a spirit as well.

Many visitors and staff experience cold spots, sensations of being touched, disembodied voices, and phone lines that light up as if they are being used when they are not. Late night security often encounters strange smells and objects that move on their own. One security guard, making his rounds after closing, wit-nessed a backdrop suspended above the stage descend slowly as if on cue. Thinking someone was behind the stage's curtain, he called out, but no one answered. Exploring the auditorium and stage carefully, he found no one. The odd fact he noted was that in order to drop the scenery, a crank needed to be turned manually by hand.

The Majestic Theatre is located at 1925 Elm Street, Dallas, Texas 75201. For more information, visit them online at www.dallassumermusical.org.

PLEASANT GROVE CHRISTIAN CHURCH

The Pleasant Grove Christian Church began in November of 1875, when the area was nothing more than a small rural community east of Dallas. Initially, the building acted as both church and schoolhouse and was named after the groves of cottonwood trees that grew in the area. Today, the church prides itself on continuing much the same as it did over one hundred years ago; with a few ghosts thrown in that is.

Visitors to the church claim to have seen children run by them as if playing tag and then disappearing into thin air. Strange howling and banging noises are heard throughout the building at times, and in one empty hallway, orbs and the face of a child have appeared in photographs. Although the ghosts of the children seem malign, the apparition of a man wielding an axe is also seen and appears much more threatening.

Pleasant Grove Christian Church is located at 1324 Pleasant Drive, Dallas, Texas 75217. For more information, visit them online at www.pgccdallas.org.

PRESTON ROAD

This is a congested stretch of road, beginning around the city's Highland Park area and shooting straight as an arrow to the northern suburbs of Plano, Frisco, and beyond. Origi-nally a pre-Columbian trade route winding its way through central Texas, it became known as Preston Trail in the 1840s and then later, Preston Road.

Motorists speeding down this busy thoroughfare claim to see groups of phantoms in early pioneer clothing making their way north, as if the cars speeding by didn't exist. Oth-ers describe the forms as something more indistinct and grayish in coloration; caught only out of the corner of the eye.

The haunted section of Preston Road runs north of Dallas's downtown district bordered by the cross streets of Spring Valley and Belt Line roads.

SAMMONS CENTER FOR THE ARTS

Completed in 1909, the fancifully ornate building designed by the prominent architectural firm of C. A. Gill and Sons was known as the Turtle Creek Pump Station and acted as the sole source of clean drinking water for the city until 1930. After the pumps were shut down, the station continued to house other functions of the Dallas Water Utility System for another twenty years, at which time it was abandoned. Then, in 1988, the former station reopened as The Sammons Center for the Arts and now hosts nonprofit arts organizations, events, rehearsals, auditions, and meetings.

Since its reopening, however, strange events have plagued the old station. Employees locking up for the night often hear the elevator come to life and begin to transverse the floors on its own. Those familiar with its quirky behavior believe it to be haunted by a ghost they refer to as Otis; a name taken from the company that built the center's elevator system. Another unusual pattern noticed by workers is that Otis seems to have a thing for the ladies. On some occasions, the elevator doors will open when a young, attractive woman walks by almost as if it were an invitation. Otis also likes to make an appearance from time to time, although mostly to women and is described as a young man, wearing overalls, a jacket, and a workman's cap. Many believe the ghost is that of a young man in his early twenties who was killed in the basement during an accident involving some of the station's machinery.

The Sammons Center for the Arts is located at 3630 Harry Hines, Boulevard, Dallas, Texas 75219. For more information, visit them online at www.sammonsartcenter.org.

SIXTH FLOOR MUSEUM AT DEALEY PLAZA

On November 22, 1963, the world watched in horror as shots rang out from the sixth floor of the Texas School Book Depository killing President John F. Kennedy. Hours later a suspect named Lee Harvey Oswald was arrested in connection with the shooting, but as he was being transferred from the city to the county jail two days later, he was shot to death by a local night club owner named Jack Ruby. Oswald never admitted to the crime, and even today, the question of who killed President Kennedy is hotly debated.

The 80, 000 square foot Texas School Book Depository is now the Dallas County Administration Building. In addition, the sixth floor of the building is a museum dedicated to the life and times of President Kennedy, with displays, interactive exhibits, audio tours, and what some say are the spirits linked to its tragic past. Those passing by the building on the street have seen a dark phantom figure in the window from which the shooting took place, called the sniper's nest. Visitors to the sixth floor have also seen a dark shadowy presence out of the corner of their eye or just as it's rounding a corner. Often, photographs taken on the sixth floor capture glowing orbs or phantom mists and some report an unnatural sense of sadness near the sniper's nest exhibit.

The Sixth Floor Museum at Dealey Plaza is located at 411 Elm Street, Dallas, Texas 75202. For more information, visit them on the web at www.jfk.org.

SNUFFER'S RESTAURANT

Opened on June 28, 1978, it began as a one-room building capable of holding only fifty-five customers. After a year, the owner, Pat Snuffer, decided to expand the business into an adjacent section of the building called the "Back Room," which doubled the seating capacity, but as renovations to connect the two sections began in 1979, so did the haunting.

All of the sightings describe a dark hazy figure with no distinct features and no sign that it is aware of its surroundings or of other people in a hallway that connects the two sections. Other apparitions are also encountered, with most of the occurrences transpiring after the place is closed for the night. One waitress reports that, one night, she entered the main restaurant section to find a woman sitting atop the cigarette machine. Knowing the place was locked tight, she went to get the manager, but when they returned together, the woman was gone and no trace of her presence could be found. Other employees have felt the touch of an invisible hand on their shoulder while going about their duties or heard their name whispered in a harsh sounding voice three times when they were alone. In one of the more ominous sightings, some have seen a pair of glowing red eyes peering out at them from under table number seven in the dining section.

Snuffer's Restaurant is located at 3526 Greenville Avenue, Dallas, Texas 75206. For more information, visit them online at www.snuffers.com.

SONS OF HERMANN HALL

Erected in 1911, the simple two-story box-like structure served as a lodge for the Sons of Hermann Order; a fraternity dedicated to preserving the heritage of the German immigrants in Texas. Now a local music venue, the building has for many years rang with tales of the spirits that inhabit it.

Board members have heard the sounds of children laughing and playing after the building was closed for the night. Doors are known to open and slam shut even after being locked tight. Pictures framed on the walls topple off without explanation and many frequenting the hall get the eerie feeling they're being watched. On more than one occasion, employees complained that after cleaning up for the night they returned the next morning to find their work undone and the place in complete disarray. One psychic touring the hall experienced a shortness of breath as if something were wrong with her chest near an open doorway leading to the outside parking lot. It was later learned through a July 6, 1897, *Dallas Daily Times Herald* article that on that date, in that location, a man named William Hardbrecht shot Walter Stover in the chest on the street outside the building where he died.

The Sons of Hermann Hall is located at 3414 Elm Street, Dallas, Texas 75371. For more information, visit them online at www.sonsofhermann.com.

TRAILS OF WEST FRISCO COMMUNITY

Named after a series of walking trails that course through the area, the new upscale community rests between White Rock Lake and the North Dallas Tollway. Many of the residents that live there today believe that the community was built atop an old settler's cemetery. There have been reports of infants crying in the night and the apparition of an old settler woman has been seen in several of the homes. Some also claim to have seen a hazy, unidentified apparition floating through the streets at night. In September of 2006, construction along the North Dallas Tollway temporarily halted after several bodies were unearthed from unmarked graves.

The Trails of West Frisco Community is located between White Rock Lake and the North Dallas Tollway.

WHITE ROCK LAKE

Comprised of ten twisting miles of shoreline, the lake is surrounded by well-kept parkland, filled with jogging paths, wooden pavilions, and scenic overlooks. Completed in 1910, the man-made reseviour pumped its contents into the city's water mains and was used as a coolant in steam-electric plants. By 1927, it became so popular among the city's residents that it was dubbed "The People's Playground."

Yet along with its popularity came the story of the phantom hitchhiker, and to this day, those traveling along the lake roads at night report run-ins with her. Legend says that she appears along the side of the roads dripping wet. When the motorist stops to help, she asks to be taken home and gives directions to a house near the lake. Once they arrive at the destination, however, the driver turns to let her out only to find she has disappeared. Upon inquiring at the house, the driver is then informed that the girl did indeed once live there, but that she died many years ago. Despite the heavy urban legend factor here, many deaths have occurred on and around the lake and numerous spectres of drowned or murdered victims have been sighted at various points along the lakeshore. In one encounter, a young couple was parked along a secluded section of the lake one night. As the two sat listening to the radio and gazing up at the stars, an iridescent form appeared over the water's surface. As the figure approached their vehicle, it changed into the glowing, white form of a woman with her arms outstretched as if reaching for them. Shaking off his terror at the last moment, the young man drove off just as the apparition reached for the handle of the car door.

White Rock Lake is located in northeast Dallas between Garland Road and Mockingbird Lane. For more information, visit them online at www.whiterocklakefoundation.org.

Denton

UNIVERSITY OF NORTH TEXAS

Joshua C. Chilton founded the school as a private college in 1890 when Denton was a rural hamlet of 2,500. The institution had its name modified six times before becoming the University of North Texas in 1989. Several of the student dormitories that occupy the campus have a history of unexplained phenomena.

Bruce Hall

The first building is Bruce Hall, which opened as an all-female hall in 1946 and is the oldest remaining residence hall on campus. It was named after Dr. William Herschel Bruce who died in 1943 and served as the university's president for some time.

The ghost that's believed to haunt the building is that of a former student from the 1950s named Wanda. The story is that Wanda became pregnant while a resident, and although she hid the truth as long as she could, the day came when her condition started to show. Deciding it was too shameful for anyone to find out, Wanda crawled into the dormitory's attic and hid until she gave birth. By the time anyone discovered the truth, it was too late, and Wanda was found sitting in a chair by the attic window dead. The baby she gave birth to was stillborn and found in a shoebox next to her. Residents of the dorm today report a number of ghostly occurrences they attribute to the tragic Wanda's restless spirit, including footsteps, voices, and heavy dragging sounds coming from the attic. Others passing by the dorm at night report seeing the silhouette of a woman staring out from the attic window. Her apparition has also been seen wandering the building's halls at night.

Maple Street Hall

Maple Street Hall is the second oldest resident hall on campus and the ghost said to haunt this building is a female spirit the students have playfully named Brenda. Brenda's true story may have been lost to time and so the tales of her death sound almost exactly like Wanda's in Bruce Hall. Her story, however, is one popular enough to be repeated in the Winter 2001 issue of the online alumni magazine *The North Texas Online.* In it there are tales of such strange happenings as doors opening and closing by themselves, lights turning on, and shower faucets starting and stopping.

The University of North Texas is located at 801 North Texas Boulevard, Denton, Texas 76201. For more information, visit them online at www.unt.edu.

Euless

CALLOWAY CEMETERY

Two of the earliest graves in the cemetery belong to Richard and Joseph Calloway, two brothers that owned the land in the 1860s. Richard's widow, Catherine, deeded the land as a public burial site in 1886 and has since come to be the final resting place for many of the area's early pioneer families. In 1908, a wooden tabernacle for burial services was added to the grounds. Those venturing into the burial grounds at night report cold spots, whispering voices, and great balls of glowing light.

You can visit Calloway Cemetery at 12600 Calloway Cemetery Road, Euless, Texas 76040.

FORT WORTH

BACK DOOR BOOK SHOP

Opened by Bert and Alice Barber in 1925 as Barber's Bookstore, the three-story art deco building lays claim to being the oldest continual bookstore in Texas. Erected in 1908, the building first served as a walk-up hotel and brothel known as the Adam's Hotel, and sometime later, the Starlight Café. During its time as a brothel, at least one murder was known to occur in the building.

The story goes that a working girl fell in love with a cowboy and the two planned to elope. When her father heard of it, he decided to end the relationship and gunned the cowboy down as he was leaving the girl's room. In a fit of depression the girl is believed to have taken her own life.

Over the years owners of the bookstore have run into a number of events they are unable to explain. On one occasion, when the owner was restocking shelves by himself, he heard the sound of papers turning rapidly. Moving through the maze of shelves to the section where the sound was coming from, he found all of the books thrown into a pile on the floor. The owner's son later reported, that while working after hours, he witnessed the apparition of a man in blue jeans and a white tee-shirt walk by his office door. Others have heard the sounds of footsteps on the interior stairwell where the murder occurred and seen shadows climb the stairs.

The Back Door Book Shop is located at 901 Throckmorton Street, Fort Worth, Texas 76102.

DEL FRISCO'S DOUBLE EAGLE STEAKHOUSE

Located in what was once the hell's half acre section of the city, known for its saloons, gambling houses, brothels, and unrestrained lawlessness, the two-story building now houses an upscale steakhouse.

Local legend holds that the building was once a bathhouse in the 1800s, and that one day, as a gentleman lay soaking in one of its tubs, an unknown gunman crept in and shot him in the back of the head. Even though the building's rowdier days are behind it, there are those that insist that the long ago murder victim still haunts the restaurant's banquet hall and upstairs bar, waiting to take revenge on his killer. Employees often feel they are being watched as they go about their duties and have encountered cold spots throughout the building. On more than one occasion, a worker has been touched by an invisible presence.

The Del Frisco's Double Eagle Steakhouse is located at 812 Main Street, Fort Worth, Texas 76102. For more information, visit them online at www.delfriscos.com.

FORT WORTH ZOO

Opening to the public in 1909, the Fort Worth Zoo is considered the oldest zoo in the state of Texas. Beginning with only one lion, two bear cubs, an alligator, a coyote, a peacock, and a few rabbits, the zoo now houses over 5,000 species of native and exotic animals. There are some zoo keepers, however, that would venture to say that the zoo holds even more than just, lions, and tigers, and bears. It might even hold a few ghosts. In the 1980s, it's said that a careless zookeeper was crushed in the elephant pen by one of the massive pachyderms and that now his apparition can be seen occasionally roaming the walkway between the elephant pen and the zebra corral. In addition, the apparition of a woman in a late nineteenth century white dress, carrying a parasol, is periodically spotted walking slowly back and forth near the zoo's café.

The Fort Worth Zoo is located at 1989 Colonial Parkway, Fort Worth, Texas 76110. For more information, visit them online at www.fortworthzoo.com.

Del Frisco's Double Eagle Steakhouse.

Jett Building

Constructed in 1902 as the Northern Texas Traction Company Office's main terminal and ticket station, it operated the first inner city rail service from Fort Worth to Dallas until 1934. Since that time, the rectangular, 3-story building has served a number of businesses, including a candy factory, bookstore, bar, and now a Jamba Juice and a country radio station called *The Ranch*.

Over the years, various owners of the building have had to contend with a number of odd occurrences. Cold spots, items moving, lights turning on, and feelings of being watched have all been reported. One employee told local news papers that as he was closing for the night on Halloween, he looked into a mirror and saw the apparition of a woman staring back at him. Others have heard what they can only describe as the sounds of a child's ball rolling across the deserted third floor and the clump, clump, of a woman's high heels. Recently, the current proprietors have gone on record with their own stories and claim to have seen the apparition of a man dressed in black cowboy boots and suit with dark hair and a pale complexion.

The Jett building is located at 400 Main Street, Fort Worth, Texas 76102.

Log Cabin Village

This living history museum is comprised of six log houses dating back to the mid 1800s and arranged over the museum grounds as if it were an actual pioneer village. Selected from all over the North Texas region and moved to the museum complex in the 1950s, each cabin has been lovingly restored to its former condition.

Although the museum opened as early as 1966, it wasn't until the addition of the Foster cabin in 1974 that claims of the paranormal began to surface. Numerous staff members and historical re-enactors have seen what they believe to be a female apparition in the upstairs corner bedroom of the Foster cabin. She is often described as an attractive woman in her thirties, with a long, black skirt, and a mauve-colored shirt with puffy Leg O Mutton sleeves. Usually, there is a heavy, overpowering presence when she manifests, the temperature drops, and the room fills with the scent of lilacs. After the spirit startled several visitors, the room was closed by the museum and turned into a staff office.

The Log Cabin Village is located at 2100 Log Cabin Village Lane, Fort Worth, Texas 76109. For more information, visit them online at logcabinvillage.org.

Miss Molly's Bed and Breakfast

Perched atop the Lone Star Café, Miss Molly's is the oldest functioning bed and breakfast in the city. Built in 1910, it was designed as a rooming house for the cowboys and traveling salesmen brought in by the stockyards. In 1920, it was called the Palace Rooms, but by the 1940s, as the neighborhood changed and the streets were flooded with servicemen, it was bought by Miss Joise King and turned into a bordello named the Gayette Hotel. Eventually, this too closed, and in 1989, it was converted into a bed and breakfast, where the owners say that the spirits of its wild past still come back to play.

Cold spots, the scent of perfume, and objects that move on their own are all common place here. One local reporter staying in the Cowboy Room was awakened in the middle of the night to find the apparition of a young, blonde woman staring at him seductively. On another occasion, an Englishman visiting the city was staying in what is called the Cattle Baron's Room. About 2:30am, he awoke to find an elderly woman in a sunbonnet and period dress staring at him intently. As soon as he switched on the light, however, she vanished.

Miss Molly's Bed and Breakfast is located at 109 West Exchange Avenue, Fort Worth, Texas 76106. For more information or to book your stay, visit them online at www.missmollyshotel.com.

MITCHELL-SCHOONOVER HOUSE

Constructed in 1907 by prominent jeweler James Mitchell, the Victorian style home of buff-colored brick sits in what used to be an affluent section of the city known as the "silk stalking" district. The house changed hands numerous times, with the Schoonover family residing in it the longest—from 1945 to 1979. In the 1980s, the home was divided and renovated into suites for small businesses. During this renovation, workers encountered cold spots, sensations of being touched on the shoulder, and dank, overpowering smells in the basement. In one frightening incident, a worker in the attic was confronted by a glowing orb of light that zipped around him. Even after the tenants moved in, the manifestations continued, with the sounds of phantom piano music, items that disappeared off of desks, doors that opened on their own, and electronic devices that turned on by themselves. Some staff members even witnessed a man in a dark suit from the corner of their eyes, but when they turned to address him he vanished.

The Mitchell-Schoonover House currently owned by the Art Brender Law Firm and is located at 600 South 8th Avenue, Fort Worth, Texas 76104.

OAKWOOD CEMETERY

Originating as a donation of land in 1879 from John Peter Smith, one of the city's first settlers, Oakwood Cemetery is actually three separate burial grounds that grew into one sprawling necropolis over the years. Houses bordering the grounds have had a long history of strange activity, including odd sounds and moving objects. In addition, cars passing late at night are often plagued by disturbing power failures that drain their batteries. Finally, a woman in white has been seen roaming among the headstones from a distance wailing out as if in agony.

Oakwood Cemetery can be visited at 701 Grand Avenue, Fort Worth, Texas 76106. For more information, visit them online at www.oakwoodcemetery.net.

PETER BROTHERS HAT COMPANY

Beginning in 1911 with two brothers, Tom and Jim Peters, the business of handmade-quality-western-hats has remained in the family for over 100 years.

Today, family members believe that Tom Peters, who died in 1991, has come back to make sure the business is being run as it should. Objects are known to move around on their own or disappear altogether. At other times, the hats, displayed on long safety hooks, are thrown to the ground and an unexplained knocking can be heard. Employees have also heard the sound of low moaning from the basement stairs, which they link to a former worker who tumbled to his death many years ago.

The Peter Brothers Hat Company is located at 909 Houston Street, Fort Worth, Texas 76102. For more information, visit them online at www.peterbros.com.

STOCKYARDS HOTEL

Erected in 1907 by Colonel Thomas Thannish, the hotel was the crown jewel of the city, hosting everything from traveling cowboys to foreign dignitaries. It was also in a rough section of town with outlaws and shootouts aplenty. Famous lawman "longhaired" Jim Courtwright met his end right outside the hotel in a showdown with Luke Short, and even the notorious pair of Bonnie and Clyde stayed in a room while casing a nearby bank.

Staff at the 100-year-old hotel reports two apparitions haunting the building. The first is an apparition they've affectionately named Jesse, who appears on the staircase landing in a cowboy hat and spurs. During his brief appearances, he is said to pay no attention to those around him, and at night, the sound of his spurs can be heard walking through the hallways. The second spirit is thought to be a former employee named Jake, who died after many years of service to the hotel. He is often blamed for the elevator traveling between floors for no reason and late night calls to the front desk from a nonexistent extension that cannot be transferred or put on hold.

The Stockyards Hotel is located at 109 East Exchange Avenue, Fort Worth, Texas 76106. For more information or to book your next stay, visit them online at www.stockyardshotel.com or call 800-423-8471.

Swift Meat Packing Building

Sitting on a low hill overlooking the Fort Worth Stockyards, this former administration building is all that remains of a complex of warehouses, meat processing plants, and auction houses. Built in the early 1920s, the plant flourished, then struggled, and finally closed its doors in the 1970s. Two massive fires swept through the complex destroying all but the administration building after its closing and several years later it was purchased and turned into an Italian eatery called the Spaghetti Warehouse.

Although the restaurant in turn closed its doors in 2003, it was during this period that tales of a haunting were most frequent. Footsteps were often heard on the empty second floor, and late at night after closing, workers sometimes noticed the figure of a man staring at them from a second-story window. In one close encounter, a manager closing for the night witnessed the dark, shadowy figure of a man sitting at the bar, which vanished as soon as he approached it.

At the time of this writing, the building is in the process of being converted into office space and is located at 600 East Exchange Avenue, Fort Worth, Texas 76106.

Texas Wesleyan University

Founded by the Southern Methodist Episcopal Church in 1890, it was originally named Polytechnic College, meaning "many arts and sciences." In 1914, the school had become a women's college, but in the hardship of the great depression, it merged with Texas Wesleyan Academy and became coeducational.

On the southeast side of the campus sits the Ann Waggoner Fine Arts Building and the legend of a ghost said to haunt it. The phantom was first spotted during a musical rehearsal in 1955 sitting in the audience watching the performers. Over the years, she has made many appearances and is always described as a woman in Victorian dress from the 1890s with puffed sleeves and a broach ending at a high collar. Each time, she appears in exactly the same seat, number thirteen, and the theater students have come to call her Georgia. When the university remodeled the theater in 2002 they recovered all of the seats but one, number thirteen, in honor of their resident ghost.

The Ann Waggoner Fine Arts Building is located at 1309 Wesleyan Street, Fort Worth, Texas 76105.

Texas White House Bed and Breakfast

Built in 1910 and purchased by William B. Newkirk, the beautiful old home remained in the Newkirk family until Mrs. Newkirk died in the home in 1967. Mr. Newkirk had also passed there a few years before her. After a series of small businesses, the home became a bed and breakfast in 1994. Women staying alone in the Lone Star Room (the former Newkirk bedroom) have been startled by a strong male presence that attempts to lay down next to them just before they drift off to sleep. When this occurs, the mattress and pillows depress as if the bed contained another person, and although the sensation is unmistakable, is does not seem to be threatening. Electrical devices also act strangely in the room and one woman watched as the blades of the ceiling fan above the bed began rotating quickly, even though the power was off.

The Texas White House Bed and Breakfast is located at 1417 Eighth Street, Fort Worth, Texas 76104. For more information or to book your next stay, visit them online at www.texaswhitehouse.com.

Thistle Hill Mansion

Known as the "Castle of Cowtown," the three-story, Georgian mansion is composed of thick, brick walls and massive limestone columns. Built in 1904 by legendary cattle baron William T. Waggoner as a wedding gift for his daughter Electra, the house remained a private residence until the 1940s when it was used as a dormitory for the Girls Service League of Fort Worth. By 1976, it was empty and awaiting the wrecking ball when a citizen's group stepped in and saved it from demolition. It is currently under the care of the Texas Heritage Corporation and open to the public for tours and events.

During renovations in the 1970s, workers began to report the sounds of music from the closed off third-story ballroom. Two apparitions were spotted during that time also, including a woman dressed in white on the landing of the grand staircase and a man in tennis clothes with a long, handlebar moustache. On October 3, 1997, a group of reporters and ghost hunters stayed the night and encountered the sounds of footsteps and disembodied voices. In the upstairs ballroom, a ninety-seven-year-old rocking chair moved on its own and one ghost hunter awoke to find a dark, shapeless mist above her, which vanished as soon as she turned her flashlight on.

W. E. Scott Theatre

Located in the city's cultural district, the 500-seat theatre built in 1966 is graced with an Italian chandelier, eight feet in diameter and weighing 575 pounds, as well as murals depicting the history of theatre architecture from as early as the Greek and Roman periods.

The basement of the building is said to be haunted by the spirit of a young stagehand named Ken Yandle, who hanged himself from a basement pipe in January of 1970. Since his death, his apparition is seen about the building wearing a brown suit. One light designer even claims to have seen his face in a stairwell door window. Another witness to the haunting included a wardrobe woman, who was so frightened by a bizarre cackling laughter coming from the stage, that she left and never returned.

The W.E. Scott Theatre is located at 1300 Gendy Street, Fort Worth, Texas, 76107. For more information, visit them online at www. fwcac.com.

Thistle Hill Mansion is located at 1509 Pennsylvania Avenue, Fort Worth, Texas 76104. For more information, visit them online at www. thistlehill.org.

Thistle Hill Mansion.

Garland

Garland Mills Cemetery

Also referred to as Mills Cemetery, this small burial ground just east of Dallas has developed an interesting tale over the years. In the cemetery lies a tombstone stone belonging to the Smiley family. The unusual thing is that all five them are listed as having died on May 9, 1927. Stories abound over how an entire family was wiped out in one day, including one in which the father, Chas Smiley, murdered the entire clan in a fit of insanity and then took his own life. The truth of the matter is that on the day of their death a terrible tornado ravaged the town of Garland killing fifteen and injuring forty and is most likely the true cause of their demise.

Local legend, however, states that if you lay on the grave at midnight on May 9th, the anniversary of their death, you can feel the sensation of phantom hands gathering around you to keep you from rising.

Garland Mills Cemetery is located at the intersection of Commerce Street and East Centerville Road, in Garland, Texas, 75040.

Gatesville

Mountain View Correctional Facility

Located three miles north of Gatesville, this sprawling complex of cell houses and guard towers started in 1889 as the Gatesville State School for Boys. In 1971, a class action lawsuit was filed against the state *(Morales vs. Turman)* claiming a pattern of cruel and unusual punishment in the school. Accusations ranged from beatings and solitary confinement to the use of chemical crowd control methods and psychotropic drugs. In response, a judge ordered the closing of the Mountain View unit. In 1975, the state of Texas began sending female prisoners to the ninety-seven-acre prison and today it also houses the female death row section.

Both prisoners and guards alike have witnessed the apparitions of little boys in the cell houses. On one occasion, a correctional officer working the third shift walked into a cell house day room and noticed in one of the mirrors the image of some one moving behind her. She quickly turned to investigate, but the room was empty. Another guard making her rounds encountered a spirit when a small ghost-like figure darted from out of one of the empty cells and disappeared. It's said she was so frightened by the experience she quit the next day.

The Mountain View Correctional Facility is located at 2305 Ransom Road, Gatesville, Texas 76528.

Driftwood Theatre 6

Resting near the shores of Lake Granbury, the Driftwood is well known for the spirits that haunt it after hours. Many times, employees working after closing hear the sounds of children laughing and playing and the apparition of a woman in white has been seen floating through the upstairs offices and projection room. In addition, objects are always being moved or are vanishing and doors open and close by themselves.

The Driftwood Theatre 6 is located at 1201 Old Cleburne Road, Granbury, Texas 76048. For more information, visit them online at www.driftwoodonline.com.

El Tesoro Camp

Meaning "The Treasure" in Spanish, El Tesoro is a 228-acre camp offering swimming, canoeing, horseback riding, and other activities to boys and girls grades 1-10.

Both campers and counselors tell of seeing the apparitions of Indians at night walking, crying, or on horseback. One of the more frequent phantoms is an Indian brave on a horse in full headdress.

The El Tesoro Camp is at 7710 Fall Creek Highway, Granbury, Texas 76049. For more information, visit them online at www.campfirefw.org.

Granbury Opera House

Playing to a host of traveling vaudeville acts, bands, and drama companies, Henry Kerr constructed the theatre in 1886, and named it Kerr's Hall. During its heyday, a rather unusual story developed involving the infamous John Wilkes Booth who assassinated President Abraham Lincoln on April 14, 1965. Although it was thought that Booth died in a barn fire while being surrounded by Federal troops eleven days after the assassination, others believe he may have traveled to Granbury and taken a part time job as an actor in Kerr's Hall, under the name Mr. St. Helen. Eventually, things would get too hot for Booth here, and after a few years, the questionable Mr. St. Helen disappeared one night for good. By 1911, the theatre closed, a victim of the temperance movement, and instead served a variety of businesses. In 1974, it was purchased by the Opera House Association and once again opened as a live theater.

In the time since its reopening, actors report the sounds of phantom footsteps pacing one of the balconies, props have been known to move on their own and something likes to play with both the lights and the doors. The apparition responsible for these occurrences may be that of a man wearing a white shirt, dark pants, and tall, heavy boots, which is seen from time to time.

The Granbury Opera House is located at 116 East Pearl Street, Granbury, Texas 76048. For more information, visit them online at www.granburyoperahouse.net.

Grande Prairie

HANGAR LOWE ROAD

Not far from the shores of Joe Pool Lake, Hangar Lowe Road runs straight as an arrow between Coastal Boulevard and Lake Ridge Parkway.

Along this strip, a ghostly jogger has been seen lying in the roadway as if struck by a vehicle. When a passing driver stops their car to help, however, the apparition disappears before their startled eyes.

PALACE OF WAX & RIPLEY'S BELIEVE IT OR NOT MUSEUM

Opening first as the Southwestern Historical Wax Museum in 1963, the exhibit with is collection of wax figures was moved to its present location in 1972. The 41,000-foot building that now houses the macabre collection is fashioned in the shape of King George IV's royal pavilion at Brighton. However, since coming to Grande Prairie, the museum has been plagued with enough mystery and tragedy to leave more than a few ghosts wandering its dark corridors.

Some of the bizarre events include two fires of unknown origin, two employees poisoned to death with strychnine, and a third man gunned down during an attempted robbery. Employees of the museum are often afraid to work alone in some sections and report strange smells such as burning wood or dark shadowy figures out of the corner of their eye creeping around. Security also seems to have difficulty with the motion detectors setting off the alarm system after the buildings is closed for the night and empty.

The Palace of Wax & Ripley's Believe it or Not Museum is located at 601 Palace Parkway, Grande Prairie, Texas 75050. For more information, visit them online at www.palacofwax.com.

Palace of Wax & Ripley's Believe it or Not Museum.

Grapevine

Lake Grapevine

Created in 1952 when the U.S. Army Corps of Engineers damned the Denton Creek, the 7,000-acre lake acts as both a water reservoir for the town and a place for its inhabitants to recreation.

Among the roads that snake their way along its shoreline is one lane known as Shady Trail, where the apparition of a little girl is seen. Eyewitnesses report she appears soaking wet and crying for her mother, but when motorists stop to assist her she disappears.

Located just north of the Dallas/Fort Worth Airport near Highway 121.

Haslet

Blue Mound Hill

The locals say that Blue Mound Hill was once a lookout and gathering place for Indian tribes in the 1800s. As more and more white settlers flooded the land, tensions flared between the two groups. One day, representatives from the tribes met at the hill to discuss the problem, but were ambushed by the white settlers who were waiting for them.

Legend now holds that on nights when the moon is full, their phantoms can be seen circling the hilltop chanting and screaming out for revenge.

Blue Mound Hill can be found by taking Highway 287 to Blue Mound Road. Once there, follow Blue Mound Road until you see a hill with a white shed atop it.

Hillsboro

Tarlton Bed and Breakfast

This three-story mansion was built by the Tarlton family in the stately Queen Anne Victorian style in 1895. It included such grand luxuries as hand-carved mantels, stained glass windows, and a speaking tube between the kitchen and the third-floor bedroom. Depressed over the death of his second wife in 1931, from cancer, and crippling losses in the stock market crash, Mr. Tarlton hung himself on the third floor of the mansion. He was seventy-one years old at the time. For years the building sat vacant, falling prey to vandals until it was purchased and restored to its former glory in 1972 and is now used as a bed and breakfast.

Guests staying at the Tarlton report phantom footsteps walking through the hallway as well as the sound of a woman gently singing. Mr. Tarlton seems to pop up from time to time also and has been witnessed bending over as if to reach down to a small child.

The Tarlton Bed and Breakfast is located at 211 North Pleasant Street, Hillsboro, Texas 76645. For more information or to book your next stay, visit them online at www.tarltonhouse.com or call 254.582.3422.

Keller

Green Olive Interiors

Built in 1888, the house that now serves as an interior design company is one of the oldest homes in the city of Keller. It was originally located in the Bear Creek Park area, but after moving several times, it came to rest at its present location. Over the years, the two-story, clapboard farmhouse has served as a home, doctor's office, and a variety of small stores. The current owners believe that Dr. Read and his wife, who once owned the building, haunt the place. In fact, the wife is said to have died in what is now the kitchen. The owners claim the house is plagued by strange noises, footsteps, floating balls of orange light, and odd smells. Neighbors have even reported seeing the apparition of an older woman in the window of the building. During one investigation, ghost hunters watched as a whiskey bottle tipped over by itself, and later that evening, dowsing rods were pulled from a ghost hunter's hands.

Green Olive Interiors can be found at 139 Olive Street, Keller, Texas 76248. For more information, visit them online at www.greenoliveinteriors.com.

Luling

Seton Edgar B. Davis Memorial Hospital

Edgar B. Davis, oilman and philanthropist from Brockton, Massachusetts, strolled into town one day in 1919 with the idea that God had sent him to the town to deliver it from economic hardship by finding oil. True to his vision, he discovered a number of oil fields and donated most of their proceeds to local charity. Although he died in Galveston on October 14, 1951, the town never forgot their benefactor, and in 1966, the Edgar B. Davis Memorial Hospital was built on the site of his home, including his grave site which rests on the hospital grounds.

Some at the hospital believe that he loved the town so much he has returned to haunt the hospital. Doctors and nurses report doors opening and closing by themselves, medicine falling from shelves and tables to the ground, and the sounds of invisible footsteps following them during their rounds.

The hospital can be located at 130 Hays Street, Luling, TX 78648. For more information, visit them online at www.seton.net/locations/edgar_davis/.

Mansfield

Farr Best Theater

The Farr Best Theater opened its doors as a motion picture house on October 10, 1917, when movies were still shown with hand cranked projectors. The theater continued to be operated by the Farr family until 1975, when it was sold and renamed The Old Bijou Theatre and then served the St. John's Lutheran Church congregation as a meeting place in 1980. Eight years later, the congregation moved down the street and the building was purchased by a community theater group named the Main Street Theatre, Inc, who has continued putting on live productions ever since.

The feisty spirit said to haunt the place has been named McDougal by the staff and began appearing after a portion of an old Scottish pub was donated to the theater as a concession stand. From then on, lights have been known to flip on and off by themselves and items disappear and reappear sometime later in a different location.

The Farr Best Theater is located at 107 North Main Street, Mansfield, Texas 76063. For more information, visit them online at www.mainstreettheatre.org.

McKinney

Londoner Pub

Known for its frosty pints of beer, this bar and grill is said to be haunted by a mischievous spirit that loves to play with the supplies in the storage area. Most of the reports stem from when the pub was a Buffalo Joe's Bar and Grill. Employees noticed items such as toilet paper strung out or thrown around or that they would walk into the storage room and find silverware impaled in the wall. The workers were so frightened by these and other occurrences that they agreed at the end of the night shift they would always leave at the same time. It seems no one wanted to be alone in the building by themselves.

The Londoner Pub is located at 100 North Tennessee Street, McKinney, Texas 75069.

McKinney Performing Arts Center

Built in 1874 by the architect Charles Wheelock in the style of the French Second Empire, the building served as the Collin County Courthouse until 1979 when a new courthouse was built just blocks away. In 1927, it underwent extensive remodeling and a more restrained, Neoclassical Revival look was added. The 480-seat facility now hosts ballets, theatrical performances, and other performing arts with the once stately courtroom transformed into an auditorium and stage.

Passersby at night often claim to see the figure of a woman in white staring down at them long after the building has closed for the evening and local legend claims that she is a suicide victim who hung herself in the early days of the courthouse.

The McKinney Performing Arts Center is located at 111 North Tennessee, McKinney, Texas 75069. For more information, visit them online at www.mckinneyperformingartscenter.org.

Mesquite

Eastfield College

In 1856, the Motley family moved to the area from Kentucky and built a Victorian, wood-framed mansion on the site. They continued to live in the home for some time, establishing a family cemetery nearby. On June 15, 1967, the old mansion, which by then was already the source for many haunted tales, was vandalized and burned to the ground. In 1970, the Eastfield Community College was founded on the site of the Motley estate and has since reported unusual activity in the Cowan Fine and Performing Arts Center, which includes the apparition of an unknown man that appears in the audience during rehearsals. Although the mansion no longer stands, the cemetery does and includes both unknown graves and graves containing body parts, such as an arm or foot.

Eastfield Community College is located at 3737 Motley Drive, Mesquite, Texas 75150. For more information, visit them online at www.efc@dcccd.edu.

Milford

Baroness Inn Bed and Breakfast

Starting as a girl's dormitory for the Texas Presbyterian Girl's College in 1850, it became the city's hotel after the college moved to Sherman, Texas. After its stint as a hotel, the building sat abandoned for many years before being purchased by Evelyn Williams who began intensive restoration efforts that took five years to complete. During its period of reconstruction, the first strange events started surfacing.

Workers claim that the radio changed stations by itself on many occasions, and that each night, no matter the precautions they took, two of the house's windows would be found open the next day. Events such as these became so frequent workers refused to work in the house at night. Once the guests started to arrive, other phenomena was reported, including the sensation of being touched on the shoulder by an invisible entity and the apparition of a woman in her late twenties sitting on a bed in one of the rooms. One guest even reports hearing a woman's voice whispering instructions on how to lace a pair of ladies boots.

The Baroness Inn Bed and Breakfast is located on 206 South Main Street, Milford, Texas 76670. For more information or to book your next stay, visit them online at www.baronessinn.com or call 972.493.9393.

Mineral Wells

Baker Hotel

Opening on November 22, 1929, the fourteen-story hotel claimed 452 rooms, two complete spas, and the first Olympic-size swimming pool in the United States. Many celebrities stayed at the Baker, including Clark Gable, Judy Garland, and even Bonnie and Clyde. The final guest checked out in 1972 and the structure quickly fell into disrepair.

Over its history there have been several events that may have led to a host of hauntings. The first ghostly encounter was recorded in the 1950s when a porter claimed to have seen the apparition of a woman on the seventh floor. Many think she may have been the hotel manager's mistress, who, distraught from the affair, jumped from the top of the building. In 1948, a young bellboy named Douglas Moore was killed when an elevator accident severed his body in half. Some have seen his apparition in the basement where the elevator shaft terminates and say only the upper portion of his body can be seen. One final tale concerns a prostitute working out of a room on the fifth floor named Candy, who was strangled in the bathtub by her pimp. To this day, she is said to appear in the room she died in.

Ghost hunters have recorded a large number of paranormal manifestations here, including cold spots, disembodied voices, EMF fluctuations, photographic anomalies, and apparitions. Psychics brought in claim as many as forty-nine different spirits inhabiting the old hotel.

The Baker Hotel is located at 200 East Hubbard Street, Mineral Wells, Texas 76067.

Fort Wolters

Established as Camp Wolters in 1925, it was named after Brig. Gen. Jacob F. Wolters, commander of the Fifty-sixth Brigade of the National Guard. During the Second World War, the camp became an important infantry training center cycling through as many as 25,000 soldiers. During the war, the camp was also used to house 300 German prisoners of war, which were located in the center of the camp surrounded by a high mesh fence and sentry towers at intervals around the compound. Some German soldiers were buried there and later the bodies were exhumed and sent back to their homeland. Shortly after the war, the camp was deactivated. In 1951, the camp reopened as Wolters Air Force Base and became the Primary Helicopter Center directed by the United States Army. By 1975, however, the camp was once again closed and this time the land and facilities were parceled out to various private and city interests. Several of the fort's structures remain standing today, including a series of military barracks and training buildings.

Those that have paid the old fort a visit claim that the spirit of a soldier haunts one of the deserted buildings. The story surrounding his death is a tragic one and instead of shipping out to fight the Germans in the Second World War, he committed suicide by hanging himself from the barrack rafters.

Fort Wolters is located at 517 Grant Road Mineral Wells, Texas 76068.

Palo Pinto

Palo Pinto Cemetery

Tracing its history to the original land survey for the township in 1855, the burial grounds came to house some of Palo Pinto's most prominent citizens. One day in the 1920s, a man named Earl Allen developed a phobia for being buried alive. To remedy his fear he had a telephone installed in his mausoleum with instructions that if he did not call within three days of his burial, the line could be disconnected.

Now, visitors to the cemetery at night say they have heard the sound of a telephone ringing, but when they attempt to locate the noise, no source can be found. The apparition of a young woman is also seen in the cemetery at night. Tales claim that she approaches cars parked near the cemetery and vanishes just as she looks in the window.

Palo Pinto Cemetery can be visited by traveling north on FM 4 from Highway 20 for thirteen miles. The cemetery gate will appear on the right hand side of the road.

Red Oak

Reindeer Manor

The land that the manor now sits on was first owned by James Sharp, a wealthy banker, who built a two-story wooden house on the site and leased it to a family of Swedish immigrants. In 1915, the homestead caught fire during a lightening storm killing everyone inside, including several small children. Undaunted by the loss of his poor tenants, James Sharp was quick to begin construction on a second house—this time a stately manor designed to be entirely fireproof. Before the completion of the manor, however, James Sharp died in Oak Cliff, Dallas, shot in the head by a women rumored to be his mistress. In 1917, Sharp's son moved into the newly completed manor house with his family and was rumored to engage in "unholy pursuits." By the 1930s, amid tales of insanity, he was found hanging from the rafters of the barn and his wife, dead from poisoning, in the dining room. The manor then sat empty until 1974 when it was converted into a Halloween theme house and has become one of the most popular attractions in North Texas.

Those working in the manor, however, feel that not all the ghosts have rubber masks. Footsteps are heard following staff members around the manor and a painful moaning is heard from the room in which Mrs. Sharp was poisoned. In the attic where the actors get into costume, an invisible presence touches the workers on the shoulder and whispers something that sounds close to "are you here to…" or "have you come to…."

Reindeer Manor is located at 410 Houston School Road, Red Oak, Texas 75154. For more information, visit them online at www.reindeermanor.com.

Rome

Deep Creek Cemetery

Named after the creek and steep banks, the first settlers to the area built their homes next to this cemetery in 1854; the cemetery began when residents built a Baptist church and burial grounds in 1860.

Local legend claims the cemetery contains a tombstone that glows at night and that the apparition of an unknown woman in white wanders among the headstones. Ghost hunters conducting investigations at the site have recorded magnetic disturbances causing compass needles to spin erratically.

Deep Creek Cemetery can be reached by traveling north on FM 4227 from Highway 114 approximately four miles.

Sherman

Woodman's Circle Home

Constructed in 1930 by the Supreme Forest Woodman's Circle, its purpose was to act as a home for the orphans and widows of the Woodman's fraternal organization. The original grounds covered 240 acres, but when the building closed in the 1970s, it was leased to a Reverend Sherman and his cult-like following. After racking up massive debts with the city of Sherman, the cult skipped town and was never heard from again. As the 1980s approached, the building and remaining grounds were purchased by an investment group, which allowed it to fall into ruin. Today, what is left of the gutted structure is owned by a local businessman and regular police patrols help deter trespassers.

For those that have made it inside, they return with tales of strange noises, voices, screams and gunshots. A woman in white wandering through the halls is seen and there are numerous occult symbols spray painted throughout the building.

The Woodman's Circle Home can be found on US 56 and FM 1417 in Sherman, Texas.

Springtown

Carter Ghost Town

Originally known as Carterville, the town sprang up along the banks of the Clear Fork River and was a well-used watering hole for thirsty herds of cattle traveling to market. Like many small frontier towns in Texas, skirmishes with hostile Indians and gunfights between cowboys were not an uncommon occurrence. In time, however, the herds stopped passing through, the flourmill burned, and the population dwindled to nothing. By the 1920s, the only sign that Carter ever existed was an old church with an adjacent tabernacle, the charred foundations of the flour mill, and a series of historical markers recounting the town's colorful history. Yet for the many ghost hunters that have explored the site something else still resides there.

Audio recording of the voices of a little girl and boy have been captured as well as cold spots, orbs, ectoplasmic mist, and feelings of being watched and touched. One ghost hunter was struck by a freezing electrical sensation as if something passed through his body momentarily.

Carter Ghost Town can be found by traveling five miles south on Highway 51 from Springtown. Once you reach Carter Road turn west and travel one mile.

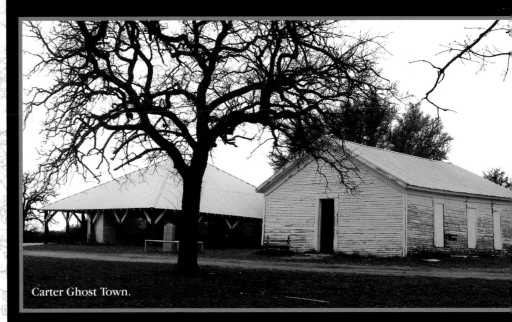

Carter Ghost Town.

VEAL STATION CEMETERY

Veal Station was founded in the 1850s when William Veal first opened a general store in the area. It grew slowly over time and was continually in danger from Indian attacks. To warn the settlers of attack, a giant bronze bell was placed atop the town meeting hall to be sounded when threats were present. Although the town survived repeated Indian skirmishes, it would not survive a lack of commerce, and when the railroad bypassed the settlement, its fate was sealed. By 1936, the only thing remaining of Veal Station was a historical maker and its cemetery.

Over the years, stories began to surface that deep within the lonely burial grounds there is a tombstone that glows with an eerie, greenish light at night—so brightly that it can be seen from the nearby road. The apparition of a woman in white is also said to prowl the grounds and is known to chase out anyone who trespasses on the hollowed soil. Ghost hunters investigating the cemetery report cold spots, photographic anomalies such as orbs and mists, and the fact that the tombstone in question really does glow at night.

The cemetery is located by traveling four miles south of Highway 51 from Springtown. Turn west on Veal Station road and continue for one mile.

THURBER

THURBER GHOST TOWN

The town was founded in 1888 by the Texas and Pacific Coal Company to service mines located in the surrounding hills. Everything from the church to the saloon was owned by the coal company and mineral deposits were so rich throughout the area that, at one time, Thurber supplied half the United States with soft coal. The town continued to prosper until the 1920s when the mines began to lose money. By 1926, the mines had closed for good and the workers moved on to other prospects, leaving behind a ghost town. Residents living near the town are all too familiar with the ghosts said to haunt its deserted streets. The first is the phantom of a woman seen strolling down what was once Main Street singing opera songs. True to form the town once boasted an opera house and the ghost is said to belong to a beautiful opera singer who died following a performance one night. The second is the phantom of another young woman, seen sitting atop a large smokestack that once belonged to the brick-making factory. Legend has it that she died of pneumonia shortly after becoming engaged and that her fiancé dug her body up one night and cut the ring from her finger. From that point on her ghost haunted the area, angry over the desecration of her body.

Thurber is located just off Interstate 20, seventy miles west of Fort Worth.

Waco

BAYLOR UNIVERSITY

Founded in 1845, Baylor is the oldest university in Texas operating under its original name. It is also the home of the Armstrong Browning Library and what some believe is a very famous ghost. The three-story building first opened on February 25, 1950, and was designed as a research library devoted to the works of Robert and Elizabeth Browning. With magnificent stained glass windows, marble columns, and intricate ceiling designs in the Italian Renaissance fashion, it has come to house the world's largest collection of books, letters, and manuscripts related to the two Victorian poets.

Students and faculty have encountered the ghost of what they believe to be Elizabeth Browning floating through the halls at night holding a candle and wearing a white gown. In the October 28, 2005, edition of the university's newspaper, *The Lariat*, Kathryn Brogdon, the library's public relations and facilities supervisor, recounts phantom sounds of footsteps shuffling through the shelves, the feeling of people creeping around, and doors that seem to lock by themselves.

The Armstrong Browning Library is located at 710 Speight Avenue, Waco, Texas 76706. For more information, visit them online at www.browninglibrary.org.

Lindsey Hollow Road

Along the tree-lined road that borders the southwest section of Cameron Park is the story of two horse thieves named the Lindsey brothers and how they met there fate. According to the late historian Roger Conger, in 1880, a group of lawmen arrested the two and were bringing them back to Waco to stand trial when the party was ambushed by a group of vigilantes. The brothers were shot and strung up in a tree 100 feet from the roadway. For those passing by the tree-shrouded lane today, flickering lights, loud bangs, and the sounds of moaning can be heard. Some have even encountered the shadowy images of the two brothers hanging from a tree in the area.

Lindsey Hollow Road lies on the southwestern edge of Cameron Park intersecting North Park Avenue in Waco, Texas.

Waxahachie

Bonnynook Inn Bed and Breakfast

Built in 1887, the Victorian Gingerbread house was first occupied by a Doctor West and his family. In 1895, Mrs. West was mysteriously killed when the kitchen stove exploded; to everyone's surprise, Mr. West in turn married her sister only three months later. The house changed hands many times until 1983 when it became a bed and breakfast. When the current owners began remodeling the house they discovered that one room had remained unexplainably locked and never opened since 1910. The first thing they did of course was unlock it and ever since the room has been plagued by strange happenings.

Guests staying in what is now the Morrow Room report faint voices at night and the image of a person that fades in and out. One guest reports that, during her stay, she heard the sound of a woman singing lullabies in Czechoslovakian.

The Bonnynook Inn Bed and Breakfast is located at 414 West Main Street, Waxahachie, Texas 75165. For more information or to book your next stay, visit them online at www.bonnynook.com or call 972.938.7207.

Catfish Plantation

Built in 1895, the Victorian home with its large porch, bay windows, and white picket fence first belonged to a farmer named Anderson. It remained a private residence until the 1970s, at which time it briefly held a doctor's office and then a series of short-lived restaurants. In 1984, it became the Catfish Plantation, and although it has changed owners over the years, its name and southern cuisine have remained the same. A trio of spirits is thought to haunt the old eatery. The first is known as Caroline, who likes to throw silverware around the kitchen area. Caroline is a former owner who died in the house and still feels she is in charge of the place. The second is an old farmer named Will, a spirit known for his flirtations with the ladies. Will is popular for placing his hand on the knees of young ladies and also moving the salt and peppershakers around on the tables. The final spirit is called Elizabeth, who was murdered on her wedding day by a former lover. She appears in one of the bay windows at night looking out onto the street. Numerous ghost hunters have experienced cold spots, EMF fluctuations, footsteps and glowing balls of light.

The Catfish Plantation is located at 814 Water Street, Waxahachie, TX 75165. For more information, visit them online at www.catfishplantation.com.

Rose of Sharon Bed and Breakfast

In 1892, an attorney named F. P. Powell moved to the small hamlet with his wife and two daughters and built a beautiful two-story home. Business was good for Mr. Powell, and in 1912, he accepted a better position with a firm in Austin and the family moved. The house changed hands many times over the years, even becoming a boarding house in the 1940s. In 1991, renovations began to covert the house into a bed and breakfast.

The current owner of the bed and breakfast, Sharon Shawn, reports that the old house is haunted by a spirit that leaves a warm, comforting impression on those who witness it. She has also witnessed the apparitional image of a family of four in the bathroom area standing together as if they were posing for a portrait. The father is described as wearing a top hat and gray suit, the woman, a long flowing dress from the 1800s, and two little girls in white dresses. Most of the activity seems to center on a room known as Kathleen's Room and guests staying the night report the sound of soft music floating through the house.

The Rose of Sharon Bed and Breakfast is located at 205 Bryson Street, Waxahachie, Texas 75165. To book your next stay, call 972.938.8833.

SOUTHERN PLAINS REGION

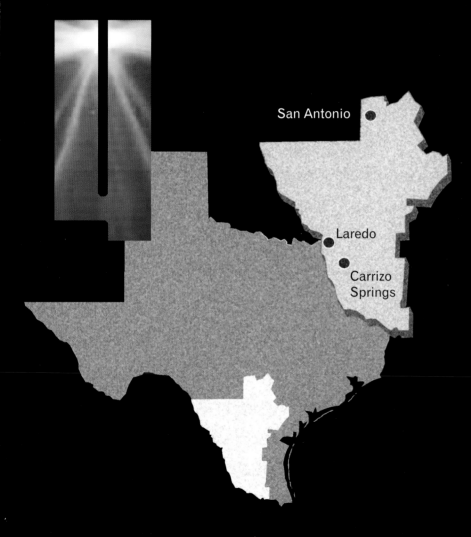

San Antonio

Laredo

Carrizo
Springs

From the rolling edges of the hill country to the humid subtropical reaches of the lower Rio Grande valley lies unbroken plains filled with scraggly mesquite trees and prickly cacti. At night the wind carries the sounds of coyote howls, and when the sun is high overhead, jack rabbits and roadrunners dart from one piece of shade to another. More than other portions of the state, the Southern Plains resemble their Mexican neighbor to the south. Both, after all, share not only a close history, but are linked by a distinct Spanish heritage influencing their customs and traditions as well as their cuisine and architecture. In fact, many Tejanos and Mexicans living in South Texas have families that date back many generations before the U. S. annexation of their lands following the Mexican American War in the 1840s.

One of the first European explorers to visit the area was a man named Alvar Nunez Cabez de Vaca, who stumbled across the area with the aide of local tribes after being shipwrecked. Soon after Alvar filed his report with King Charles V of Spain, the plains saw a new type of visitor as Franciscan monks began establishing missions throughout the region. In addition to the missions, Spanish soldiers constructed presidios or forts to protect their new holdings. The Presidio La Bahia del Espiritu Santo, built in 1721, is in fact one of the oldest forts in the United States. Years later, another Spanish mission became the ground upon which one of the most celebrated battles in the fight for Texas independence took place when a few staunch defenders held out against the overwhelming forces of Santa Anna's army at the Alamo in 1836.

Today, the region continues to be sparsely populated with widely spaced small towns and ranchland. The city of San Antonio remains the area's greatest attraction as the second largest city in the state. Famous for its River Walk, the Alamo, and other attractions, it's often considered by many to be the cultural gateway to the southwest.

Weaving its way through the rich culture of the Southern Plains, are numerous tales of spectral monks wandering through ancient monasteries, of phantom soldiers that still guard the crumbling walls of the Alamo, and of cursed railroad crossings where the dead still linger. The ghostly traditions of the region are in fact so ingrained in the landscape today, that the San Antonio Chamber of Commerce advertises ghost hunts and tours alongside such popular attractions as the Alamo or Six Flags.

Alton

Alton Bus Crash

On September 21, 1989, a school bus collided with a delivery truck at the corner of Five-Mile and Bryan Roads. The collision sent the bus into a forty foot, rain filled, gravel pit and claimed the lives of nineteen children in what was the worst school bus accident to date in Texas history. The incident inspired the Russell Banks' story and movie *The Sweet Hereafter* as well as a few ghost stories.

For those traveling past the scene of the accident at night, the sounds of screams are heard rising from the now fenced-in gravel pit. Others claim to see the apparitions of children sitting on the pit's ledge with their feet dangling over the side.

The site of the crash is located next to a memorial to the victims at Five-Mile and Bryan Road.

Eagle Pass

Eagle Pass Army Airfield

Opening in July of 1943, the facility was used by the United States Army Air Force as an advanced single engine flying school. In the 1950s, the base became the home of a long range radar station until it was closed in 1963. Then, sometime between 1991 to 1994, it operated for a short time as a private airfield named Bowles Airfield.

Yet since the military's final closing of the base, local teens exploring the area have encountered hazy, grayish apparitions and strange noises, such as footsteps and laughter. In addition, the phantom sounds of propeller-driven aircraft has been heard to fill the skies even though they were empty.

Eagle Pass Army Airfield is located eight miles north of Eagle Pass just off Highway 277.

Carrizo Springs

Dimmitt County Courthouse

First built 1884, the imposing gray-colored courthouse remained unchanged until 1926 when it underwent renovations. Although improvements have continued over the years, including the addition of an elevator, it remains much as it did in the 1920s.

Employees working late into the night report the sound of footsteps on the second floor accompanied by the rattling of keys. Many believe the sounds are the manifestation of a former sheriff who worked in the courthouse for many years and was murdered at his home by two men.

Dimmitt County Courthouse is located at 103 North Fifth, Carrizo Springs, Texas 78834.

George West

Live Oak County Courthouse

Built in 1919 by architect Alfred Giles in the Texas Renaissance tradition of red brick and white columns, the three-story structure is well known for the spirits that haunt it. Often visitors to the courthouse report the sounds of children playing and laughing through the halls when they are alone. The south hall of the second floor seems most active, however, with phantom footsteps and the apparition of the city's founder, George Washington West, who is said to occasionally make an appearance. Others believe that a picture in the District Courtroom of an exdistrict judge is haunted and that the eyes follow you wherever you go.

The Live Oak County Courthouse is located at 301 Houston Street, George West, Texas 78022. For more information, visit them online at www.co.live-oak.tx.us.

Laredo

Circle K Convenience Store

For sometime now, clerks and customers alike have spotted the apparition of a little girl wandering through the aisles of the store. Although no one knows her identity, she is described as wearing a sundress and carrying a carton of milk and other groceries. The apparition only lasts a moment or two before disappearing without a sound.

The Circle K Convenience Store is located at 5301 McPherson Road, Laredo, Texas 78041.

Fire Station No. 2

Although there is nothing sinister about the relatively new, red brick building that houses the fire station, the firefighters who live and work there claim it is haunted by a former comrade named Lupito, who in both life and death loved to play jokes. One of his favorite pranks seems to be pulling their legs off the bed while they are trying to sleep. One sleeping firefighter was even levitated completely off the bed one night. Other ghostly acts attributed to Lupito include the violent shaking of furniture and the movement of smaller objects.

Fire Station No. 2 is located at 2200 Zacatecas, Laredo, Texas 78046.

Hamilton Hotel

Built in 1900 as a three-story hotel in the Spanish Colonial design, later additions in various phases during 1924 to 1949 sent it soaring to twelve stories and made it the tallest building in the city at 151 feet. For years the building sat empty after the hotel closed down, but in the 1990s, the city converted the building into apartments for low income elderly residents, naming the complex Hamilton Housing.

The old building has many stories associated with it over the years. One legend states that a series of murders occurred in the hotel, one of which involved the death of a priest who was pushed out of a window. The Padre's death was to have occurred sometime in the 1960s when a local racketeer spotted what he thought was a rival gang member. Acting quickly, the racketeer pushed the man out of an open window to his death, only later to learn it was a case of mistaken identity.

Today, residents of the complex claim to hear the phantom sounds of children playing and running through the halls even though they are empty. In the apartments, furniture moves by itself and lights turn on and off for no reason. Even the apartment elevator functions strangely and moves between floors opening and closing on its own.

The old Hamilton Hotel is located at 1401 Farragut Street, Laredo, Texas 78040.

La Posada Hotel

Built on the foundations of the city's first government—the Casa Judicial—it originated as a Spanish Colonial style convent in 1916. After the convent closed, the building was the city's first high school until 1961 when a former graduate purchased the building and converted it into a luxury hotel named *La Posada,* which means "the inn" in Spanish.

Guests staying the night here are known to witness the apparition of a nun, which roams the halls late at night. Employees also encounter a strange spirit they claim takes on the form of fellow workers and although it appears in every way like the person it mimics, it refuses to utter a word or make a sound. Other spirit-like manifestations include cold spots, objects moving or falling without explanation, and a disembodied voice that calls out your name. Most frequent, however, is the sound of footsteps and running in the St. Augustine Ballroom when it is empty.

The La Posada Hotel is located at 100 Zaragoza Street, Laredo, Texas 78040. For more information or to book your next stay, visit them online at www.laposadahotel.com.

La Posada Hotel. *Courtesy of the La Posada Hotel.*

LAREDO CHILDREN'S' MUSEUM

Occupying what used to be the 1910 chapel hall for Fort McIntosh, the building now hosts exhibits for children, including a computer lab, science displays, and play areas. Before its role as base chapel, the first floor was said to have acted as the fort's morgue and may have given rise to the present haunting. Shadowy figures are sometimes seen moving through the exhibits, disembodied voices can be heard after hours, and cold spots in the shape of bodies can be felt on the floor.

The Laredo Children's' Museum is located at P-56 Fort McIntosh, Laredo Community College, Laredo, Texas 78040.

LAREDO CITY HEALTH DEPARTMENT

Although no one yet knows who or what is haunting the offices of the city's health department, both former and current employees working late at night have witnessed the ghostly forms of apparitions moving through the rooms. Lights turn on and off by themselves and cold spots are felt. Most unnerving, however, is that janitors often find their cleaning supplies missing from their carts even though no one else is around.

The Laredo City Health Department is located at 2600 Cedar Ave, Laredo, Texas 78040. For more information, visit them online at www.cityoflaredo.com.

LAREDO COMMUNITY COLLEGE

Established in 1947 on the former site of the Fort McIntosh Military Base, the campus is well known for being the home of a number of spirits that roam its grounds. Built in 1849, the fort sat at a strategic crossing along the Rio Grande River. During the American Civil War, Confederate troops repulsed three attacks by Federal troops from behind its protective walls. The fort continued to serve the American military until 1946 when it was decommissioned. One year later, when the community college took possession, it simply used many of the fort's existing buildings for classrooms, offices, and student dormitories. Bordering the southern edge of the school's Crispin "Doc" Sanchez Baseball Field lies a plot of land that once functioned as the fort's burial ground. In fact, campus maps still list it as a historical cemetery and it remains undeveloped.

Students and campus security crossing this area have encountered vague, misty apparitions within the limits of the old cemetery as well as the phantom sounds of cannon fire and horses.

The Laredo Community College is located at West End Washington Street, Laredo, Texas. For more information, visit them online at www.laredo.edu.

LAREDO NATIONAL BANK HEADQUARTERS

Built in 1926, the ten-story building, which is the fifth tallest in the city, first served as the Plaza Hotel. In 1976, it was purchased by the Laredo National Bank and converted into their corporate headquarters.

Cleaning staff and security personnel working the night shift have experienced the sounds of people talking in empty rooms and the fleeting glimpse of apparitions moving about. One restroom in particular seems to be especially haunted and it often sounds like someone is moving around when in fact it's empty.

The Laredo National Bank Headquarters is located at 600 San Bernardo Avenue, Laredo, Texas 78040.

OFFICE OF JUSTICE OF THE PEACE OSCAR MARTINEZ

Once a Department of Public Safety office, employees claim that a former DPS officer still patrols the building. Many blame the phantom trooper for turning on and off lights and computers, slamming doors, shuffling papers around, and turning doorknobs. Cold spots are also frequent as well as the feeling of being watched.

The Office of Justice of the Peace Oscar Martinez is located at 8501 San Dario, Laredo, Texas 78045.

RIO GRANDE LEGAL AIDE OFFICE

Established in 1970 as a nonprofit organization providing free legal aid to low income and disadvantaged clients, the large white building that houses their offices are said to be haunted by dark shadowy figures from the past. One dark shadow has been seen moving through the offices to a particular desk where it's known to pause before disappearing. Many of the staff working here believes the offices are built atop an ancient monastery and that the dark shapes are phantom monks associated with the former religious site.

In an effort to capture evidence of the haunting, one employee left a tape recorder on a stairwell over night. When recovered, it was found to have captured the sounds of someone walking up and down the stairs, a pause, and then what sounds like the tape recorder being kicked down the stairs where is was found the next day.

The Rio Grande Legal Aide Office is located at 1702 Convent Avenue, Laredo, Texas 78040. For more information, visit them online at www.tria.org.

RIO GRANDE PLAZA HOTEL

Built in 1975, it was formerly known as the Hilton Hotel. At fifteen stories tall, the tower shaped hotel is one of the few buildings in the city to have a thirteenth floor, which is contrary to the superstitions of most builders in the industry.

Perhaps because of this, the ghost of a former employee is said to have returned to the unlucky thirteenth floor and is seen in a number of rooms as if in the act of cleaning them as he did in life. He is described as wearing a brown hotel uniform, but seems not to be aware of others around him. Also, on the fifteenth floor, scratching sounds in the rooms and stairwell can be heard, objects fall as if from nowhere, and mysterious calls to the front desk late at night that cannot be traced.

The Rio Grande Plaza Hotel can be located at 1 South Main Avenue, Laredo, Texas 78040.

ZACATE CREEK

Along a stretch of the small creek that runs through the La Azteca section of the city, an unusual apparition has been seen out for late night strolls. Although her origins are shrouded in mystery, she is described as wearing a white dress covered in mud. Worse yet, a terrible odor seems to accompany the specter whenever it appears.

She can be seen along the creek bed where Grant Street intersects with San Eugenio Avenue.

Roma

LA MINITA CREEK

The story goes that, in the 1950s, a vehicle traveling across the creek during a storm lost control and plunged into its swollen waters. In it was a family of three, and although the mother and father survived, their eight-year-old daughter did not and her body was never recovered.

Today, motorists traveling across the creek at this exact spot have sighted the misty apparition of a little girl walking along the banks. Others, such as local dove hunters, claim she runs through the field bordering the water's course. Even illegal aliens crossing the border where La Minita Creek flows into the Rio Grande have their stories about her.

The area of the haunting can be found on Old Highway 83, seven miles north of Roma.

MAIN PLAZA OF THE HISTORIC DISTRICT

Surrounded by Spanish colonial structures from the 1840s, the historic cobblestone plaza was once used as the backdrop for the 1953 Marlon Brando movie *Viva Zapata*. Residents of the town are well acquainted with the ghost of a little girl in a beautiful white dress walking through the plaza. Many link her to the accidental death of a young girl in the 1940s, who, while playing in the plaza right before her first communion, struck her head in a fall and died.

The historic plaza is located at 77 Convent Avenue, Roma, Texas 78589.

San Antonio

Alamo Historic Site

Originally named Misión San Antonio de Valero, the *Alamo*, Spanish for "cottonwood," served as home to missionaries and Indian converts for nearly seventy years. During its time as a mission, what is now the Alamo Plaza, was once a burial ground from 1724 to 1793, with historical records showing as many as 1,000 graves. In the early 1800s, the Spanish military stationed a cavalry unit at the mission and later it became a Mexican military post. In 1835, during the Texas Revolution, Ben Milam led a group of volunteers against Mexican troops quartered in the city. After five days of fighting, General Marín Perfecto de Cós and his soldiers surrendered and Milam's men occupied the Alamo. On February 23, 1836, General Antonio López de Santa Anna's army arrived outside San Antonio and laid siege to the old mission for thirteen days. When the smoke cleared, almost 200 rebel Texans and Tejanos, including famous personalities such as David Crockett, Jim Bowie, and William B. Travis, lay dead among the mission's walls.

One of the first ghostly sightings associated with the Alamo occurred almost immediately following the battle. As General Santa Anna marched off to meet his fate with Sam Houston at the Battle of San Jacinto, he ordered some of his men to stay behind and demolish the mission. Those assigned the task reported that, on the first day of the demolition, six *diablos,* or "devils,"

The Alamo. *Courtesy of Todd Toney.*

poured from the gate as they approached, waving flaming sabers and screaming at them. The next day, when the soldiers returned, an apparition again confronted them—this time of a man on one of the walls with ghostly fire in his outstretched hands. The soldiers again fled, never to return, and the Alamo remained standing.

Since that time, a number of paranormal manifestations have been encountered in and around the mission. Visitors to the historic sight have experienced the sounds of screams, explo-

sions, and the faint sound of the *El Deguello,* the Spanish tune for "no quarter." Numerous apparitions are also reported, including a man in soaking wet clothes, a monk kneeling in prayer, a white horse, and a man in buckskin walking through a wall.

The Alamo is located at 300 Alamo Plaza, San Antonio, Texas, 78205. For more information, visit them online at www.thealamo.org.

Bexar County Juvenile Detention Center

Legend has it that portions of the monolithic compound are built on the site of an early Spanish mission and burial grounds. Juvenile detainees wake in the night screaming about Indians in their cell with them as well as fires that do not exist. Even detention officers have had their share of run-ins with the supernatural while working here, reporting the smell of smoke and burning wood when there were no fires. Others have seen the image of an apparition in an older fashion of officer's uniform reflected in the glass of the windows.

The Bexar County Juvenile Detention Center is located at 600 Mission Road, San Antonio, Texas 78210.

Brooks City Base

Located seven miles southeast of the city, the airfield was originally named Brooks Air Force Base after Sidney Johnson Brooks. Brooks was the first flying cadet to lose his life in San Antonio during training prior to the First World War. Brooks Field was used to train cadets in balloon and airship training during the First World War and then later B-52 pilots in the Second World War. Today, it is home to the Aerospace Medical Center, which includes the School of Aerospace Medicine. President John F. Kennedy dedicated the School of Aerospace Medicine in November of 1963, one day before he was assassinated in Dallas, Texas.

Those working at the base claim that, on nights when fog rolls onto the grounds, a mysterious young woman is seen wearing a backpack and moving silently between the buildings. No one knows her identity, but it's said that if the base guards fall asleep on the job, she will wake them up by taping them on the shoulder.

Brooks City-Base is located at 1 BDA Crossing, San Antonio, Texas 78235. For more information, visit them online at www.brookscity-base.com.

Cadillac Bar

This Tex-Mex restaurant has been serving customers for over twenty-five years and boasts that a number of ghosts reside within its walls. Employees of the eatery are convinced that one of the former owners of the business haunts the basement storage area, which they are reluctant to enter at night alone. A second presence, which haunts the kitchen, is thought to be the negative spirit of a former employee named Beatrice, who appears as a thin woman with long stringy hair. She's known to turn the faucets on, throw utensils, knock plates off shelves, and set the alarm off. Two other unknown apparitions have been seen as well, including a man on the back steps and a woman near the party room.

The Cadillac Bar is located at 212 South Flores Street, San Antonio, Texas 78204. For more information, visit them online at www.cadillacbar.com.

Church Bistro and Theatre at King William

Located in the King William Historic District of the city, the gray brick mission-style building was constructed in 1912 and served as the Alamo Methodist Church until 1968. After this period, it sat vacant until 1976, when it was purchased and turned into a restaurant with home-style cooking and a buffet. A short time later a portion was also transformed into the Green Room Dinner Theatre, offering live performances.

The current owners believe that the haunting began after renovations in the 1970s and have counted a number of ghosts in the building. One of the more frequent seems to be a woman in a white flowing gown in the old choir loft that loves to watch the stage rehearsals. Many believe she is the ghost of Margaret Gething, an ailing actress who died in her home a few blocks away in 1975. The second spirit is that of a young boy the staff has named "little Eddie," who delights in playing pranks on the cooks, moving objects, turning lights on and off, and running up and down the theatre aisles. His spirit is said to have come attached to an old rattan wheelchair brought in as a prop for a theatrical performance. One of the final spirits known for making a showing is that of an elderly man in a dark suit who likes to hangout in the belfry and wave to passersby on the street below.

The Church Bistro and Theatre at King William is located at 1150 South Alamo Street, San Antonio, Texas 78210. For more information, visit them online at www.churchbistroandtheatre.com.

COMANCHE LOOKOUT PARK

This ninety-six-acre park filled with native juniper, Texas buckeye, hackberry, and mesquite, was once a lookout point for Apache and then later Comanche Indians. The hill was also a prominent landmark for early settlers traveling along the Old Spanish Road from San Antonio to Bastrop and Nacogdoches in East Texas. In 1923, retired Army Colonel Edward H. Coppock purchased the land, and with the help of his two sons, constructed an impressive compound on the hill, which included a four-story, medieval-style stone tower. In the 1990s, it was purchased by the city and converted into a public park.

For some hiking along the trails that weave their way to its top, the apparitions of Indians have been seen near the summit still spying out the land below.

Comanche Lookout Park is located at 15551 Nacogdoches, San Antonio, Texas 78283.

EMILY MORGAN HOTEL

Named after the woman Texas folklore claims distracted Santa Anna before the Battle of San Jacinto, helping to win the fight, the hotel is one of the most recognizable landmarks in downtown San Antonio and only steps away from the Alamo. Built by architect Ralph Cameron in 1924 as a medical arts building, the Gothic Revival structure rises thirteen stories and is festooned with gargoyles depicting various ailments, such as toothaches and other medical themes. In 1974, the building was converted into modern office space, and ten years following that, it became a hotel.

A number of strange happenings have occurred in the grand old building over the years that have led many to believe it is haunted. Guests staying on the ninth floor often complain of slamming doors and toilet lids and objects that move on their own. In the lobby, cold spots are encountered, and in the basement, which once served as a morgue, dark figures are seen moving about. One of the more frequent manifestations involves a mischievous poltergeist-like entity, which plagues the hotel's elevators. The staff claims that it seems to delight in making calls to the front desk from the elevator phone and pushing the buttons that make it run up and down between floors. Many also think that the hotel is the site of mass burials that followed the fall of the Alamo, which may account for the haunting.

The Emily Morgan Hotel is located at 705 East Houston Street, San Antonio, Texas 78205. For more information or to book your next stay, visit them online at www.emilymorganhotel.com or call 210.225.5100.

FORMER SAN ANTONIO STATE HOSPITAL

Local stories persist that the sounds of screaming and moaning can be heard at night coming from the crumbling ruins of this old mental hospital. Doors slam by themselves, and in the adjacent cemetery, figures can be seen roaming about.

The hospital first opened as the Southwest Lunatic Asylum, in 1892, on the southern edge of the city. Surrounded by pecan trees, the sprawling hospital, which sat on 500 acres, was a self-contained community with its own crops, livestock, and cemetery for the burial of patients whose families failed to claim their bodies. Today, the abandoned structures are only a shell of what they used to be and entering the grounds is both dangerous and illegal if permission is not first sought out.

The Former San Antonio State Hospital is located on South Presa Street, San Antonio, Texas 78201.

MARRIOTT PLAZA SAN ANTONIO

The 246-room hotel is surrounded by lush gardens, courtyards, fountains, and free roaming pheasants and peacocks. It also has the unique distinction of having five historic buildings on the property, which have been renovated and are now used as meeting rooms.

Guests and staff have both encountered the apparition of an unknown woman in a long white dress holding a cat in her arms as she glides through the garden, basement, and upper levels of the hotel. A clue to her identity may be the fact that a former owner of one of the historic buildings that now occupies the grounds hung her cat and then herself in a fit of insanity. Lights are also known to turn on and off by themselves in certain rooms and the drawers at the front desk open on their own.

The Marriott Plaza San Antonio is located at 555 South Alamo Street, San Antonio, Texas 78205. For more information or to book your next stay, visit them online at www.marriott.com/hotels/travel/satpl-marriott-plaza-san-antonio or call 800.421.1172.

McNay Art Museum

Founded by painter and art collector Marion McNay in the 1950s, the museum stands on twenty-three acres of fountains, lawns, Japanese gardens, and fishponds. Once the home of Mrs. McNay, the museum today is rumored to be haunted by her ghost. Night security personnel reports the transparent figure of a woman in the first floor women's bathroom as well as the sound of a female's voice humming in the west wing library. Others have seen what they now call "Old Lady McNay," floating down the art filled halls or passing between buildings.

The McNay Art Museum is located at 6000 North New Braunfels Avenue, San Antonio, Texas 78209. For more information, visit them online at www.mcnayart.org.

The Menger Hotel. *Courtesy of Miller, Hartel & Tharp, Inc and the Menger Hotel.*

MENGER HOTEL

Built in 1859 by William A. Menger, the hotel was constructed on the site of Menger's brewery, the first in Texas. The hotel quickly became a center for the city's social elite as well as hosting such figures as Robert E. Lee, Ulysses S. Grant, Dwight D. Eisenhower, Mae West, and Oscar Wilde. The hotel bar was even used in 1898 by Teddy Roosevelt to recruit his famous Rough Riders for the Spanish-American War. Over time, the hotel continued to grow with new additions to the original structure, increasing its size from a two-story building to a five-story hotel with over 300 rooms.

In addition to its historic past, the Menger boasts that it is haunted by as many as thirty-two spirit entities. One of the most often sighted is that of Sallie White, a chambermaid who was shot by her jealous husband inside the hotel on March 28, 1876. Today, her ghost appears at night in the Victorian Wing, wearing a long, gray skirt, a bandana around her forehead, and carrying a load of towels. Another figure that likes to make his rounds belongs to Captain Richard King, the owner of the King Ranch in South Texas—the largest ranch in the world. King died in the Menger in 1885, and since that time, has been witnessed entering his old suite through a spot in the wall where the suite's door once stood. Another ghostly guest appears in various rooms throughout the older portions of the hotel as an apparition dressed in a buckskin jacket and gray pants. Those encountering this spirit describe it as having a heated conversation with another unseen presence, demanding, "Are you gonna stay or are you gonna go?" three times before vanishing. The Menger's most famous spirit, however, is that of former President Teddy Roosevelt, who has been spotted in the hotel bar as if he were having a drink.

The Menger Hotel is located at 204 Alamo Plaza, San Antonio, Texas 78205. For more information or to book your next stay, visit them online at www.mengerhotel.com or call 800.345.9285.

REGAL ALAMO QUARRY STADIUM 16

Borrowing its design from the surrounding shopping plaza's quarry theme, legend has it that the theater was built on the site of an old cement factory and that there are bodies within the foundation. Staff working in the projection room late at night has seen a young boy running by and disappearing into thin air. On the second floor of the buildings, moviegoers often complain of bone-chilling cold spots. Employees have also noticed that the light within the auditorium slowly dims, and then shines brightly at times for no explainable reason.

The Regal Alamo Quarry Stadium 16 is located at 255 East Basse Road, San Antonio, Texas 78209.

ST. ANTHONY HOTEL

Opening in 1909, the lavish hotel is filled with French Empire antiques, bronze statues, and art from around the world. For all of its elegance, however, some believe it may also be filled with the spirits of long dead employees and guests.

One of its most famous spirits is that of an old woman, whose black shoes have been seen under the stall door in the public restroom. Open the door, however, and there was no one there. Word of the apparition spread and curiosity seekers visiting the restroom to witness the phenomenon became too much for the hotel, which installed a full-length door effectively ending the sightings. A second apparition seen at the hotel is that of a man standing in the doorway to one of the rooms near the elevator. When spotted, he quickly turns and walks through a solid door into one of the guestrooms. In the elevator, a transparent woman in a red dress and a man in a top hat and tails has been known to pop up from time to time. Perhaps the most amusing haunting in the building, however, has to be the ghostly newlywed couple that can still be heard enjoying their wedding night in one of the rooms when it's empty.

The St. Anthony Hotel is located at 300 East Travis Street, San Antonio, Texas 78205. For more information or to book your next stay, visit them online at www. wyndham.com/hotels/satst or call 210.227.4392.

SCHILO'S DELICATESSEN

Serving German-style delicatessen lunches since 1945, its roots run back to Papa Fritz Schilo's 1917 saloon. Just a few steps from the city's river walk, the deli's huge dining room is filled with aging beer signs, German flags, and as some have come to believe, an invisible presence. Lights periodically turn on and off on their own, objects such as utensils and plates move when no one is looking, and employees often catch the glimpse of unusual shadows out of the corners of their eyes. Whatever the presence is, it must like the ladies, because several report being pinched by the entity.

Schilo's Delicatessen is located at 424 East Commerce Street, San Antonio, Texas, 78205.

SHERATON GUNTER HOTEL

Opening its doors on November 20, 1909, the historic Gunter Hotel began as the Frontier Inn in 1837, one year after the fall of the Alamo. At the turn of the century the small inn attracted the attention of a man named Jot Gunter, who purchased the property and added six more stories of steel, concrete, and buff colored brick, making it the largest building in the city at the time. The hotel quickly became a landmark that drew the likes of Mae West, Roy Rogers, John Wayne, Gene Autry, and Presidents Franklin Roosevelt and Harry Truman.

In the 1960s, a grisly murder occurred in the Gunter hotel leading to what maybe a haunting. Records indicate that on February 2, 1965, a man in his late twenties checked into Room 636 under the alias Albert Knox. For the next few days, he was seen in the company of a mysterious and sophisticated blonde woman. On February 8th, a maid entered the room to find Mr. Knox standing next to the bed with the entire room covered in blood from the carpet to the walls. Racing past the frightened maid, the man quickly escaped, but police later tracked him to the St. Anthony Hotel a few blocks away. The suspect, whose real name was Walter Emerick, had taken his own life with a bullet to the head. The woman's body was never found, but to this day, staff and guests report strange occurrences near Room 636. Sounds of hammering are heard coming from the room when it is unoccupied and some have witnessed the brief apparition of the blonde woman with her arms outstretched. Certain members of the maid staff have even quit after cleaning the room and experiencing the phantom for themselves.

The Sheraton Gunter Hotel is located at 205 East Houston Street, San Antonio, Texas 78205. For more information or to book your nest stay, visit them online at www.gunterhotel.com or call 210.227.3241.

SPANISH GOVERNOR'S PALACE MUSEUM

Built in 1749 to protect the Alamo and surrounding colonies from French incursions, the adobe residence with its tree-shaded, cobblestone courtyard, and stone fountain was the seat of government for the Spanish in Texas. A keystone above the building's entrance bears the date of construction and the Hapsburg coat of arms. As Spanish sovereignty ended, the building became a tailor shop and then later a barroom, restaurant, and finally a schoolhouse, until it was restored by the city as a public museum in 1931.

One of the more unusual attractions on the museum grounds is known by the locals as the "tree of sorrow," so named because during its history forty-six convicted criminals were hanged from its branches. Lore has it that the faces of the condemned men can be seen in the patterns of the tree's trunk, grotesquely contorted with pain and agony of their execution. Another source of unusual activity comes from a well in the courtyard, where long ago bandits killed a woman and dumped her body down its shaft to hide the evidence of their misdeed. Workers at the museum claim that, on some nights, the murdered woman's sobs are heard rising from the well. Within the palace itself odd noises are heard, and when the museum staff opens in the morning, they often find the chairs in the hallway rearranged from their previous positions the night before.

The Spanish Governor's Palace is located at 105 Plaza De Armas, San Antonio, Texas 78205.

The Lambermont Inn. *Courtesy of Erica Vasquez and the Lambermont Inn.*

LAMBERMONT INN

Built in 1894 by Edwin Terrell, a prominent lawyer and statesman, the Victorian home was designed to resemble the castles and chateaus Edwin fell in love with while touring Belgium and France. The Terrell family remained in the house until Edwin's death in 1910, at which time it passed through a succession of owners, finally becoming a bed and breakfast in 1986.

Many believe the house to be haunted by the former Mrs. Terrell, who can be sensed in the library and even heard walking up the parlor steps in her high-heeled shoes. The housekeeping staff also report seeing shadows of people on the floor when no one is around.

Lambermont is located at 950 East Grayson Street, San Antonio, Texas 78208. For more information or to book your next stay, visit them online at www.lambermontevents.com or call 210.271.9145.

STINSON MUNICIPAL AIRPORT AND MISSION BURIAL PARK

Many believe the cemetery bordering the northern edge of the airport is haunted by strange blue lights. These spirit lights are said to be so bright that motorists passing along Mission Road have witnessed them on many occasions. Also on Mission Road, which runs through the 1915 airfield founded by the aerial stunt flying Stinson family, is an old corrugated metal hanger used by the airport as storage. Workers at the facility claim that years ago a man was killed there when he accidentally walked into the spinning blade of an airplane propeller. Now his ghost is said to haunt the hanger in the form of cold spots, the sound of footsteps, and the eerie feeling that people get as though they are being watched. The Stinson Municipal Airport is located at 8535 Mission Road, San Antonio, Texas 78214. For more information visit them online at www.nps.gov/nr/travel/aviation/sti.htm.

VICTORIA'S BLACK SWAN INN

Surrounded by a landscape of lush gardens and 100-year-old oak and pecan trees, the southern plantation house with its Greek Revival Colonial architecture is now home to such events as concerts, weddings, and other formal gatherings. Filled with period antiques, crystal chandeliers, and expansive hardwood floors, the 1867 mansion has seen more than its share of history. Archeological evidence suggests that the site once held an early Native American encampment around 1000 AD. Later, in 1842, when the Mexican army attempted to invade Texas a second time, it was at this location that 200 Texans repulsed 1,500 Mexican soldiers under the command of French mercenary Brigadier General Adrián Woll in a skirmish known as the Battle of Salado Creek. Most of the paranormal activity associated with the home surfaced in the 1990s when the current owner, Jo Ann Rivera, purchased the property. For many nights after moving in, she reported waking to the dark figure of a man standing at the foot of her bed, which vanished after a few seconds. Although in time the apparition stopped appearing, other strange occurrences flared up, including lights turning on and off, music coming from the walls, doors locking and unlocking, and unexplained knocking. Once, during renovations to the basement, a workman fearfully complained about the apparition a child that taunted and poked him. A final apparition seen with some frequency is a young woman in 1920s attire walking down the staircase followed by an intense feeling of cold.

Numerous television shows, such as *Sightings*, have featured the house and its ghosts on their program, during which many experienced unusual equipment malfunctions and drained batteries. Ghost hunters investigating the property have also captured what they believe to be EVPs of a man exclaiming, "Oh, shut up."

Victoria's Black Swan Inn is located at 1006 Holbrook Road, San Antonio, Texas 78218. For more information or to book your next stay, visit them online at www.sawhost.com/victoriasblackswaninn or call 210.590.2507.

VILLAMAIN RAILROAD CROSSING

Said to be the location of a tragic accident in the 1930s in which a train struck a stalled school bus killing the ten children inside; the debate over the details and legitimacy of the haunting have raged for years.

Legend has it that if you park your vehicle on the tracks and leave it in neutral, the ghosts of the dead children will push it off to safety. To validate the claim, many coat their bumper with talcum powder and say that afterwards child size handprints can be seen as evidence of the experience. As San Antonio's most famous haunting it has aired on many television programs over the years, including *Unsolved Mysterious* and the *Discovery Channel.* This has led to a massive influx of curiosity seekers every Halloween requiring local law enforcement to direct traffic at the crossing. Even worse, some unsavory characters have used the legend to perpetrate carjackings and other crimes on those venturing out to the location at night.

The Villamain Railroad Crossing is located at the tree lined intersection of Villamain and Shane roads, where the two meet at the railroad tracks not far from the San Juan Mission.

WILLOW RUN APARTMENTS

Once called the Caribbean Apartments, this huge complex is said to have had a high crime rate over the years, resulting in what maybe several hauntings. One unconfirmed report is that a woman was once raped and murdered in an apartment on the north end of the complex. Residents today say that, during the middle of the night, a woman's cries can be heard echoing through the corridors near that area. Others state that somewhere in the complex a young mother died from an overdose of pain medication leaving her two-year-old baby to starve to death before the two were discovered. Those living under the scene of the tragedy report that, when the apartment is empty, they can hear the sounds of a woman crying, toilets flushing, loud thumps, and that the lights often turn on and off by themselves. Although no one seems to know just which apartment it is, they all claim it never stays occupied for long.

The Willow Run Apartments is located at 7543 Sea Lane, San Antonio, Texas 78216.

The Witte Museum. *Courtesy of the Witte Museum.*

WITTE MUSEUM

Opening in 1926, the museum hosts exhibits and interactive learning activities of South Texas history, culture, and natural science. Many working in the museum have come to think the ghost of former founder and director Ellen Schultz Quillen haunts it. Footsteps and the sound of a chair being dragged across the floor are heard in the museum attic and a shadowy figure lurks about some of the displays. In the offices, paperwork disappears from desks and is found in other locations and doors lock and unlock by themselves.

The Witte Museum is located at 3801 Broadway, San Antonio, Texas 78209. For more information, visit them online at www.wittemuseum.org.

HILL COUNTRY REGION

Fredericksburg

Austin

Kerrville

Formed approximately thirty million years ago, when the earth heaved and buckled pushing up a stratum of limestone, the formation eventually wore down into the series of rugged hills now comprising the central portion of the state. Over time, lakes and rivers filled the region as oak, ash, and juniper brakes sprouted among the hillsides. Wildflowers also came to flourish in the region and are today a popular roadside attraction for tourists looking to get a good picture.

The region first began intense settlement in the 1840s when an influx of immigrants from central Europe poured into the area searching for a new home. Many newcomers were of German Hessin and Lower Saxon descent, which established picturesque little towns throughout the region bearing names such as Frederiscksburg and New Braunfels. This led to a cultural fusion of Spanish and European influences on the food, beer, music, and architecture of the area, giving it a distinction all its own. Not to be outdone by the rest of the state, the hill country also emerged as a leader in Texas wine production. Now each year, thousands of tourists flock to the grape-covered slopes of the hill country vineyards for a tour of the wineries and a chance to taste some of the best wines Texas has to offer.

The heart of the region, however, remains the state capital of Austin, which was named after Stephen F. Austin, the "Father of Texas" when the city was chosen to become the capital of the newly independent Republic of Texas in 1839. In addition to becoming a center for business and technology, the city has adopted the official slogan of the "Live Music Capital of the World" and has more live music venues per capita than any other U. S. city.

However, when the sun sets behind the hills and their slopes run from twilight red to darkest night, stories of the dead returning to walk the earth again come to life. From the tales of tragic spirits in the State Capitol Building to the moonlit cemeteries of small German towns, the hills are filled with the sounds of its ghosts.

Austin

Austin's Inn at Pearl Street

Built in 1896, the Greek Revival home first appeared on records in 1914, as the private residence of 26th Judicial District Judge Charles A. Wilcox and his family. In the early 1980s, the home was used as a movie set before being abandoned until 1993, when it was purchased and refurbished as a bed and breakfast.

It was during the renovations that signs of a haunting were first known to have occurred. Workers reported strange noises and the feeling of being watched. Several refused to stay the night out of fear that ghosts inhabited the house. One carpenter on the project witnessed the apparition of a woman carrying a small child from one room to another. On another occasion, the same man also spotted her sitting in a rocking chair, swaying the small child back and forth.

The inn's owner, Jill Bickford, has also had a few encounters of her own. One night during the renovations, she arrived to find a light on in an upstairs window. This surprised her because the home had yet to be wired for electricity. Circling to the back of the house for a better view, she was more taken aback when the light suddenly extinguished.

Austin's Inn at Pearl Street is located at 1809 Pearl Street on Judge's Hill, Austin, Texas 78701. For more information or to book your next stay, visit them online at www.innpearl.com or call 800.494.226.

Austin Pizza Garden. *Courtesy of owner Brian Abart.*

Austin Pizza Garden

James Andrew Patton first constructed the building in 1898 in the style of the early German rock buildings found in central Texas. Patton, a Texas Ranger and fierce Comanche fighter, settled here and operated a general store out of the building for many years. Later the structure housed a local Woodmen of the World lodge on the second floor before becoming a family run pizzeria.

During the many years it served as a restaurant, both the employees and the patrons report seeing the images of faces appearing and disappearing on its stone walls. Although they appear as a hazy, grayish image, the faces are said to be definitely male. Cold spots also felt in the dining area and one manager witnessed silverware flying across the room.

The Austin Pizza Garden is located at 6266 Highway 290 West, Austin, Texas 78735. For more information, visit them online at wwwaustinpizzagarden.com.

CARRINGTON'S BLUFF BED AND BREAKFAST

Carrington's began in 1877 when a shopkeeper named L. D. Carrington purchased twenty-two acres on a tree-covered bluff in central Austin and built an English country house. Today, the bed and breakfast sits on one acre of land and includes both the main house and a small cottage added in 1920, decorated with English and American antiques.

Guest staying the night in this charming inn often feel as if they are being watched by an invisible presence and footsteps can be heard coming from empty parts of the house. In addition, guests often return to their room after an outing to find their possessions moved from where they left them and the televisions have the odd habit of turning on by themselves precisely at midnight. One guest reports that while shampooing his hair in the shower, he felt an invisible hand gently massage his scalp.

Carrington's Bluff Bed and Breakfast is located at 1900 David Street, Austin, Texas 78705. For more information or to book your next stay, visit them online at www.carringtonsbluff.com or call 888.290.6090.

DAVID GRIMES PHOTOGRAPHY

Records indicate the building first began in 1874 when an Italian immigrant named Michael Paggi opened a blacksmith and repair shop on the site. In 1911, a rather "dapper" black businessman and funeral director named Nathan Rhambo purchased the building and operated a funeral parlor. Fate would conspire against Rhambo, however, and in 1932, he was lured from his place of business by an unknown man and murdered.

When David grimes took the place over in 1993, and converted the old structure into a photography studio he found many relics from the building's past, including a few ghosts. Most of the activity began when the building was first converted into a studio. Electricians complained that each day they returned to the studio, they found the work they accomplished the day before completely undone. In some cases, heaps of electric wiring would be found piled on the floor. Objects also had a way of acting strangely in the studio. Once, when David placed an empty pint glass on the table, he was amazed when, a few moments later, it split in half vertically. A small remote control car is also known to take off through the studio by itself as if possessed—even after the batteries have been taken out. Finally, the apparition of a woman is occasionally seen standing in the doorway that leads to where the bodies were kept on ice while it was a funeral home. Mostly seen from the corner of the eye, she immediately disappears as soon as the witness turns to look directly at her. A psychic recently toured the building and noted that it was occupied by as many as three ghosts; a black man, a woman, and a little girl.

David Grimes Photography is located at 503 Neches Street, Austin, Texas 78701. For pictures of the apparitions captured by photography check out www.davidgrimes.com.

DRISKILL HOTEL

Built by the wealthy cattle baron Jesse Driskill, the ornate, sixty room, Romanesque style structure opened on December 20, 1886, and was known at the time as "The finest hotel south of Saint Louis." In short order, Driskill lost his fortune in bad cattle drives, and according to legend, he lost the hotel in a hand of poker. The hotel continued to change hands over the years and periodically underwent modernizations.

The one thing said to stay constant over time is the large number of spirits rumored to haunt it. One is thought to be the four-year-old daughter of a U. S. Senator, who fell down the hotel's grand staircase to her death. Many have heard the sound of her laughter and that of a bouncing ball on the stairs. Another apparition is that of Peter J. Lawless, who lived in the hotel from 1886 to 1916. He is mostly seen on the fifth floor near the elevators looking at his watch. A third ghost, known as Mrs. Bridges, is believed to be a former employee who worked the front desk. At times, she is spotted in a Victorian dress walking from the vault to the middle of the lobby where the front desk once stood. One of the more interesting stories involves a Houston socialite who fled to the hotel after her fiancé broke off their engagement in the 1990s. It's said she booked a one-week stay, went on a shopping spree with his credit card, and then shot herself in the bathtub of her room. She is known to appear coming out of the elevator on the fourth floor with a large number of packages in her arms. One final manifestation involves the painting of a little girl holding flowers on the third floor. Some standing in front of it claim that an invisible force tries to lift them up into the air, leaving them feeling strange for hours afterwards.

Driskill Hotell. *Courtesy of Cynthia Maddox and the Driskill Hotel.*

The Driskill Hotel is located at 604 Brazos Street, Austin, Texas 78701. For more information or to book your next stay, visit them online at www.driskillhotel.com or call 800.252.9367.

NEILL-COCHRAN HOUSE MUSEUM

Built in 1855 by Abner Cook, who also built the Texas Governor's mansion, this elegant example of Greek Revival architecture with its towering Doric columns first served as a school for the blind after the initial owners were financially ruined by its construction. At the close of the American Civil War, General George Armstrong Custer used the house as a headquarters for troops and later as a hospital for soldiers stricken with yellow fever. Many of those who died from the epidemic were buried on the grounds of the estate. In 1876, it was purchased and occupied by Colonel Andrew Neill, and in 1895, by Judge Thomas Beauford Cochran, both of whom give the house its name today. In 1958, it was purchased by The National Society of the Colonial Dames in America in The State of Texas and is open to the public for tours.

Many of the residents living near the house report seeing the apparition of Colonel Neill riding a white horse on the grounds that surround the house. Others have seen his figure sitting on the balcony or even at times on the front porch. The sounds of invisible booted footsteps are also heard both in the house and on the surrounding grounds.

The Neill-Cochran House Museum is located at 2310 San Gabriel Street, Austin, Texas 78705. For more information, visit them online at www.neill-cochranmuseum.org.

The Haunted Grand Lobby.

OMNI HOTEL

Located in the heart of downtown Austin, the luxury hotel has been plagued by reports of a haunting since the death of one of its guests. Little is known about the man in question, other than that his name was Jack and that he appeared to commit suicide by jumping from the balcony of his suite. In a bit of macabre irony, because he died without paying his hotel bill, his name still registers in the hotel computer as staying in the room. Members of the hotel staff claim to hear his spirit moving around the room when it is empty and guests staying in the room report other bizarre sounds as well.

The Omni Hotel is located at 700 San Jacinto Blvd, Austin, Texas 78701. For more information or to book your next stay, visit them online at www.omnihotels.com or call 512.476.3700.

PARAMOUNT THEATRE FOR THE PERFORMING ARTS

The site of the Classical and Baroque Revival style theatre was once home to Sam Houston's office, the War Department of the Republic of Texas, and later the Avenue Hotel. As Austin's oldest surviving theatre, it opened its doors on October 11, 1915, under the name Majestic Theatre, which hosted vaudeville acts, silent movies, and Broadway hits. Even the legendary escape artist and spiritualist debunker Harry Houdini graced its stage for a performance.

According to her book *Haunted Texas Vacations,* Lisa Farwell writes that actors and employees have witnessed ghostly lights in the projection room, felt a presence behind them on the stairs, and watched props move across the stage on their own. In one story, a stagehand fell asleep on a couch near the stage. When he awoke, it felt as if someone was holding him down and an electrical charge was passing through his body.

The Paramount Theatre for the Performing Arts is located at 713 Congress Avenue, Austin, Texas 78701. For more information, visit them online at wwwaustintheatre.org.

ST. EDWARD'S UNIVERSITY

Founded in 1873 by the Reverend Edward Sorin of the Holy Cross Fathers and Brothers, the main building of the private Catholic University is a four-story Gothic structure constructed with local white limestone. In the spring of 1903, a mysterious fire destroyed the main building, but by the fall of that year it was restored to its original condition. In 1973, the building was added to the National Register of Historic Places. A second major disaster occurred in 1922 when a tornado swept through Austin damaging buildings on the campus and killing one student. In the end, the university weathered these storms and today has a student body of about 5, 000. The campus is said to contain several buildings that are haunted by what might be former students and faculty.

The first is Doyle Hall, which opened in 1960 and although it was at times an all men's dorm and later a girl's dorm, it is now coeducational. Many believe the dorm is haunted by the spirit of a nun who walks the halls late at night. She is also known to turn the showers on when no one is around.

The second location is Premont Hall, a recently renovated office building for faculty and staff. It's said that one spring break when the hall was an all-male residence, a student returned to the dorm earlier than most, and while taking a shower, slipped on the wet tile and died. An entire week went by before the other students began returning and discovered his body. His spirit is now said to violently slam doors and windows throughout the building.

The final building is the 180-seat Mary Moody Northern Theatre, where the spirit of a former suicide is rumored to remain. The story is that a young man hung himself from one of the weighted ropes that holds props above the stage. Some claim that they have seen his apparition swinging from a noose, complete with the sounds of a creaking rope.

St. Edward's University is located at 3001 south Congress Ave, Austin, Texas 78704. For more information, visit them online at or www.stedwards.edu.

SPAGHETTI WAREHOUSE RESTAURANT

Located in what was once the warehouse district of the city, the 1870s brick building was once a brothel when the area was a red light district called "Guy's Town." After the famous Italian eatery moved in to the building, employees began to experience strange events. Much of the activity seems to center on the second floor, where the employees have their break room. Strange noises are heard when walking up the stairs and the lights often flicker on and off by themselves. On the first floor, the apparition of a little boy is seen running and laughing in the direction of the restrooms. Also many employees refuse to go down to the basement because of a strong presence of someone watching them and cold spots.

The Spaghetti Warehouse Restaurant is located at 117 West Fourth Street, Austin, Texas 78701. For more information, visit them online at www.meatballs.com.

TAVERN RESTAURANT AND BAR

According to historical records, the building was built in 1916 as a grocery store on the outskirts of town. R. Niles Graham hired architect Hugo Kuehne, who brought the building plans from Europe and modeled the house after a German Public House. The Enfield Grocery Store, as it was known, continued until 1929 when it moved next door so that a steak restaurant could open. Steaks were sold there for fifty cents and legend tells that the second floor included a speakeasy and brothel. When prohibition ended in 1933, the restaurant became a bar and today continues to function as such with over fifty television sets mounted on the walls throughout.

Many patrons believe that the ghost of a prostitute they've named Emily and her daughter haunts the place. It's thought the two were killed when a fight broke out between customers in the 1940s. The apparition of Emily has been spotted walking through the kitchen late at night and is blamed for breaking plates and glasses as well as switching the stations on the television sets. Her daughter is also seen looking out the windows at night after closing.

The Tavern Restaurant and Bar is located at 922 West Twelfth Street, Austin, Texas 78703. For more information, visit them online at www.austintavern.com.

TEXAS GOVERNOR'S MANSION

In 1854, the Texas Legislature appropriated $14,500 for construction of a "suitable residence" for the Governor of Texas. Built by an Austin architect named Abner Cook, the mansion adopted a style of Greek Revival architecture, including a deep veranda, floor-length windows, sixteen-foot ceilings, and twenty-nine-foot Ionic columns. Two earthbound specters are thought to be responsible for the haunting. The first is none other than the state's third governor himself, Sam Houston, who stepped down from the governorship after refusing to support the Confederacy. His apparition has been seen in a corner of the Houston bedroom and was reported by both the wife and daughter of Governor Mark White in the 1980s. The more frequent phantom, however, belongs to the nephew of Governor Pendleton Murrah, who in 1864, committed suicide after his marriage proposal to a young woman was refused. Soon after his death, doors began to open on their own, cold spots appeared, and a terrible moaning rose from the bedroom where he killed himself. Servants refused to enter the room, and just after the American Civil War, Governor A. J. Hamilton had it sealed. The haunting seemed to die down after that, but when the room was reopened in 1952 it began again.

The Texas Governor's Mansion is located at 1010 Colorado Street, Austin, Texas 78701. For more information, visit them online at www.txfgm.org.

Texas State Capitol Building

The domed structure that rises above East Eleventh Street is the state's fourth capitol building. Constructed between 1882 and 1888 by Abner Taylor, the building was designed in the Renaissance Revival style and modeled after the national capitol in Washington. Upon completion, the Capitol building contained 392 rooms, 18 vaults, 924 windows, and 404 doors. From the ground floor to the statue of the Goddess of Liberty atop the dome, the building is 311 feet tall. In February 1983, a fire badly damaged the east wing of the Capitol calling for extensive renovations.

From its very beginning the grounds and Capitol building are thought to have been haunted. A story predating the Capitol building appeared in print in 1898, and tells of an army scout and a Comanche girl who fell in love and planned to run off one night. Before they could make their getaway, however, they were discovered by the girl's father, who killed the scout on the grounds where the Capitol was later built. In her grief, the Comanche girl committed suicide and the two have been spotted ever since wandering the grounds late at night.

Some think the building may also be haunted by the former state comptroller, Robert M. Love, who on June 30, 1903, was shot to death at his desk by a deranged coworker named W. G. Hill. Since the shooting, the figure of a man wearing clothing from that period has been recorded on security cameras walking through the halls. When police approach the figure, he turns and vanishes into the wall. One final ghost that inhabits the rooms of the Capitol may belong to a man named Mathew Hansen, a horse trainer for the daughter of the former Lieutenant Governor. In the 1983 fire that swept through the building, Hansen became trapped while staying in the Lieutenant Governor's apartment. Although he tried to escape through a window, which had been sealed shut, he died from smoke inhalation. After the apartment was restored, cleaning crews continued to report fingerprints on the glass window right after they'd cleaned it. EVPs taken throughout the building include voices saying "Senator, let's run him," "Thank you Frank," and the word "half-breed."

The Texas State Capitol Building is located at 112 East Eleventh Street, Austin, Texas 78701. For more information, visit them online at www.senate.state.tx.us.

University of Texas at Austin

Founded in 1883, it currently has the largest enrollment of all colleges in the state of Texas with 50,000 undergraduate and graduate students and over 16,000 faculty and staff members. Two structures occupying the campus grounds have over the years developed a reputation for being haunted. The first and most well known is the university's main building with its 305-foot-tall tower. Built by Paul Cret of Philadelphia, it was completed in 1937 and attracts over 20, 000 visitors a year. Although a distinctive landmark at the university, it has also been the site of much tragedy. In 1935 a construction worker plummeted twelve stories to his death and in the years that followed numerous suicides have occurred from the tower's top.

Its most publicized tragedy, however, occurred in 1966, when Charles Whitman climbed to the tower's observation deck with a rifle and began firing on the students below. The shooting raged for ninety-six minutes before he was shot dead by Austin Police. In all, seventeen people died, including Whitman, his mother, and his wife, whom he murdered before climbing the tower. Those visiting the tower today claim to feel cold spots on the observation deck and the sensation of being watched. Campus security also reports strange sounds in the tower and lights that turn on and off on their own.

On the west side of the campus is a second location known as the Littlefield House. Built in 1893 by cattle baron, banker, and southern Confederate officer, Major George Littlefield was a large contributor to the university in its early years. The rambling structure is an eclectic example of Victorian architecture with a deep veranda, intricate iron grillwork, and blue-gray marble columns. It's also a place of great mystery where numerous ghost stories abound. Legend holds that whenever the Major was away from home, he locked his wife, Alice, in the attic to protect her from Union soldiers. On one such confinement, bats attacked Alice, and to this day, her screams are said to occasionally echo through the house. Other stories claim that towards the end of Alice's life she became depressed and was afraid to leave the house. After her death in 1935, the home was donated to the university and has served as its music hall, Navy ROTC, and today is used for special presidential functions. Some report witnessing the apparition of Alice roaming the attic of the house and looking out of its windows. Other reports include the sensation of being watched and objects moving on their own in the house.

The University of Texas at Austin is located at 2400 Inner Campus Drive, Austin, Texas 78712. For more information, visit them online at www.utexas.edu.

Brady

McCulloch County Courthouse

Built in 1899 by the architectural firm of Martin and Moodie in the Romanesque style from native limestone, this towering structure may be haunted by several specters from its past. In the county clerk's office, the record vault often closes by itself, and on some occasions, ledgers that were locked in over night have been found taken out and opened the next morning. One judge working in the building alone at night also claims that the elevator moves between floors by itself and that muffled voices and cold spots are not uncommon. Finally, after a picture was taken of the building's exterior one night, it revealed the image of an older man in the window of the sheriff's office wearing 1800s clothing and a badge.

The McCulloch County Courthouse is located at 104 North College Street, Brady, Texas 76825. For more information, visit them online at www.co.mcculloch.tx.us.

Soldier's Waterhole

During the 1800s, this watering hole and natural rock fortification served as a way stop for early settlers traveling west before the American Civil War. U. S. Soldiers under the command of Robert E. Lee also used the site while patrolling the nearby military road for hostile Indians. The "Soldier's Waterhole" as it became known was also the site of a terrible massacre in which twenty-seven Indians surprised a group of settlers bedding down for the night. In all, eighteen men, women, and children were killed, their wagons were burned, and their horses stolen. Shortly after the attack, the U. S. Calvary buried the bodies in unmarked graves at the location and today a historical plaque marks the site.

Those who have visited the waterhole at night report the sounds of screams and battle as if the massacre were being replayed right before them. Others claim to see camp fires at the site as they approach, which disappear the closer they get to it.

The Soldier's Waterhole is located at 2120 Farm Road 412, Brady, Texas 76825.

Brownwood

Flat Rock Park on Lake Brownwood

Also known as the Brownwood Reservoir, the 7,300-acre artificial lake rests eight miles north of Brownwood, in north central Brown County on the Pecan Bayou. On the southern shores of the lake lies Flat Rock Park, a small recreational area popular with local boating enthusiasts.

Legend tells of a small girl who drowned in the Pecan Bayou before the lake was created in 1933. Some have heard her laughter at night in the park, while others have witnessed her apparition running down the dock and vanishing. Over the years, numerous drowning deaths have occurred in this portion of the lake and boaters report unexplained malfunctions with their watercraft while attempting to use the boat ramp.

Flat Rock Lake is located at 332 Flatrock Road, Brownwood, Texas 76801. For more information, visit them online at www.flatrockpark.net.

Fischer

Stage Stop Ranch Bed and Breakfast

Located at the base of the Devil's Backbone region near Highway 32, the Ranch has been a stagecoach stop for weary travelers making their way between San Antonio and Austin since the 1860s. Legend has it that to the left of the ranch's main plaza is a tree that was used to hang a man for killing the sheriff's deputy. His corpse was left to hang in the hot Texas sun until the buzzards picked him clean. Now, there are those who say that if you approach tree at midnight, you can see the apparition of the man hanging from one of the branches and hear the sound of wagon wheels passing by.

The Stage Stop Ranch Bed and Breakfast is located at 1100 Mail Route Road, Fischer, Texas 78623. For more information, visit them online at www.stagestopranch.com.

FREDRICKSBURG

National Museum
of the Pacific War.

NATIONAL MUSEUM OF THE PACIFIC WAR

Once a steamboat-shaped hotel owned by Fleet Admiral Chester W. Nimitz' grandfather, a former seaman in the German Merchant Marine, the museum is the only institution in the United States dedicated to telling the story of the Pacific battles of World War II. The complex includes the National Museum of the Pacific War, the George Bush Gallery, the Admiral Nimitz Museum, the Japanese Garden of Peace, the Pacific Combat Zone, the Plaza of the Presidents, the Surface Warfare Plaza, the Memorial Wall, the Veterans Walk of Honor, and the Center for Pacific War Studies. The 34,000 square feet of exhibit space includes displays of Allied and Japanese aircraft, tanks, and guns from the Pacific War.

Employees working late into the night report seeing the shadows of men in World War II military uniforms roaming the exhibits and hearing the invisible tread of footsteps. Lights have also been known to turn on and off when now one is around.

The National Museum of the Pacific War is located at 340 East Main Street, Fredericksburg, Texas 78624. For more information, visit them online at www. nimitz-museum.org.

KERRVILLE

SCHREINER UNIVERSITY

Founded by a former Texas Ranger, Captain Charles Schreiner, and the Presbyterian Church, the school first began in 1923, as a military academy for young boys. By 1971, however, military training was discontinued and the school became fully coeducational. Today it stands as a private liberal arts university of about 1,000 students.

Many of the students who attend the university are well aware of the rumors that one dormitory on campus, named Delaney Hall, is haunted by the spirits of those who have died here over the years. Some are said to have died by accident, such as one student who fell down the stairs and died in the 1950s; others supposedly died by their own hand, with at least one student known to have committed suicide in the dorm in the 1960s. Now, hazy apparitional figures are seen in the hall at night. Cold spots are felt in certain rooms and televisions and radios turn on by themselves. In one incident when the building was empty campus security watched lights in the hall turning on and off rapidly. When the police department arrived, the lightshow stopped and the building proved to be empty.

Schreiner University is located at 2100 Memorial Boulevard, Kerrville, Texas 78028. For more information, visit them online at www.schreiner.edu.

Y.O. Ranch Resort Hotel and Conference Center

Now a historic hotel, the land was part of Captain Charles Schreiner's immense Y.O. Ranch in 1880, which encompassed over 600,000 acres of the Texas Hill Country and more than 300,000 head of Longhorn cattle. Filled with dark, rich wood, exotic game trophies, and Old West memorabilia, the hotel stands as a tribute to Texas's frontier heritage.

Staff and guests alike report seeing the apparitions of cowboys sauntering through its courtyard at 3 am near the swimming pool. Any attempt to approach these phantom cowpokes, however, causes them to vanish into thin air. Another curious apparition can be encountered in the hotel's Branding Iron Restaurant. Restaurant wait staff report a phantom patron that approaches them asking where the bathroom is. The manifestation appears so life like that the employee directs them to the bathroom, but after the patron doesn't return, the bathroom is checked and found to be empty.

The Y.O. Ranch Resort Hotel and Conference Center is located at 2033 Sidney Baker, Kerrville, Texas 78028. For more information, visit them online at www.yoresort.com.

Killeen

Hastings Books, Music, & Video

Managers of the store report seeing a misty, human-like figure floating through the store's offices and merchandise aisles. The unknown ghost is known to knock magazines off their racks and cold spots can be felt in the manager's office. When the building was previously a Randall's Food Store, there were stories of workers opening up in the morning to find cans of food mysteriously stacked in pyramids in the middle of the aisles.

Hastings Books, Music, & Video is located at 2200 East Veterans Memorial Boulevard, Killeen, Texas 76543.

Lockhart

Caldwell County Historical Museum

Built in 1908 as the Caldwell County Jail, the five-story, red brick structure is a rare example of the Norman castellated style of architecture. Containing nine cells divided into smaller sections on the upper three floors, the building also contains a basement for storage and a ground floor once used as the residence of the County Sheriff. Originally, the jail began as a log cabin, which burned down in 1858. Prisoners were then kept in the courthouse basement until 1873 when increased outlaw activities forced the county to build a stronger limestone structure downtown. Later this too was replaced by the current building, which in turn closed in the 1970s and became a museum in 1991.

Many deaths are said to have occurred here during its history, which may have left strong residual impressions from the past. Visitors to the museum claim the upper three floors where the prisoners were kept gives off such strong feelings of sadness and pain, and that for some, it becomes hard to breathe.

The Caldwell County Historical Museum is located at 315 East Market Street, Lockhart, Texas 78644. For more information, visit them online at www.lockhart.net/history/.

Maxdale

Maxdale Cemetery

Established in the 1860s for the small community of Pleasant Grove, this cemetery is one of the oldest in Bell County. Of the 260 known interments, the earliest grave is that of Louisa Marlar (1849-1867). Others include pioneer settlers and veterans of the American Civil War, World War I, World War II, and Korea.

Legend has it that the burial grounds are haunted by the apparition of an older man that moves with a limp, who some believe may have been the former undertaker. Before reaching the cemetery, there is a small iron bridge which shares in the legend. It's said that if someone parks their car on the bridge at night, turns off the head lights, and counts to ten, that when they turn them back on the ghost of the old undertaker will appear in front of them. Ghost hunters visiting the area report strange anomalies such as glowing orbs in their photographs. Unfortunately, this quiet country cemetery has also been plagued by vandalism recently, with over twenty century-old headstones smashed or tipped over.

Maxdale Cemetery is located at the intersection of Maxdale and Wolf Ridge roads south of FM 2670.

New Braunfels

ADOBE VERDE RESTAURANT

Located in the Gruene Historic District, the Tex-Mex restaurant is a wooden building with corrugated tin siding covered in colorful signs. Before it became a spicy eatery the building was the town's electric cotton gin in the 1920s. During that time, a groundskeeper named Frank hung himself from the rafters after losing a loved one. Now the spirit of Frank is thought to roam the restaurant playing practical jokes on the employees. Some of the antics include turning the lights off, throwing objects off of the counter, and knocking glasses together. Others have heard the sound of booted feet running back and forth across the upstairs dinning area, but when they investigate the sounds they find no one there.

The Adobe Verde Restaurant is located at 1724 Hunter Road, New Braunfels, Texas, 78130. For more information, visit them online at www.adobeverde.com.

FAUST HOTEL

Walter Faust Sr., a New Braunfels' businessman, first opened the doors to this four-story hotel in 1929, calling it the Traveler's Hotel. Throughout the Great Depression, the hotel remained open, and in 1936, it was renamed the Faust Hotel. After World War II, the hotel was purchased by Arlen Krueger, who was unsuccessful at running it, and for the first time since its opening, it closed its doors in 1975, falling into ruin. In 1977, it was purchased and renovated and today maintains its elegance with finely crafted furniture, a mirrored elevator, artwork from the 1930s, an antique grand piano, and a vintage microbrewery known as the Faust Brewing Company.

Besides its obvious charm, the hotel is said to sport a few ghosts as well. One is thought to be former owner Walter Faust Sr., who is spotted roaming the halls on the fourth floor. Known for always being a practical joker he is now blamed for opening and closing doors, rearranging furniture, and turning the faucets on in Room 218 late at night. One employee reports seeing a portrait of Mr. Faust in the hallway leading to the basement glowing at night, even though a thunderstorm had cut the power to the hotel. Another employee who worked there for many years remembers that each night, at the same time, the elevator opened its doors, even though it was empty. Other ghosts said to haunt the hotel include a little girl nicknamed Christine. One night, a hotel maid walked into the hallway and noticed a small girl standing next to her cleaning cart. When she approached the cart, the little girl turned and ran into a solid wall, vanishing from sight. It was later discovered that, at that exact spot, there was once a door leading to a series of suites.

The Faust Hotel is located at 240 South Seguin Avenue, New Braunfels, Texas 78130. For more information or to book your next stay, visit them online at www.fausthotel.com or call 830.625.7791.

KARBACH HAUS BED AND BREAKFAST

A wealthy dry goods merchant named George Eiband and his wife, Hulda, first built the two-story home with its expansive wraparound porch, shaded by ancient pecan, cypress, and magnolia trees. In 1938, a prominent doctor and his wife named Karbach purchased the house and renovated the structure. Today, the home is a bed and breakfast owned by Ben and Kathy Kinney, who take great pride in tracing their roots to one of the first German families to settle the area.

Since converting the home into a bed and breakfast in 1987, the owners report a number of strange occurrences they attribute to both spirits of deceased relatives and some of the former owners of the home. Many times while guests are sleeping, the sounds of children running through the house laughing and playing can be heard. Also, lights left on, often turn off by themselves, and items left out, are put back where they belong. Kathy believes this spiritual house cleaning may be the activity of her deceased mother, who she says was always so meticulous in life. Finally, some have seen the apparition of an older woman in a rocking chair on the front porch and claim she is the spirit of former owner Hulda Eiband, still looking after the house.

The Karbach Haus Bed and Breakfast is located at 487 West San Antonio Street, New Braunfels, Texas 78130. For more information or to book your next stay, call 830.625.2131.

San Angelo

Angelo State University

The history of the university can be traced to 1928 with the establishment of San Angelo College. In the 1960s, the first baccalaureate degrees were awarded and the name of the institution was changed to Angelo State University. According to a 2007 issue of the *ASU Ram Page,* a young freshman named Leandra Morales was murdered in Room 200 of the Hardemann Building on April 27, 1978. Her body was found strangled with numerous stab wounds made by a pair of scissors. A sophomore acquaintance named Robert Wagner was arrested for the crime, and an investigation revealed that after Morales spurned Wagner's romantic advances, he murdered her in cold blood.

The Journalism Department now occupies the building and some of those working late into the night swear they have heard the sounds of invisible footsteps walking down the halls. Others have heard what sounds like a faint argument between a man and a woman and some have even seen the ethereal apparition of a woman on one of the staircases. The room where the murder took place is now the Residence Life office. Local ghost hunters investigating the claims experienced unplugged radios suddenly coming to life and blaring music, and an elevator that operates on its own.

Angelo State University is located at 2601 West Avenue N, San Angelo, Texas 76909. For more information, visit them online at www.angelo.edu.

Fort Concho National Historic Site

Established in 1867 along the banks of the Concho River, the fort was created to protect early settlers and quell hostile threats by local Comanches. Constructed of native limestone, Fort Concho consisted of forty buildings covering more than 1,600 acres. Some of the most famous frontier units of the time were stationed here during its active period, including the 4th and 10th cavalry units as well as all four regiments of Buffalo Soldiers. During one action in September of 1872, troops from the fort attacked a large Comanche camp catching them completely by surprise. When the smoke cleared, twenty-three Comanches were dead and many women and children taken captive. The captives were taken back to Fort Concho where they were kept in horse corrals over the winter before moving to the Indian reservation near Fort Sill, in Oklahoma. For over twenty years the military post continued in its role until it was deactivated in June of 1889. Today, Fort Concho is a National Historic Landmark and includes twenty-three of the original fort's structures, restored and operated by museum staff.

Although, the soldiers that once garrisoned this post marched away many years ago, there are some who believe a few might have stuck around.

In Officer's Quarters No. 3, the ghost of the fort's former commander, Colonel Mackenzie, is reported by both visitors and staff. One staff member claims that, while closing up one evening, she heard the sound of footsteps behind her. Turning around, she was knocked against the wall by a violent blast of cold air, accompanied by what sounded like someone cracking their knuckles, a trait Colonel Mackenzie was well known for.

Another structure known for being haunted includes Officer's Quarters No. 1, which was once the home of Colonel Gierson, commander of the 10th Cavalry. History tells us that the Colonel's young daughter died in an upstairs bedroom on her twelfth birthday and has been seen many times after. She is seen playing jacks on the floor of the bedroom where she died accompanied by cold spots.

The Fort Concho National Historic Site is located at 630 South Oaks, San Angelo, Texas 76903. For more information, visit them online at www.fortconcho.com.

Officer's Row,
Fort Concho.

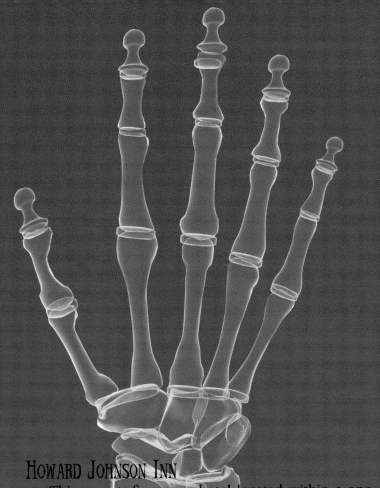

Howard Johnson Inn

This seventy-five-room hotel located within a one-mile radius of such attractions as Historic Street One, Fort Concho, and the River Walk, is well known for the ghosts that haunt it. In one room on the second floor, guests are startled by a pair of glowing red eyes watching them at night. In the same room, hotel staff has heard the sounds of someone moving around, even though the room is vacant. The figure of a cowboy has also been seen roaming through the lobby, bar, and pool area, but any attempt to approach him causes him to vanish. Doors open and close by themselves and a misty figure is reported flying down the hallways.

The Howard Johnson Inn is located at 415 W Beauregard Avenue, San Angelo, Texas 76903. For more information or to book your next stay, call 325.659.4393.

San Marcos

Gary Job Corps Center

As the largest Job Corps center in the United States, the grounds cover 775 acres with facilities for 1,600 students and industrial buildings offering training in over two dozen vocational specialties. The center initially began after the bombing of Pearl Harbor, in 1942, as a training site for pilots under the name the San Marcos Army Airfield. By 1964, the base closed in the face of governmental cutbacks, and shortly thereafter, President Lyndon B. Johnson announced the formation of the Job Corps Center in its stead. When the change took place, the center simply utilized many of the former barracks and other buildings for its housing, offices, and vocational needs, which may explain the hauntings that occurs there today.

Many of the students who live on campus encounter the apparitions of men in military uniform wandering between the rows of barrack houses. In some buildings, strange noises are heard, including invisible footsteps and whispered conversations.

The Gary Job Corps Center is located at 2800 Airport Highway 21, San Marcos, Texas 78666. For more information, visit them online at www.gary.jobcorps.gov.

San Marcos Bridge

Legend has it that the bridge (also known as the Thompson Island Bridge) is haunted by the ghosts of Confederate soldiers stationed there during the American Civil War. For those driving across the structure late at night, when the fog rises from the water below, spectral sentries can be seen pacing back and forth across the span of the bridge. Most describe them as wearing gray and yellow uniforms with a cap and cape, and armed with Kentucky Long Tom rifles held at attention.

The San Marcos Bridge is located forty-seven miles northeast of San Antonio on Interstate 35 where it crosses the San Marcos River.

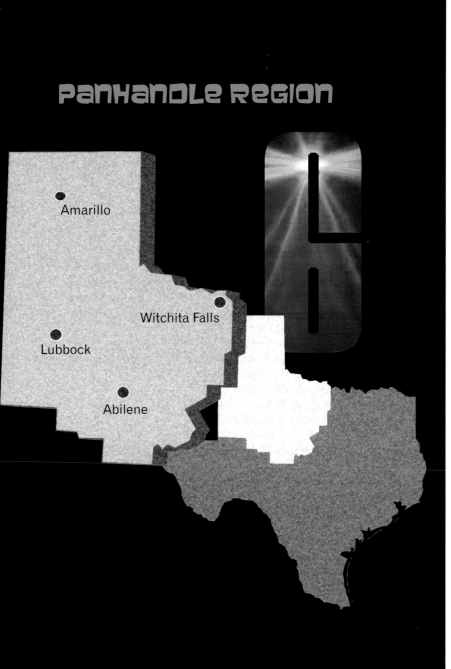

PANHANDLE REGION

Amarillo

Witchita Falls

Lubbock

Abilene

Shaped by the convergence of Oklahoma and New Mexico, the rolling plains that make up the topography extend east almost to Fort Worth. Along its western edge, the land is divided into deep canyons carved by flowing rivers, such as Palo Duro Canyon, whose 800-foot walls make it the second largest canyon in the United States. When Francisco Vazquez De Coronado first made his way across the endless plains in search of the fabled golden city of Cibola, he wrote in a dispatch to the King of Spain in 1541, "I reached some plains so vast, that I did not find their limit anywhere I went, although I traveled over them for more than 300 leagues…with no more landmarks than if we had been swallowed up by the sea…there was not a stone, nor a bit of rising ground, nor a tree, nor a shrub, nor anything to go by" (Winship, 215).

By the 1700s, these endless tracts were tightly controlled by fierce mounted Comanche warriors, whose territory reached across the Great Plains and further south. Their supremacy, however, would meet its greatest challenge in the 1870s when professional buffalo hunters invaded the land slaughtering the vast herds of bison the plain's tribes relied upon for survival. In retaliation, resentful warriors led by Chief Quanah Parker attacked several buffalo hunter camps sparking the Red River War of 1874-75. By the end of the conflict, the powerful Comanche and their allies were either pushed further south or forced onto reservations.

With the plains subdued, cattle ranching and cotton farming took over, destroying the last of the grasslands. The discovery of oil also played a role in changing the landscape, bringing a wave of industrialization that created towns where none stood before and making Amarillo the hub for the west Texas oil industry.

Most of the ghostly tales that come from this region sound almost as if they were created to be told by cowboys around a campfire at night to the sound of a lone coyote howling in the distance. Many include stories of long-dead Indian braves returning for revenge or phantom herds of cattle led by solitary horsemen cursed to roam the plains forever.

Ghost hunters and curiosity seekers alike have for years found a wealth of haunted places to explore in both the cities and towns that dot the landscape and in the long desolate plains that stretch between. Places filled with the history of the land and the men and women who came here to make their mark. A small few found the fortunes they sought and some even found a little fame along the way as well; many more, however, found hard lives of toil and uncertainty and six feet of hard Texas earth with a simple wooden cross.

ABILENE

FORT PHANTOM HILL

Built in the 1850s to protect settlers moving westward from hostile tribes of Indians, the location of the post was a poor one from the start and had little access to wood or water. Stone for the fort's construction had to be shipped from two miles away and oak logs for the officers' quarters and hospital traveled by ox wagon from as far as forty miles. The guardhouse, magazine, and commissary storehouse were built entirely of stone, while other buildings were built of adobe. Officially, the fort was named the "Post on the Clear Fork of the Brazos," but after a nervous sentry shot at what he thought was the phantom of an Indian on the hill one night, most began to call it "Fort Phantom Hill." Life in the fort was difficult and soldiers died from scurvy, fever, dysentery, pneumonia and lack of proper supplies. On April 6, 1854, the fort was abandoned and as the troops marched away, they noticed the post was on fire, which many believe was started by disgruntled soldiers. In 1858, the remaining structures of the fort were repaired and used as a way station for the Southern Overland Mail Stagecoach Line. During the American Civil War, it was also used as a base of operations by Confederate forces, and in the 1880s, a small town briefly sprouted among its buildings. In 1972, the fort was opened to the public and maintained by the Fort Phantom Hill Historical Foundation. Today the twenty-two acre site includes three intact stone buildings including the powder magazine, guardhouse, and commissary.

Numerous sightings are reported of phantom Indians still stalking the ancient grounds at night. One visitor to the fort said that he watched the old officers' quarters change into its former condition while standing in it. Two men in officer's uniforms stood before him, glaring as if unhappy with his intrusion. When he turned to flee, the apparitions and the building faded. Ghost hunters encounter strange equipment failures (including drained batteries), cold spots, and photographic anomalies of orbs and mist during their visits to the site.

Fort Phantom Hill is located by traveling eleven miles north of Interstate 20 on FM Road 600.

The remains of Fort Phantom Hill.

LAKE FORT PHANTOM HILL

The reservoir was built in 1937, two miles south of the old military post of Fort Phantom Hill and supplies water for about 100,000 people in Taylor and Jones counties. Some have seen the phantom of a woman dressed in a long gown wandering around the lakeside. Others described the apparition as floating over the lake's surface, sometimes carrying a lantern and surrounded by a glowing light. One of the many legends meant to explain the spectral presence tells of a husband and wife who built a small cabin in the woods where the lake now stands. Indians often attacked the cabin, and to guard against the threat, the couple made a pact that no one could enter the cabin without the secret password. If it wasn't given, they were to shoot anyone that tried to enter. One day, the husband went hunting and was ambushed by Indians. Suffering from severe wounds he clawed at the cabin door for help. Unable to recite the password, his wife shot him through the door, and from then on she is said to wander the area, cursed for killing her husband. Ghost hunters prowling the shoreline at night encounter cold spots, phantom mists in photographs, and the apparition of a young girl.

Lake Fort Phantom Hill is located nine miles north of Interstate 20 on FM 600.

PHANTOM HILL CEMETERY

Next to the Fort Phantom Baptist Church lies a small, well-maintained burial ground situated among the hilly shrub land of the countryside with the earliest tombstones reading from 1889. Although unrelated to the earlier military post of Fort Phantom Hill, it may have serviced the town that briefly sprang up in the ruins of the fort in the 1880s. Some believe that the same spirit lady that haunts nearby Fort Phantom Lake wanders through these tombstones as well and that her body may actually be buried here.

Ghost hunters conducting investigations here encounter temperature fluctuations and orbs or ectoplasmic mist in their photographs.

Phantom Hill Cemetery is located by traveling north of FM 600 approximately ten miles from Interstate 20.

WHITTEN INN

Formerly the Travel Lodge Motel, this clean, quiet, modern hotel has three connecting rooms known for their paranormal activity. The light in the bathroom turns on and off late at night and something is known to rearrange the belongings of guests staying in these rooms, who often find their credit cards and driver's licenses spread out under the bed like a poker hand. In addition to this, one of the rooms each night between 12 midnight and 2 am, fills with an unexplainable stench. In other parts of the hotel, the apparition of a man wearing green workman's clothes is seen. Witnesses state that he wears a cap, which hides most of his face with the exception of a bright red beard. He has been mistaken for a hotel employee on numerous occasions and is even known to have checked a few guests into their rooms.

The Whitten Inn is located at 840 East Highway 80, Abilene, Texas 79601. For more information or to book your next stay, visit them online at www.whitteninn.com or call at 800.880.7666.

Amarillo

Gebo's

Formerly known as the Bonanza Super Market in the 1980s, it's said by many that an employee died one night in the meat department. Since the death, strange things are known to occur after the store closes for the night and the employees begin the task of cleaning and stocking the shelves for the next day. No matter how orderly they arrange items on the shelves, when they return the following morning, they find them misplaced or moved. Although the ghost has never actually been seen or heard from, many get the creepy feeling they are being watched while doing inventory in the meat section.

Gebo's is located at 2500 East 3rd Avenue, Amarillo, Texas 79104.

York Tire Company

For years, employees of the company reported strange events they could not explain in the three-story building from the 1920s. One assistant manager named Montie Townsend claims that he first encountered the ghost of the building when he began working for the company many years ago. According to Townsend, workers would unload the trucks and stack the tires in back. The next day, every stack was knocked over. This continued until one day Townsend barked out "Knock it off," and it never happened again. On another occasion Townsend witnessed a man walk into the break room counting change in his hand as if he were about to purchase something from the vending machine. The odd thing was that he was wearing a gray uniform similar to what the Westinghouse elevator repair people used to wear. When Townsend entered the break room to see what the man needed, there was no one there. Interestingly enough, the only death to occur in the building was that of an elevator repairman, who fell down the elevator shaft in the building's early days. Psychics visiting the building have communicated with not one, but seven different entities.

The York Tire Company is located at 714 East 10th Avenue, Amarillo, Texas 79101.

Andrews

Shafter Lake

Surrounded by scrub brush and mesquite trees, the shallow body of salt water was named after Colonel William Shafter, who discovered it in 1875 while chasing a band of renegade Indians. For a time, a short-lived settlement sprang up along its southern shore in 1908, but all that remains of it today are a few half-buried foundations and a small cemetery. Legend holds that if a person parks their car just off the road that runs along the lake near a set of large rocks and flashes their lights three times, a woman in a white gown carrying a lantern will appear and approach the vehicle. Others claim that the lake was once sacred to the local Indians and that somewhere along its shores lies a lost burial ground from which the sound of drumming can be heard at night.

Shafter Lake lies seven miles north of the town of Andrews west of Highway 385.

Anson

Anson Ghost Lights

For years, locals flocked to the site of the mysterious ghost lights in hopes of catching a glimpse of the unusual light show. Over time, the phenomenon has become so popular that it has been featured on such television shows as *Unsolved Mysteries.* In order to see the lights, curiosity seekers must drive past the Mt. Hope Cemetery to a deserted country crossroad at night. After turning the car around to face the direction of the cemetery and turning the engine off, it's said the driver must flash his lights three times. In no time at all, a light will appear at the end of the road moving towards the crossroad. As it moves closer, it changes colors and even dances about, however, any attempt to approach the light will cause it to disappear.

Area legend attributes the lights to the spirit of a grief-stricken mother. It's said that during the depression, a young child wandered away from his home one cold winter night. When his mother realized the child was missing, she grabbed a lantern and frantically ran along the road calling out his name. Although the child was never found, the mother's spirit returns each night still looking for her little lost boy.

To view the Anson ghost lights travel east from Anson on Highway 180, turning right on CR 387 next to the Mt. Hope Cemetery. From there travel south to the crossroad of CR 387 and CR 376.

Baird Cemetery

Located just a short distance north of the town, the quiet country burial grounds have developed a rather peculiar tale about its nocturnal inhabitants. Local stories tell that there was once a woman in the 1880s, so grief stricken by her husband's death that at night she patrolled the cemetery where he lay buried with a shotgun and lantern, in fear that grave robbers would desecrate his resting place. A short time later, she too passed away and the townsfolk buried her next to her beloved husband. If they thought that giving her a proper burial was all it took to end her nightly guard duty, they were wrong, and soon after her death, a ghostly light was seen wandering through the cemetery. To this day, many of those brave enough to venture into the burial grounds at night report seeing a ghostly light moving about in the shape of an old lantern and believe her spirit still guards her husband's grave.

Baird Cemetery is located one mile north of Baird on Highway 283.

Ballinger

Texas Grill

Sitting just across from the Coppini Cowboy Statue in the Courthouse Square, the two-story stone building was constructed in 1901, and began as a saloon until prohibition shut it down in 1913. It then became a department store until 1954, when it was converted into a 24-hour restaurant, which has thrived ever since. Not only do they serve up good food here, but as some patrons will tell you, a few ghosts as well.

Small items such as glasses and silverware are known to move on their own and footsteps are heard coming from the empty second floor which is used as storage. Most of the staff have taken to calling the ghost Norton, and claim to have seen him on several occasions. Usually, he appears as a white misty figure with a recognizable face and a broad brimmed hat. At least on one occasion, a patron mistook him for a living person and followed him down the back hallway; when the witness looked away briefly, the man disappeared completely. A psychic who recently visited the restaurant claims to have communicated with the spirit and says he was a fugitive from justice who lived off the land in a tiny shack in 1901 before the building was constructed. His life ended when the law finally caught up with him and shot him on the spot.

The Texas Grill is located at 700 Hutchins Street, Ballinger, Texas 76821.

Big Spring

Center Point Road

On foggy nights, it's said the headlights of a phantom truck appear behind motorists traveling down this roadway. The lights seem to match speed with the vehicle it's following and only disappear if the driver turns off the road. During the chase, the drivers often feel as if someone is in the back seat of their car watching them from behind.

Center Point Road is located north of Big Spring, east of Highway 87 for a stretch of about eleven miles.

Federal Correctional Institution (FCI) Big Spring

The maximum-security federal prison has changed hands many times over the years. Initially, it began as a state prison, but even before its buildings were completed, unusual happenings began to occur. It started with building materials that seemed to disappear each night from the construction site. Thinking thieves were at work, a guard was posted to watch over the area. One night, the guard radioed the prison control center frantically calling for help. A figure was prowling the site, yet each time the guard thought he was closing in on the would-be thief, it disappeared before his eyes. As the call was coming in to control, loud music erupted from the prison mess hall, but as soon as the guards entered the room to investigate, the music stopped. Following that night, strange noises, balls of light, and whispering sounds began to occur. In response, the guards were doubled and told not to go anywhere alone. While making their rounds, many logged instances of an apparition of an old woman in the prison's education wing where she was seen walking the halls at night, and after giving the startled witnesses a quick glance, would disappear. Those encountering her say that she leaves behind an unidentified white powder as evidence of her presence. Another entity inhabits the mess hall where items move about on their own and pots and pans rattle together. A shadowy figure is seen walking through the cell house wings at night and the apparition of a small boy haunts the prison's fence line. The small child has appeared on several occasions in the back of the patrol truck looking in at the passengers and has caused a number of accidents.

The Federal Correctional Institution (FCI) Big Spring is located at 1900 Simler Avenue, Big Spring, Texas 79720.

Borger

Plemon's Crossing

Once the scene of clandestine Ku Klux Klan meetings, the crossing consists of an old, rickety bridge that spans the Canadian River along the road to what remains of the ghost town of Plemons. Several lynchings have taken place on the bridge as well as a horrible car accident that left one teen dead and which some believe may have led to the bridge being haunted.

Local legend holds that on nights when the mist rises from the water's surface below, the phantoms of the hanging victims appear on the bridge seeking to drag unwary travelers into the water's depths in revenge for the injustices committed against them. Cars passing over the bridge at night also experience strange electrical problems, such as the headlights flashing on and off. As soon as the car crosses the bridge, however, everything seems to return to normal.

Plemons Crossing is located by traveling approximately seven miles northeast of Borger on Plemons Road.

Canyon

Panhandle-Plains Historical Museum

When the uniquely designed art deco museum first opened in 1933, it was a 12,500-square-foot building dedicated to displaying the historical, cultural, and scientific heritage of the Panhandle-Plains region. Today, it has grown to 285,000 square feet and sees an average of 100,000 visitors a year. There are close to a million artifacts on display, from Chief Quanah Parker's eagle feather to collections of historic art from the southwest.

One permanent exhibit in the transportation section of the museum, featuring a wide range of vehicles from ancient wagons to modern cars, is said to be haunted by the ghost of a woman named Sarah Jane. According to the *Amarillo Globe News,* she was first spotted by Ann Bacon the museum custodian in 1970, standing next to a WWI ambulance display in a long calico dress as if waiting for someone. Since that time, she has been seen on numerous occasions in the exact same location. Others claim that while passing the ambulance, they experience headaches, feelings of panic, and the smell of blood.

The Panhandle-Plains Historical Museum is located at 2503 4th Avenue, Canyon, Texas 79015. For more information, visit them online at www.panhandleplains.org.

Coleman

Hord's Creek

Running along the eastern and northern limits of the city, the stream meanders west where it's damned to create Hord's Creek Lake. On the northern section where the old Abilene Highway once spanned its watery course, local residents claim to spot a white, hazy mist in the shape of a man wandering the banks where a shootout occurred in the 1930s. Records from that period reveal that there were three outlaw brothers, Dave, Luke, and "Doc" Trammell, who were terrorizing the countryside at the time committing robberies and car thefts. During one crime spree, a night watchman was killed in the town of Blackwell, and fearing they had finally gone too far, the three brothers decided to hideout at Hord's Creek till things blew over. On July 7, 1933, Sheriff Frank Mills caught wind that the deadly trio was held up in his jurisdiction and quickly gathered a posse together and surrounded the outlaws under a pecan tree on the creek bed. A brief shootout followed leaving one brother, "Doc," dead and another, Luke, in handcuffs. The third brother Dave isn't mentioned after that, but Luke later went on to be executed at the Huntsville Penitentiary for the killing of the night watchman.

In the 1940s, the U.S. Army blew the bridge that spanned the creek, but the abutments still remain to mark the location. Many who have found the old pecan tree where "Doc" Trammell died that fateful day say the area is deathly quiet and it feels as if they are being watched.

The haunted section of Hord's Creek is on the north side of the city where Highway 84 crosses the stream.

Floydada

Lamplighter Inn Bed and Breakfast

Opening in 1913, the hotel was operated for three long generations of the Daily family before becoming a bed and breakfast in 1991. Recently, however, the inn closed and the new owners are undecided as what to do with it.

Shutting the doors and locking the windows, though, hasn't seemed to diminish its reputation for being haunted by what many report are the ghosts of a man and a woman. The former staff of the inn claim to encounter the ghosts so many times they've named the male Floyd and the female Ada, in honor of the town. Both are said to leave distinctive odors when they are present. Floyd often smells of Old Spice when he is manifesting, while Ada smells of sweet magnolias. On different occasions, the two are spotted as apparitions. Ada appears as a woman in a purple 1930s style dress and is seen in both the dining room and looking out from the upstairs windows. Floyd, on the other hand, only appears as the partial form of a man's shoes and trouser clad legs dashing up the lobby stairs before disappearing at the top.

Over the years, there have been several deaths at the hotel that may or may not have contributed to the strange reports coming from within. The first death recorded was of an elderly man known as Mr. Cornelius, who passed away in a room that he rented. The second death occurred in the 1970s when a man caught wind that his cheating wife was to meet her lover at the hotel one night. The husband confronted the two in their room and the men began to fight. The rival unfortunately bested the husband, who died while being rushed to the hospital.

The former Lamplighter Inn Bed and Breakfast is located at 102 South Street in Floydada, Texas 79235.

Kalgary

STAMPEDE MESA

In 1889, this area was a favorite stop for tired cattle herds making their way to the beef markets further east. The mesa was actually a small peninsula that jutted out into what is now known as the White River Reservoir and provided not only a high vantage point to spy the layout of the land, but also plenty of water and grass. One day, a trail boss inadvertently drove his herd across a farmer's property mixing his cattle with that of the farmer. Upon reaching the mesa, the farmer caught up with the trail boss and his men and demanded the return of his property. In the growing darkness, an argument ensued over which cattle belonged to which party and an agreement was reached that the farmer would return the next day when there was light enough to fairly divide the herds. As the trail boss and his men bedded down for the night, the cows suddenly stampeded towards their camp and the steepest part of the mesa. Although the trail boss managed to save some of the herd, by morning two men and hundreds of steers lay at the bottom of the cliff. Some of the weary cowboys claimed they thought they saw the old farmer on his horse driving the herd toward the cliff when the stampede occurred. In revenge, the trail boss had the farmer dragged up the mesa, tied to his horse, and driven off the cliff.

In time, word spread from cowboy to cowboy that the spot was cursed and that herds bedding down for the night became spooked and stampeded off the cliff. Even today there are some that claim to have seen a phantom herd of cattle on the mesa being driven off its cliff by a solitary dark rider without making a single sound.

The stampede mesa can be found by traveling north on FM 3385 from FM 261near Kalgary to the White River Reservoir. The mesa is a small peninsula on the northern side of the Reservoir thrusting out into the water.

Levelland

FM 1490

Running north from the town through fields of farmland, this quiet stretch of county road is home to an unusual spectacle. Locals using the road at night report an ambulance suddenly appearing either behind them or coming head on toward them with its sirens blaring and lights flashing. Only when they pull to the shoulder of the road to let the ambulance pass do they notice something is not right. In each case it is described as an older model ambulance of the type no longer used today. Even more chilling is the fact that as soon as it roars by, it disappears without a trace—lights and sirens included.

The haunted section of road can be found on FM 1490 just north of the town limits.

Lubbock

TEXAS TECH UNIVERSITY

Created by a legislative act in 1923, the university is the only one in the state that includes a major university, law school, and medical school all on one campus. Originally known as Texas Technological College, it opened in 1925 with six buildings and an enrollment of 914. Now with over 1,800 acres, it has grown to become the second largest campus in the United States and one of the most haunted in Texas.

Holden Hall

One of the first buildings with a bit of ghostly history is Holden Hall. It's said that, in the 1960s, a well-liked professor at the university began a chemistry tutoring program in the hall. Years later when the professor died, many of the students he had mentored were saddened by his loss. Soon after his burial, however, students in the hall began reporting that a well groomed professor in a moustache, beard, and cowboy hat appeared from behind them and offered to help them with their studies. The figure is said to be a perfect match to that of the beloved former professor.

The Steam Tunnels

Because of its size, the campus is honeycombed with a labrynth of tunnels that carry water pipes and electrical cables to various buildings throughout the university. One story told on campus is that, in its early days, a young man used the tunnels to visit his sweatheart at night in Horn Hall, the all girls' dorm. When the dorm warden found out about the secret rendezvous, she had the maintaince staff weld shut the subterrainan gates leading to the hall. When the young man next tried to enter the hall he found himself locked out, and as he tried to retrace his steps, he became lost in the dark tunnels and was found dead weeks later. Some belive that his ghost still haunts the network of steam tunnels and workers report seeing his figure at the end of different tunnels. He always appears far off, and if approached, will vanish.

Horn/Knapp Hall

Another building rumored to be haunted is the Horn/Knapp Dining halls, where the spirit of a little boy is said to occupy a storage closet on the third floor. Those who encounter the playful little spirit say he can be heard throwing a ball down the stairs and laughing. Students familiar with the story further claim that if you knock on the storage door he will knock back. Some students reason that the child must have died in the building many years ago or possibly even on the property before the halls were built.

Knapp Hall, Texas Tech University.

Merket Alumni Center

One of the most widely reported buildings on campus has to be the Merket Alumni Center. Built in 1925 to house the school's first president, Paul Whitfield Horn, many today think it's still haunted by his ghost. Horn died in the building from a heart attack on April 13, 1932, in a second-story bedroom now coverted into office space. Cold spots, footsteps, and voices are reported coming from rooms that were empty, as well as the pungent smell of cigar smoke in what is now a smoke-free building. Numerous custodians have even quit after working a few nights in the old building claiming that they hear the sounds of keys jingling when they are alone, and on many occasions, they find the cleaning supplies rearranged when they weren't looking. On Friday 13, 2004, a reporter with the *Avalanche-Journal* named John Davis stayed the night in the building to see if he could witness for himself the strange goings on reported by so many. During his night vigil, he encountered unusual noises, cold spots, electrical equipment failures, and shadows that moved from the corner of his eyes.

National Ranching Heritage Center

The Heritage Center, which is also located on the university's campus, is a twelve-acre complex exhibiting thirty-one historical structures moved from sites around the state depicting the history of farming and ranching from 1830 to 1917. One two-story white farmhouse at the southwest end of the complex is said to be haunted by the wife of the rancher who originally built it. Her figure is seen looking out one of its upper windows at night so frequently that police no longer bother to respond to calls of her sighting, knowing that when they arrive the house will be empty.

Thompson Hall

Yet another building, Thompson Hall, is also believed to be haunted by an unknown spirit that may be tied to its past as a gross anatomy lab and morgue as part of the university's medical school. A figure is seen roaming the floors at night, which are restricted to public access requiring a key to enter or exit. Strangely enough, the doors are electronically monitored and fail to alert security that there has been any movement in or out of them the following day of the reported sighting. Security also reports that the elevator doors sometimes open near the security desk late at night, followed by the sound of phantom footsteps exiting and walking down the hall. Finally, the apparition of a woman in a nurse's uniform is spotted looking out of the fourth floor window above the main entrance.

The Biology Building

The university's biology building is also known to be haunted by the ghost of a murder victim from the 1960s. In 1967, a custodian named Sarah Morgan surprised a student named Benjamin Cach stealing the answer sheets to the biology exams from one of the 3rd floor lab rooms. In a fit of rage at the discovery, Cach seized Sarah Morgan and nearly decapitated her with a scalpel. Shortly after the grisly murder, Sarah's apparition began appearing in the building's hallways during student exams. Each time, she is seen looking at the students through the glass in the door and shaking her head sadly. It's said that on the anniversary of her death each year, the bloodstain that soaked into the linoleum of the lab floor where she lay dying reappears.

Texas Tech University is located at 2500 Broadway Boulevard, Lubbock, Texas 79409. For more information, visit them online at www.ttu.edu.

Muleshoe

Bailey County Jail

The old county jail that once occupied the courthouse in Muleshoe is no longer there and the prison cells that filled the building's third floor are now used as storage space for the courthouse's legal documents.

Built in 1925, in the Classical Revival style, the courthouse is still in use today and although it no longer houses prisoners the story of its haunting remains. The building's strange tale first began on April 16, 1979, when twenty-five year old Fernando Torres Alvarado hung himself in his cell while being held for the murder of his girlfriend. Shortly after the suicide, odd noises, including mumbling and talking came from his old cell after lights out. A dark presence was also seen prowling the cell block and some claim to have witnessed it disappear into a solid wall. One inmate staying in the haunted cell told deputy sheriffs that he awoke one night to find himself held fast to his cot with the sheets drawn tight against his body. He tried to scream out for help, but found that no sound would escape his throat. The state of paralysis lasted for several moments before everything returned to normal and deputies' claim that afterwards the once trouble making inmate became a model prisoner. During the height of the haunting, the story grabbed national attention by appearing on both the *Paul Harvey Radio Show* and *Newsweek Magazine*.

The Bailey County Courthouse is located at 300 South 1st Street, Muleshoe, Texas 79347.

Olney

Hamilton Hospital

Dating back to 1908 when Dr. George Hamilton established the hospital in a wood framed building called the Cathey House, the facility was moved to a two-story brick building at its present location in 1927. Considered one of the best-equipped hospitals west of Fort Worth at the time, it was again upgraded to a 103-bed-capacity structure in 1964, taking on the name Hamilton Hospital. In time, however, declining patients and lack of funding caused older sections of the facility to close down. Today those sections have reopened to house a Physical Therapy clinic, rooms for the ambulance crews, and administrative offices.

Once these areas became accessible again, unexplained phenomena began to occur, including hot and cold spots in the hallways and lights that turn on and off in rooms when they are empty. Many of the staff also report that patient files, seen only moments before, have a tendency to disappear for periods of time, only to be seen later in their former spots.

Hamilton Hospital is located at 901 West Hamilton, Olney, Texas 76374. For more information, visit them online at www.olneyhamiltonhospital.com.

Johnson Road

Local legend claims that if you travel down this stretch of isolated road at night with your lights off (not the safest thing to do and I certainly wouldn't try this at home) that bright orbs will appear as if from nowhere and begin swarming the vehicle.

Johnson Road is a three-mile length of rural pavement twisting its way from FM 251 to Pringle Rothell Road just southeast of the town of Olney.

Padgett Cemetery

The township of Padgett derived its name from one of its first settlers, I. B. Padgett, in 1875. In its prime, the settlement boasted a gin mill, post office, school, and numerous churches and small businesses. Sometime around the 1960s, the town fell on hard times and disappeared for good, leaving only the cemetery behind as a reminder of its passing.

Many that visit the cemetery today believe it is haunted by the ghost of a former grounds keeper who spent much of his life working in the cemetery and was notorious for chasing out trespassers. Even during daylight hours, his apparition is seen in the act of raking leaves on the ground.

Padgett Cemetery can be reached by traveling west on Comell Road from highway 79 for 2.5 miles. It sits on the left side of the road.

Plainview

Plainview High School

According to Docia William's marvelous book *Phantoms of the Plains: Tales of West Texas Ghosts,* the high school has held a long and proud tradition of being haunted by a ghost they have nicknamed "Herkie." Many claim he lingers in the school's auditorium and there are several versions of how old Herkie came to be. The first is that he was once a workman involved in the construction of the building, who in an unexplained fit of depression, hung himself in the auditorium. The second and more colorful tale is that he was a man named Herkemer, who owned the land the school was built upon. It's said that he became so upset when he found out the school would be constructed on his property that he bricked himself up in one of the auditorium walls in protest (where he also died as a result).

Regardless of which version is told, strange things are known to happen in the school's auditorium, including lights turning on an off, cold spots, unexplained shadows, props that move on their own, and the reports of the hands of the auditorium's clock spinning erratically.

Plainview High School is located at 1501 Quincy, Plainview, Texas 79072.

Post

Town of Post

In 1907, millionaire cereal manufacturer C. W. Post decided to create a town of his very own modeled in the form of a utopian society, which he called Post City. Purchasing 200,000 acres of ranchland on the West Texas plains, he proceeded to build trim houses, the Algerita Hotel, a gin mill, and a textile plant. Trees were planted on every street and vices such as alcohol and brothels were strictly prohibited. The town flourished, and when the railroad reached it in 1910, it changed its name to Post. On May 9, 1914, the "Father of Post City," committed suicide in a hospital in Santa Barbara, California after struggling with poor health and depression. Although Post's legacy lives on through both the town and the cereal company, citizens of Post believe he still stops in to make sure his dream town is running as it should.

Police patrolling the town at night have seen the dark image of a man walking down Main Street. When they attempt to stop the figure or speak to him, the apparition quickly turns a corner and disappears.

The town of Post is located thirty-seven miles southeast of Lubbock on Highway 84.

Shilverton

Tule Canyon

Before the Lake MacKenzie reservoir was built, archeologists found evidence of human occupation in the picturesque canyon dating back to more than 10,000 years ago. Later, when Spanish conquistador Francisco Vásquez de Coronado passed through looking for the Seven Cities of Gold, it's thought that he too used the canyon as a campground. In 1874, the 4th U.S. Cavalry, led by Colonel Ranald Mackenzie, camped in the same area before their decisive battle against the Comanche in Palo Duro Canyon. Following his victory, Mackenzie ordered 1,450 captured horses led into Tule Canyon and shot. For many years, their bones lay scattered across the western slope of the canyon in glistening white heaps until a fertilizer company eventually carted them away.

To this day, many of the plain's tribes view the canyon with superstitious veneration and the Kiowa or Comanche will not enter it for fear of being trampled by the ghostly herd of horses. Others passing through at night, especially on FM 207, catch glimpses of the phantom horses running alongside the road as well.

Tule Canyon lies twelve miles northwest of Shilverton, Texas along FM 207 near Lake MacKenzie.

Stamford

Bute Park

According to an October 30, 1985, edition of the *Abilene Reporter News,* the long forgotten grounds of this former public park are said to carry with them a sinister tale of heartbreak and murder, as well as a phantom known as the "Hatchet Lady." First opening in 1910, the park was named after local real estate developer Bernard Buie. At the time, the heavily wooded area was a popular spot for young couples to stroll hand in hand on a Sunday afternoon. Legend has it that on just such a day a newly engaged couple made their way to a more isolated section of the park to talk in private. The young man it seems was having second thoughts about their upcoming nuptials and informed his fiancée that he wished to break off the engagement. Devastated by the news, the girl flew into a rage and after grabbing a hatchet from a nearby woodpile she hacked him to death.

Although the park has been closed now since the 1960s, its overgrown grounds continue to lure area teenagers and other curiosity seekers who claim that the apparition of a woman is seen wandering the grounds with a hatchet in her hand. Ghost Hunters visiting the site have also encountered unusual activity, including the sound of footsteps following them around, EMF fluctuations, feelings of being watched, and photographic anomalies such as ectoplasmic mist and orbs.

Buie Park is located five miles south of Stamford on FM 1226.

Stanton

St. Joseph's Convent

In 1881, Carmelite monks traveled to the area in the hopes of establishing a German Catholic Colony. By 1884, they had completed a two-story adobe and brick monastery with Gothic elements followed one year later by a wooden church named St. Joseph's Catholic Church. In 1897, the monks disbanded and sold the property to an order known as the Sisters of Mercy, who operated an academy and convent on the grounds. The sisters lasted until 1938, when they abandoned the convent following a disastrous tornado on June 11, 1938. All that remains of the convent are the dormitory, cemetery, and several ruined structures.

Sweetwater

St. Joseph's Convent.

Many passing by the convent grounds at night have seen the figure of a weeping nun gliding through the ruins. Local legends hold she is the spirit of a nun that bore the child of one of the priests. To hide the misdeed, she buried the infant alive somewhere on the grounds, and to this day, returns looking for the child she killed. In addition to the phantom nun, strange, glowing lights are reported on the grounds and within the dormitory.

The Convent is located at 301 East Carpenter Street, Stanton, Texas 79782.

Mulberry Mansion

Built in 1913 by Thomas Trammell for his new wife, Mattie, who they say, was thirty years younger than him, the house later served as the city and county's only hospital from 1923 to 1926 under the name Sweetwater Sanitarium. When a new hospital was built, the mansion was converted back to a private residence until it became a bed and breakfast in 1992.

Guests staying at the mansion report a wide array of paranormal activity from items appearing and disappearing to feelings of being watched. One of the more frequent occurrences is the sound of high-heeled shoes walking up and down the carpeted staircase.

The Mulberry Mansion Bed and Breakfast can be found at 1400 Sam Houston Street, Sweetwater, Texas 79556. For more information or to book your next stay, call 325.235.3811.

Sweetwater High School

Both faculty and students alike have encountered the playful presence that haunts this high school. On a number of occasions, the ghost locks the teachers' classrooms in the morning so they cannot get in. At other times, the sound of light footsteps are heard running up and down the stairs between the upper and lower levels of the school as well as the auditorium stage. The mischievous ghost doesn't seem confined to the school, however, and players on the nearby football field have felt bone-chilling cold spots when it's present.

Sweetwater High School is located at 1205 Ragland Street, Sweetwater, Texas 79556.

Sweetwater Lake

Created in 1930, this 630-acre body of water dives as deep as forty-five feet in some places. Motorists out for a moonlight drive along the lakeshore have witnessed orange lights dancing across the water's surface for which there is no natural explanation.

Sweetwater Lake lies five miles southeast of the city of Sweetwater along FM 1856.

Texas Movie Theatre

With its sandstone colored, art modern façade, this movie house has been dishing out blockbuster movies to residents of Sweetwater for years. During its time, employees have had a lot of trouble from the ghosts that haunt the place. On some nights, money from the register drawer disappears and then reappears later, making counting at the end of the shift impossible. Strange noises and disembodied voices are also encountered as well as a dark shadowy figure in the audience seating area during movies.

The Texas Movie Theatre is located at 114 East Broadway, Sweetwater, Texas 79556.

Turkey

Hotel Turkey Bed and Breakfast

Built in 1927 as the town of Turkey sprang up next to the railroad line, the hotel provided lodging for salesmen or "drummers," as they were often called, making their way west from Fort Worth and Dallas. Since its initial opening those many years ago, the hotel remains in continuous use and is listed in both the state and national historic registries. Currently, the hotel operates as a fifteen-room bed and breakfast styled with original 1920s décor. The present owners, however, admit that there might be more going on there than one would think.

On stormy nights, the staff reports that the front desk bell will ring on its own followed by the sounds of footsteps walking up the lobby staircase to the rooms above. On nights such as these, the bed in Room 20 is always found the next day as if someone had slept in it, even when the room is not occupied. One guest went as far as to report that one night she awoke to find a figure standing in the doorway between the bedroom and bathroom waving his hand back and forth with a lantern much like a train engineer might do.

The Hotel Turkey Bed and Breakfast is located at 3rd and Alexander Streets in Turkey, Texas 79261. For more information or to book your next stay, visit them online at www.turkeybb.com or call or 806.423.1151.

Wichita Falls

F.S. White Sanitarium

Opening in 1926 under the direction of Dr. Frank S. White, who previously acted as superintendent of the state asylum in Austin, the sanitarium was a private hospital providing more pleasant accommodations that diminished the affects of asylum life on the symptoms of his patients. Designed in the Spanish style of architecture, the three-story, cream-colored stucco building with its well-manicured lawns lasted until 1939, when the building was abandoned after damage from severe flooding. For many years, the building continued to deteriorate as well as develop a reputation for being haunted. In 2002, it was purchased for a small price of $15,000 (thanks in part to investors not wanting to buy a haunted house) and efforts began to convert the building into an apartment complex.

Most of the reported paranormal manifestations occurred during the period while the building was still abandoned and included the sounds of invisible footsteps and a woman's voice calling out the name "Susan" over and over. More recent visits by ghost hunters have yielded a wide assortment of unexplained activity, including one report of an ashtray that repeatedly moved across a coffee table on its own.

The F.S. White Sanitarium is located on the corner of California and Olen roads in Wichita Falls, Texas 76301.

Dr. White's Sanitarium.

North Texas State Hospital

Dating back to 1917, the complex was originally called the Northwest Texas Insane Asylum. By 1925, its name was changed to the Wichita Falls State Hospital and was updated with laboratories, electroshock therapy, and hydrotherapy. During the depression era, the 940-acre campus the hospital had grown into was a fully self-sustaining community with farming, hogs, chicken, and cattle. By WWII, the complex consisted of thirty-five brick buildings and sixty wooden structures serving approximately 2,400 patients. On September 1, 1998, the Wichita Falls facility and another in Vernon, Texas, were consolidated to create the largest state hospital in Texas.

One of the hospital's buildings said to be haunted dates back to the founding of the original asylum in the 1920s and was for many years used as a patient dormitory before being turned into administrative offices. Lights are seen going on and off through the windows at night when the building is closed and vague, humanoid shapes are seen at the end of hallways near twilight. In addition, some of the staff has heard disembodied wails and moans coming from the third floor.

Another building known for its haunting is Building M, where at night doors are heard opening and closing on their own, cold spots are felt in the hallways, and the apparition of a woman in a white nurse's outfit is spotted wandering the halls. Staff working late at night claim that at times it feels as if an invisible hand comes to rest on their shoulders. When they turn to look behind them no one is there.

The North Texas State Hospital is located at 6515 Kemp Boulevard, Wichita Falls, Texas 76308.

BIG BEND COUNTRY

El Paso

Midland

Marfa

Presidio

Del Rio

The region derives its name from the bending course of the mighty Rio Grande River as it flows through the area marking the border between the United States and Mexico. The Spanish, however, have long named it *El Despoblado* or the "uninhabited land." Reaching from the border city of El Paso in the west to the Pecos River in the east, the landscape is composed of hot sandy plains that make up part of the Chiluahuan Desert. Cacti and sagebrush fill the barren terrain along with breathtaking desert mountain ranges that include the Chisos, Davis, and Gaudalupe Mountains. Big Bend is also home to one of the state's greatest natural wonders known as Big Bend National Park, which encompasses almost 1,250 square miles.

In the 1800s, the region lay along the path of the Great Comanche War Trail from which the fierce mounted warriors raided towns and homesteads in both Texas and northern Mexico. After the 1849 war with Mexico, the United States constructed numerous forts throughout the region to protect newly arriving settlers from attacks by the Comanche as well as Mescalero Apaches and other tribes pushed into the region from father north. By 1870, with most of the hostile tribes defeated and relocated to reservations, ranchers bringing sheep, goats, and cattle established large spreads on the range.

Today, one of the most important cities in the region is El Paso, which in Spanish means "the pass"—so named because it provided easy access between Mexico and the northern regions to early explorers and settlers. Located on the Rio Grande River across from its Mexican counterpart, Ciudad Juarez, El Paso is also the home of Fort Bliss, a major military installation, as well as White Sands Missile Range where the American V2 rocket program began.

Some may think the infernal deserts and lonely mountain passes of this land are largely uninhabited by the living, but that doesn't mean that time and circumstance haven't populated it with the spirits of the dead. In the Big Bend, phantom soldiers still parade through old frontier forts that no longer stand and spectral lights jealously guard forgotten gold mines. Even in its metropolitan areas, there are stories of haunted churches, schools, and theaters. Some might even go as far as to claim that in some parts of the Big Bend, the dead outnumber the living.

El Paso

CATHEDRAL HIGH SCHOOL

Founded in September of 1925, the school is a private, parochial, all boys high school operated by the Christian Brothers, a Catholic order founded in Rheims, France, in 1680. Two areas associated with the third floor of the massive red brick building are known to be haunted. The first is the third floor hallway where the freshman lockers are located. The story goes that a freshman was hanging out in the hallway during class when he noticed an open locker at the end of the hall. He started down the hall to see who it belonged to when the locker slammed closed and a white figure sped off in the opposite direction. The student ran after the phantom, but as soon as it turned a corner, it disappeared. The second area is a separate classroom attached to the third floor by a staircase. It's said that an unsettling presence lingers in the room and there is a strong feeling of being watched when students are left alone there.

Cathedral High School is located at 1309 North Stanton Street, El Paso, Texas 79902. For more information, visit them online at www.cathedral-elpaso.org.

CONCORDIA CEMETERY

Beginning in 1840 as a ranch settled by pioneer Hugh Stephenson and his wife, Juana Maria, the chapel and cemetery followed in 1854 with Juana Maria becoming the first interment after being gored by a deer. Stephenson lost his land after the American Civil War, and in 1882, the city of El Paso bought part of the cemetery to use as a burial ground for paupers. Over time, the cemetery continued to grow, filling with gunslingers, Chinese railroad workers, and buffalo soldiers (a term used by the Indians to describe black soldiers). Even the Mexican Revolutionary leader and ally to Pancho Villa, Pascual Orozco, was originally buried at Concordia before his remains were later moved to Mexico. Since 1990, the Concordia Heritage Association has been working to preserve and restore the historic cemetery, and to date, has counted approximately 65,000 graves within its grounds.

With all that history there is also bound to be a few ghosts, and over the years, visitors to the ancient grounds have heard the sounds of invisible horses galloping by and disembodied voices holding conversations that can not be heard well enough to understand. In addition, late at night the sounds of children laughing and playing drifts above the tombstones, victims, it's said, of a small pox epidemic that swept the area in the 1800s filling the cemetery with a large number of children's graves. Finally, there is also the story of a woman in a wedding dress that roams the grounds at night softly crying to herself. When approached she vanishes.

Concordia Cemetery is located at 3700 West Yandell Street, El Paso, Texas 79901.

CRISTO REY CATHOLIC CHURCH

Dedicated in 1972, the modern chapel is actually part of a much older mission chapel known as Our Lady of the Valley Church. Today it is part of a cloistered convent and opens to the public only during Holy Week once a year. During that time, parishioners come to pray and celebrate mass, and on more than one occasion, run into the phantom nun that haunts the chapel. Some claim to seen her enter from a side chapel and kneel before the altar's communion rail to pray. She is described as a kindly, older nun dressed in the traditional habit of the order and is mistaken for a living person. That is of course until someone tries to approach her and she vanishes.

The Cristo Rey Catholic Church is located at 8011 Williamette Street, El Paso, Texas 79907 and is only open to the public during Holy Week, the week immediately proceeding Easter Sunday.

EL PASO MUSEUM OF ART

Founded in 1959, the El Paso Museum of Art is a major cultural and educational resource for West Texas, New Mexico, and Mexico. The Museum houses a permanent collection of over 5,000 works including early American, Spanish, and European art. It's also said to house the spirit of an unknown elderly woman who is seen at various times looking out from one of the windows on the top floor of the museum. Staff also reports doors opening and closing on their own, lights that turn on and off, and eerie moaning sounds in the basement.

The El Paso Museum of Art is located at One Arts Festival Plaza, El Paso, Texas 79901. For more information, visit them online at www.elpasoartmuseum.org.

Evergreen Cemetery

Nestled in the heart of the city just south of Interstate 10, these burial grounds date back to 1894 and cover forty-seven acres. Stories abound that if you drive along Almeda Avenue in the early morning hours as it passes the cemetery, you will see a little boy standing alongside the road as if looking for a ride. If you slow down or stop to help, however, he will disappear right before your eyes. Others encounter a mysterious mist near the railroad tracks that border the northern edge of the cemetery and many claim that when it appears, it is accompanied by an overwhelming odor that is difficult to describe.

Evergreen Cemetery is located at 4301 Almeda Ave, El Paso, Texas 79905.

Fire Station No. 9

Built in the heart of the city's warehouse district in 1927, it is often referred to even on official city web sites as the "haunted firehouse." Numerous fire fighters stationed at No. 9 over the years came to believe that the spirit of one of their fallen comrades watches over the place and warns them right before a big fire. On February 14, 1934, Captain Woodard F. Bloxom, the station chief, died fighting a blaze across the street from No. 9 at the American Furniture Co. His badly burned body was carried back to the station where he died from his injuries and in honor of his sacrifice the station was later dedicated to his memory. Frequently, right before a big fire, strange things begin to happen around the station. Lights start turning on and off on their own, toilets flush mysteriously, furniture moves, footsteps can be heard creeping slowly up the firehouse staircase, and a shadowy figure is seen sulking around the engine room. These manifestations often cease completely after the alarm sounds, only to begin again right before the next big blaze.

Fire Station No. 9 is located at 275 Dallas Street, El Paso, Texas 79901.

Horizon Boulevard

Running east of the city of El Paso toward Mountain View High School is a stretch of road famous for a specter seen walking along its shoulder at night. Few reports actually describe it other than to say that it looks like a man walking by, but when drivers look back at the figure as they pass, it can be seen slowly disappearing into thin air.

The haunted stretch of roadway can be found in the vicinity of 14521 Horizon Boulevard, El Paso, Texas 79928.

Insights El Paso Science Museum

Opening to the public in 1980 in the basement of the El Paso Electric Company building, what was once a little science museum has come a long way. It now occupies a building of its own near the city hall and the El Paso Museum of Art, where its hands-on educational exhibits include a Tesla coil, centrifugal force spinner, and much more. Yet since moving to its new building, there has been a rash of unexplained occurrences that lead many to believe the museum haunted. While waiting in line for the building to open one morning, a crowd of visitors looked through the glass doors to catch a glimpse of an Indian, costumed in native battle dress, standing in the lobby with his arms crossed. After just a few moments, the apparition vanished in front of the startled crowd of onlookers. Another apparition seen from time to time is that of a little boy in a striped shirt, who disappears into the walls when noticed. Finally, the elevator travels between floors on its own and museum exhibits often turn themselves on and off without explanation.

The Insights El Paso Science Museum is located at 505 North Santa Fe Street, El Paso, Texas 79901. For more information, visit them online at www.insightselpaso.org.

LORETTO CHAPEL

Located on the campus of the Loretto Academy when the school began in the 1920s, it has for many years carried with it the strange tale of a phantom nun that resides in the chapel's bell tower. Although the church bells no longer call the all-girl student body to mass anymore, a white, misty figure, formed as if wearing a nun's habit, has been spotted moving around the top of the square Spanish style tower. Numerous stories are told about her origin, including tales of suicide and murder. The most interesting, however, was told by a family that once lived near the school and encountered the phantom nun first hand. One night, as they drove by the campus, they noticed a mist, which seemed to descend from the bell tower and follow their vehicle. Once home, the family ran inside only to find the mist waiting for them in their living room. From the mist came the voice of a woman who claimed that she had been a nun at the school long ago, and because of some unknown sin she had committed, the other nuns locked her in the tower and had forgotten her. Without food or water she died and now returns to find those responsible for her death. At the conclusion of the story, the mist vanished, but there would be other residents over the years telling similar tales of a misty figure that followed them home.

The Loretto Chapel is located at 1300 Hardaway Street, El Paso, Texas 79903. For more information, visit them online at www.loretto.org.

LOST PADRE MINE

In the early 1600s, the Franciscan priests built the Nuestra Senora de Guadalupe mission in Juarez and operated a rich gold mine somewhere in the Franklin Mountains. When the Pueblo Indians revolted in 1680 and rampaged across the countryside, the Franciscans were forced to leave the area, abandoning both the mission and the mine. Determined that no one should find their precious source of wealth, the priests had the mine filled in with red dirt and the Indian laborers killed to keep it a secret. To further safeguard the site, they left a priest behind to watch over it and a dog to keep him company. For hundreds of years, what has become known as the "Lost Padre Mine," has lured gold miners and treasure hunters to the mountains seeking their fortune. Although none have been lucky enough to discover the mine, some have run into the spectral figure of a priest and his dog, which they believe still guards the mine to this day.

In the 1960s, when the Woodrow Bean Transmountain Road cut its way through the Franklin Mountains, drivers began reporting a figure in priestly garb that suddenly appeared in the middle of the road. In many cases, the drivers swerved to avoid the apparition and found themselves fighting to stay on the roadway. The El Paso Police Department reports that although most accidents along this stretch of highway are the result of human error, some have been blamed on the phantom priest.

The haunted section of road can be found north of El Paso between Interstate 10 and Texas 54 as the Transmountain Road cuts through Franklin Mountain State Park.

McKELLIGON CANYON AMPHITHEATRE

Surrounded on three sides by canyon walls, the 1,500-seat amphitheatre in the Franklin Mountains plays host to musical performances, dances, and plays all year long. The men's dressing room of the amphitheatre is said to be haunted by the spirit of an unknown construction worker who died during the building of the structure in 1912. Lights flicker on and off and the sounds of someone frantically running around the room banging on the walls are experienced by those preparing for a show.

The McKelligon Canyon Amphitheatre is located at 1500 McKelligon Canyon Road, El Paso, Texas 79931. For more information, visit them online at www.visitelpaso.com/mckelligon_canyon.sstg.

PLAZA THEATRE

Opening on September 12, 1930, to a capacity crowd of 2,410, the Plaza was advertised as the largest theater of its kind between Dallas and Los Angeles. Although the exterior is designed in the Spanish Colonial Revival style of architecture reminiscent of early Spanish missions, the interior includes painted ceilings, mosaic-tiled floors, and antique furnishings. The Plaza continues in its grand tradition even today, offering musicals, plays, performances, and concerts to the public.

Sacred Heart Catholic Church

Built by the Jesuits in 1893 to meet the spiritual needs of the city's poor, Sacred Heart stands just a few blocks from the United States/Mexico border and is one of El Paso's oldest churches.

Some parishioners claim to hear what sounds like a low chanting or murmuring as if someone were talking to themselves. Others continue to report the apparition of a Mexican woman in a turn-of-the-century bridal gown, weeping in the side chapel of Our Lady of Guadalupe. Over the years, the story has developed that she is the ghost of a jilted bride left heart broken at the altar and still waits for her lover to return.

The Sacred Heart Catholic Church is located at 602 South Oregon Street, El Paso, Texas 79901.

Six Poles

Located on the grounds of the Mission Del Paso campus of the El Paso Community College, the site consists of six concrete pillars arranged in a circle around a stone dais or platform. There have been many sinister stories told about this location over years. Some claim that the site is the home of evil spirits, others that it is an unholy place of satanic ritual and sacrifice, and finally, that it was the site where livestock and other animals were once taken to slaughter. Regardless of the tale, many believe it to be haunted by the apparition of an unknown woman seen holding her decapitated head in her hands.

Six poles is tucked away on the western extremity of the campus at 10700 Gateway Boulevard, El Paso, Texas 79927.

For ghost enthusiasts, however, its most interesting feature may be the apparition of a man in military uniform seen near the balcony stairs smoking a cigarette, despite the Plaza being a no smoking building. Yet before anyone can approach him to ask him to put it out, he vanishes. Some claim that the spirit is of a Fort Bliss solider who died years ago of a heart attack while smoking in the men's room. Employees also hear the sound of someone choking in the basement, but no one has yet identified the source of the noise.

The Plaza Theatre is located at 125 Pioneer Plaza, El Paso, Texas 79901. For more information, visit them online at www.theplazatheatre.org.

Fabens

Cattleman's Steakhouse

Beginning as a ranch renting horses to tourists, the owner, Dieter Gerzymisch, added a restaurant in 1973. In five years time, the steakhouse became so popular that additions were built to meet the demand of its hungry customers. Today, the once simple ranch is a sprawling complex of movie sets, petting zoos, and playgrounds.

What some of its hungry customers may not know, however, is that it's also haunted by a host of unknown spirits. More than once, the wait staff at Cattlemen's has seen shadow-like figures lurking around the bar area and the Buffalo Room. Customers have also had their share of paranormal experiences here. One night, a couple reports that after finishing their meal, they returned to their car to find a little blonde girl seated in back with the doors locked. When they unlocked the door to see just how she had gotten inside, she disappeared before their eyes. Another phantom often encountered is thought to be that of a former staff member. One night, the employee in question was killed when his car overturned at a curve in the road on the way home. A short time later, other employees driving home at night began to see him standing at the side of the road near the crash site.

Cattlemen's Steakhouse is located 4.5 miles north of Interstate 10, Fabens, Texas 79838. For more information, visit them online at www.cattlemanssteakhouse.com.

Fabens Port of Entry

Five miles southeast of the city, where the borders of the United States and Mexico meet, is a U.S. Customs facility to monitor the traffic between the two countries. For years, border guards report instances of phantom horsemen charging across the border late at night. As the specters pass, they discharge firearms at the guards before fading away into thin air.

The old Fabens Port of Entry is located at Island Guadalupe Road, Fabens, Texas 79838.

FORT BLISS

FORT BLISS

In 1849, the U.S. War Department ordered the creation of a military post in El Paso to protect settlers from marauding bands of Apache and Comanche. In September of that year, several companies of the 3rd U.S. Infantry arrived and established a post in the area named Fort Bliss, in honor of Lieutenant Colonel William Bliss, the son-in-law of then-president Zachary Taylor. During the American Civil War, Confederate forces held the fort for a time and used it as a base to launch attacks into New Mexico and Arizona. Following the war, the fort returned to the original task of protecting settlers from Indian attacks until the surrender of Geronimo in 1886 ended such threats. During World War II, the size of the base increased dramatically as it trained a new generation for war. Today, at approximately one million acres of land, it is the largest military facility in the United States, weighing in at roughly the size of Rhode Island. Given the size and history of the fort, there are a number of buildings that have developed a reputation for being haunted over the years.

The Morgue

Built in 1914, the rectangular, two-story structure, simply named Building No. 4, originally served as an isolation ward for the sick and dying, and also, for a short time, as a morgue. The apparition of a man in a doctor's coat and cavalry uniform is seen pacing the second story of the building. At times, footsteps and voices can be heard throughout the building as well as a disembodied voice in the basement that calls out, "Help me move this…", followed by the sounds of something heavy being dragged across the floor. Base security has a difficult time coaxing their patrol dogs into the building while on rounds, but that hasn't stopped ghost hunters from investigating the place. Strange sounds, orbs, and unexplained EMF spikes are reported during investigations of the building.

The Barracks

Dating back to 1893, Building No. 13 was initially a troop barracks and is today one of the oldest remaining buildings on the base. Lights and vague figures are seen moving across the dark windows of the third floor late at night when the place is closed. Doors and windows are known to open and close by themselves and cold spots are felt whenever a spirit is thought to be present. According to the *El Paso Times*, a soldier named Carl Schiller of the 309th infantry hung himself in the attic with a length of wire on June 11, 1919. Schiller was just one day short of being discharged and the circumstances of his death are highly suspect.

The General's House

Occupied by General "Black Jack" Pershing between 1914 and 1916, the two-story building, known as the Pershing House, is a combination of Georgian revival and Plantation style architecture. General Pershing, for whom the building was later named, used Fort Bliss to launch punitive expeditions into Mexico in search of the revolutionary leader Pancho Villa. On one occasion, a salt shaker rose from the dining room table during a formal dinner party in the 1980s and moved across the table.

The Hospital

The William Beaumont Army Medical Center opened in 1921 as a medical complex consisting of forty-eight tile and stucco buildings, of which one building in particular is well known for its strange activity. Base security claims that in Building 7919, lights go on and off at night when it is unoccupied. Some even report the sound of a person screaming from inside, and one military personnel has seen the figure of a man hanging from the ceiling. The manifestations here are so disturbing that many MPs do not like to enter the building alone at night.

Fort Bliss is located at 1 Pershing Road, *Fort Bliss*, Texas 79916. For more information, visit them online at www.bliss.army.mil

Created in 1961 to protect what remained of the historic military post, Fort Davis is thought to be one of the best surviving examples of an Indian War's frontier post from the early southwest. Established in 1854, its duty was to protect settlers and mail coaches along the Trans-Pecos portion of the San Antonio-El Paso and Chihuahua Trail. During its service, it played a major role in the African American involvement in the west by playing host to numerous black regiments established after the American Civil War. Deactivated in 1851, the site today consists of twenty-four restored buildings and over 100 ruins and foundations. In 1961, the fort was designated as a national historic landmark and is operated by the national park service.

Numerous visitors to the site, however, report more than they initially bargained for and left the old military post believing it to be haunted. Many report the apparitions of former soldiers in the restored hospital building as well as unexplained cold spots and feeling of being watched. Others, including some of the park staff, have witnessed figures in cavalry uniforms drilling on the parade ground in the early morning hours.

The Fort Davis National Historic Site is located at 101 Lt. Henry Flipper Drive, Fort Davis, Texas, 79734. For more information, visit them online at www.fortdavis.areaparks. com.

Fort Stockton

Fort Stockton State Historical Site

Constructed in December of 1858 by soldiers of the 1st and 8th Infantry, the adobe post was named after Commodore Robert Field Stockton, a naval officer during the Mexican War. It, like many other forts in the region, was designed to protect settlers and supply lines from warring Apache and Comanche Indians. In the midst of the American Civil War, the fort was occupied by Confederate forces, whom later torched many of the buildings before handing it back over to Federal troops. Although much of the old fort now lies in ruins, a number of the buildings have been restored and are open to the public.

Most of the reported phenomena at this site comes from an adobe structure that once served as the fort's general store and later as the town hospital. During the building's colorful history, many deaths occurred within its walls. At least one murder took place here in 1902, and in 1918 when it was used as a hospital during an epidemic of the Spanish Flu, many others died as well.

Between the 1920s and 1930s, the building became the home and shop of a black smith, whom many thought was a *bujo*, or "male witch." Following this, the home was occupied by another eccentric character named George "Choche" Garcia. One day, Choche suddenly took to wearing all black, including a hat and cape. He also developed the habit of lurking around the town at night frightening the locals. Perhaps it was his reputation for strange behavior that now leads many to believe the ghost of Choche haunts the house. Area residents report a large dark phantom wearing a cape and hat near the dried up well next to the home. The town's Hispanic population calls him *El Bulto*, meaning "the shape or figure" and even local law enforcement has had their share of run-ins with the mysterious phantom. Others visiting the site report flickering lights from within the crumbling structure and what they describe as the sounds of kitchen china being smashed to bits.

The Fort Stockton State Historical Site is located at 300 East Third Street, Fort Stockton, Texas 79735. For more information, visit them online at www.tourtexas.com/fortstockton/ftstockfort.html

Marathon

Gage Hotel

Built by Alfred Gage, the hotel first opened in 1927 and doubled as the headquarters for Gage's lucrative Alpine Cattle Company. At the time of its construction, the boxy two-story building was considered the most elegant building in Texas west of the Pecos. Gage, however, died in 1928 and the hotel remained neglected until 1980 when it was purchased and renovated.

Since the restoration of the hotel, both staff and guests have experienced a host of paranormal activities. One employee reports that while working in the basement late one night he began to feel as if he were not alone. Suddenly, a hand came to rest upon his shoulder and swiftly turning around, he was confronted by the apparition of Alfred Gage, whom he recognized from a portrait hanging in the hotel. The apparition looked straight at the man and said, "I do not want you in my hotel any longer," at which the employee promptly left and never returned again.

Several rooms in the hotel are also well known for being haunted. In Room 10, the sound of music is heard when the room is unoccupied, and some guests claim that they were awakened in the middle of the night by a gentle tap on the arm and a woman's voice softly reciting poetry. In Room 25 as well, guests have awakened in the night to find the misty form of a young woman with short brown hair standing next to their bed.

The Gage Hotel is located at 101 Highway 90 West, Marathon, Texas 79842. For more information or to book your next stay, visit them online at www.gagehotel.com or call 432.386.4205.

Gage Hotel. *Courtesy of the Gage Hotel.*

Marfa

MARFA GHOST LIGHTS

The famous ghost lights are thought to be one of the strangest and most frequently sighted phenomena of this type known to exist. Often seen near Route 67 on Mitchell Flats, just east of the town of Marfa, facing the Chinati Mountains, these spectral lights have captivated on-lookers nightly for over 120 years. In most cases, the lights appear as glowing basketball size orbs or spheres floating in the air off in the distance. They are seen in numerous colors, including white, yellow, red, green, orange, and blue. At times, they seem to appear or disappear at will, in ones or twos, even blending and mixing together as they move about the night sky. The one thing that does remain constant about their character is the fact that they always vanish when approached and have so far remained unexplained.

The mysterious lights were first recorded as early as 1883, when a cowhand named Robert Reed encountered them while driving cattle through the Paisano Pass. He and his men at first thought they might be the lights of Apache campfires, but after scouring the area, no sign of the Indians or their camp could be found. Cowboys herding beef through the area continued to witness the spectral display over the years. During WWII, pilots from Midland Army Airfield just outside of Marfa reported the lights as well, but try as they might, they were unable to discover the source.

Today, watching the lights is a popular passtime for visitors, and roadside parking areas outside of town have even been erected by the state for easier viewing. Over time, as many as seventy-five different legends have developed explaining the origin of the lights—everything from St. Elmo's Fire to UFOs and phosphorescent jackrabbits have been blamed, but the most popular legend is that of the ghost of Alsate.

In the 1850s, Alsate was one of the last remaining Apache war chiefs in the Big Bend area. He and his band of warriors were known to use the deserted passes of the mountain range as a hideout when raiding across the border into Mexico. The story goes on to claim that, one day, Alsate was betrayed to the Mexicans stationed in San Carlos, just across the Rio Grande, by a man named Loenecio Castillo. As a result of the treachery, Alsate was executed and his tribe marched off in chains, but soon after, many believe the ghost of the great war chief returned to the mountains in search of the man who betrayed him. Each night his spirit and those of his enslaved tribe members return as burning lights to seek their revenge.

There are others, however, that believe the lights are not malicious entities bent on vengeance from beyond the grave, but rather helpful spirits, and there is even one record of them saving the life of a local rancher. According to Mrs. W. T. Giddons, her father was in the mountains one winter night looking for stray cattle when a blizzard struck. In the darkness and blinding snow, he was unable to find the trail leading home and was sure to perish. Suddenly, a light appeared from behind an outcropping and warned him that he was dangerously close to a steep precipice; one false move and he was sure to plummet to his death. The light then guided him to the safety of a cave where he sheltered for the night, and the very next morning, when the storm had passed, the rancher made his way safely home. During the harrowing experience, the light explained to the rancher that it was a spirit from long ago, but would elaborate no further.

The Marfa Ghost Lights may be viewed by traveling nine miles east on Highway 90, keeping an eye out for the roadside sign marking the parking lot and viewing area.

Monahans

Monahans Sandhills State Park

Consisting of over 3,900 acres of sand dunes, some reaching as tall as seventy feet, the park has become a Mecca for hikers, campers, and "sand surfers." Although the park opened in 1957, it's believed the land was occupied as much as 12,000 years ago. The early Spanish explorers were the first Europeans to record the existence of the vast sand hills, at which time they found it inhabited by various Indian tribes using it as temporary camping grounds, meeting site, and as a place to bury their dead.

Many park officials at Sandhills have come to find more than just beauty in the strange landscape; there's something else as well. For years, footprints appeared in the sand before the startled eyes of witnesses as if made by invisible feet, and figures are seen walking across the crests of dunes before abruptly disappearing into thin air. Legend has it that the Dunagan Visitor's Center near the park entrance is built atop a nineteenth century Comanche burial ground and that the restless spirits of those buried there haunt the place to this day. Doors open and shut on their own, shadowy figures are seen moving about the center at night, and the unexplained sound of a heavy object crashing to the floor is routinely heard. One park official reports being frightened by the sound of a woman screaming, but upon investigation, the source of the noise could not be found. In 1967, credence was given to the tales of a burial ground when two young boys digging near the visitor's center unearthed a human skeleton.

The Monahans Sandhills State Park is located five miles east of Monahans off Interstate 20 exit 86. For more information, visit them online at www.tpwd.state.tx/park/monahans.htm.

Odessa

Odessa High School

In the 1960s, the body of a seventeen-year-old student named Betty Jean Williams was discovered shot and weighted down with rocks in a stock pond near Motrees, in Ector County. Soon after, her boyfriend Mack Herring confessed to the crime, but stunned everyone by maintaining that Betty had asked him to do it. The murder made headlines across the southwest and was popularly known as the "Kiss and Kill Murder," which later became the subject of a book by Shelton Williams entitled *Washed in the Blood.* Betty, who was a theater student, spent a lot of time in the school auditorium and began reappearing there after her death.

The school is also known to be haunted by the ghosts of two Shelton ponies, who were former school mascots named Spirit I and Spirit II. One died from paint poisoning, when a rival high school painted the horse, and the other from natural causes. Both were subsequently buried near the school's baseball field, and on clear nights, it's said the two ponies can be seen grazing or galloping across the grounds.

The Odessa High School is located at 1301 North Dotsy Avenue, Odessa, Texas 79763.

Presidio

Fort Leaton State Historic Site

In 1848, a scalp hunter for the Mexican government named Ben Leaton built a fortified adobe trading post on the abandoned site of a Spanish mission called El Apostol Sabriag. The ruthless and deadly Leaton dominated the border trade with the Apache and Comanche tribes before succumbing to yellow fever in 1851. The fort was used for various purposes after his death until 1968 when the Texas Parks and Wildlife Department purchased the site and opened it to the public.

The first signs of a haunting began to seep out as a result of treasure hunters digging pits in search of the vast fortune in gold rumored to be buried by Leaton somewhere in the fort. One evening, two park employees were cleaning up one such hole when they suddenly fled in terror, claiming an invisible force tried to pull them into the pit they were filling in. Other park officials report the apparition of Edward Hall, a former tenant, in the room where he was shot to death in 1877. In addition, the apparition of an elderly woman has been seen several times in a rocking chair in the fort's kitchen. Finally, legend holds that on nights when fierce thunderstorms rock the fort, the headless phantom of a cowboy appears on a white horse riding around the fort's corral.

The Fort Leaton State Historic Site is located four miles southeast of Presidio, Texas 79845 on FM 170.

Terlingua

Perry Mansion

On a hill overlooking the ghost town of Terlingua sits the ruins of a two-story stucco building with a long galleried porch known as the old Perry Mansion. Built prior to 1910 by Howard Perry, the tyrannical founder of the Chisos Mining Company, the home was rarely used by Perry other than to entertain "lady friends," out of the prying eye of his wife. In 1942, the mining company filed for bankruptcy and closed its doors. The town of Terlingua, which sprang up over night with the mine's opening soon disappeared also. Two years later, Perry died on a train traveling to Florida, but the town that he built and the mansion from which he ruled it still stand.

Those curious enough to venture into the mansion at night encounter the apparition of an unknown woman wandering through the crumbling rooms and corridors of the second floor.

The Perry Mansion is located on FM 170 five miles west of Texas 118.

Part Three: Ghostly Resources

Texas Size Trick or Treats

If after wandering through all of the haunted cemeteries, ghost ships, and spooky old houses contained within this book, you still don't feel like you've had enough, then try one of these macabre events on for size. From commercial haunted houses and festivals honoring the dead to ghost hunting conferences and horror film festivals, Texas has everything you need for a frighteningly good time.

Some of the activities listed below are seasonal events happening around the month of October in celebration of Halloween, while others operate year round. So before planning your next big adventure, check their Web sites for times, dates, admission fees, and locations. Just remember that some of these attractions are not for the faint-of-heart and promise to literally scare you to death.

So be safe and have fun.

Amarillo

Center City Massacre Haunted House
www.youcantscareme.com

Dr. Haunt's Terror on Tenth Haunted House
www.drhaunt.com

Warehouse of Nightmares Haunted House
www.warehouseofnightmares.com

Austin

Austin Ghost Tours
www.austinghosttours.com

House of Torment Haunted House
www.houseoftorment.com

The Mansion of Terror Haunted House
www.mansionofterror.com

The Rocky Horror Picture Show
www.austinrocky.org

Corpus Christi

Corpus Christi Spook Central Paranormal Conference
www.ccspookcentral.com

Dallas/Fort Worth

Cutting Edge Haunted House
www.cuttingedgehauntedhouse.com

Dallas Halloween Conference and Ghost Hunt
www.ghosthuntersoftexas.com

Dungeon of Doom Haunted House
www.dungeonofdoomtexas.com

Fear Fest Horror Convention
www.txfearfest.com

Fort Worth Spirit and Paranormal Adventures
www.dfwparanormalresearch.com

Louis Tussaud's Palace of Wax Museum
www.palaceofwax.com

The Munster Mansion
www.munstermansion.com

Slaughter House Haunted House
www.weslaughter.com

Texas Frightmare Weekend Horror Convention
www.texasfrightmareweekend.com

Texas Paranormal Conference
www.metroplexparanormalinvestigations.com

El Paso

The Forbidden Sanctum Haunted House
www.myspace.com/fx4u

Houston

Ghost Tours of Galveston
www.ghosttoursofgalvestonisland.com

Houston Halloween Film Festival
www.halloweenfilmfest.org

Nightmare on the Bayou Haunted House
www.nightmareonthebayou.com

PHOBIA Haunted Houses
www.darke.com

Port Isabel Day of the Dead Celebration
www.portisabelmuseums.com

ScreamWorld Haunted House
www.screamworld.com

Walking Ghost Tours of Old Town Spring
www.oldtownspringonline.com

Lubbock

Nightmare On 19th Street Haunted House
www.nightmareon19thstreet.com

San Antonio

Alamo Ghost Conference
www.ghostweb.com

Edge Of Darkness Haunted House
www.edgeofdarkness.piczo.com

Hauntings History of San Antonio Ghost Hunt
www.alamocityghosttours.com

Louis Tussaud's Plaza Wax Museum
www.plazawaxmuseum.com

San Antonio Ghost Tours
www.alamocityghosttours.com

Tyler

Haunted Mead Manor Haunted House
www.meadmanor.com

Thrillvania / Verdun Manor Haunted House
www.thrillvania.com

GHOST HUNTERS DOT COM

Today, ghost hunting as a movement has swept across this country and others with a host of books, radio shows, television programs, and ghost hunting clubs. Many of those involved in the field have dedicate themselves to exploring the mysteries of the unknown and seeking out proof that something exists beyond the materiel world we inhabit. Texas of course is no exception to this and contains a number of ghost hunting groups ready to dash out into the night with their cameras and EMF detectors at a moment's notice. Each brings with them a unique perspective to the field of ghost hunting and various investigative techniques that range from the use of mediums to high tech equipment.

The following is a list of ghost hunting groups active in the state of Texas and open to investigation requests at the time of this writing. Not only do most of these groups work for free, but they also publish Web sites filled with a vast amount of information. If all else fails and you cannot secure the assistance of one of these groups, then by all means, start your own.

ABILENE

Central Texas Ghost Search
www.centraltexasghostsearch.com

AMARILLO

Northwest Texas Paranormal Investigators
www.mwtexasparanormal.com

AUSTIN

The Austin Ghost Hunters Meet Up Group
www.ghosts.meetup.com/52

Texas Paranormal Investigation
www.txspirits.com

CORPUS CHRISTI

Corpus Christi Spook Central Paranormal Research and Investigation
www.ccspookcentral.com

South Texas Paranormal Society
www.angelfire.com/sk2/stparanormal

DALLAS/FORT WORTH

Association for the Study of Unexplained Phenomenon
www.asup-texas.com

Carrollton Paranormal Society
www.carrolltonparanormalsociety.com

Dagulf's Ghost
www.dagulfsghost.com

DFW Ghost Hunters
www.dfwghosthunters.com

DFW Paranormal Research of North Texas
www.dfwparanormalresearch.com

Metroplex Paranormal Investigations
www.metroplexparanormalinvestigations.com

Society for Paranormal Investigation
www.paranormalghost.com

Tarrant County Investigations of the Paranormal
www.tarrantcountyparanormal.com

Texas Hauntings Society
www.texashauntsociety.com

EL PASO

Paso Del Norte Paranormal Society
www.ghosts915.com

Southwest Paranormal Investigators
www.ladystouch.tripod.com/paranormal

HOUSTON

Lone Star Spirits
www.lonestarspirits.org

Houston Ghost Research
www.houstonghost.com

Ghost Hunters of Southeast Texas (G.H.O.S.T.)
www.ghostmeetup.com/459

LUBBOCK

West Texas Paranormal Investigations Society
www.wtpis.org

SAN ANGELO

Texas Paranormal Research Team
www.tprt.org

SAN ANTONIO

Alamo City Paranormal Club
www.webspwaner.com/users/mleal

San Antonio Paranormal Network
www.ghost411.com

San Antonio Ghost Hunters Meet Up
www.ghosts.meetup.com/36

TYLER

Paranormal Society of Tyler
www.paranormalsocietyoftyler.com

Swat Paranormal
www.swatparanormal.org

Tyler R.I.P.
www.tylerrip.com

VICTORIA

Paranormal Organization of South Texas
www.myspace.com/parasouthtx

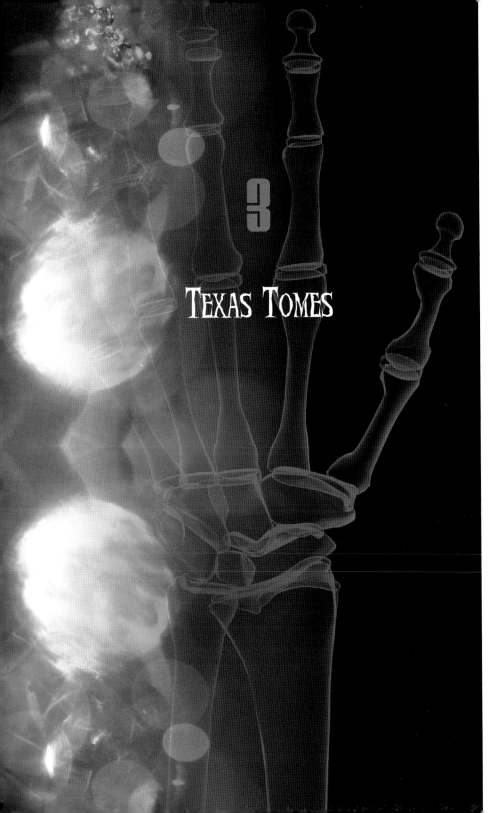

Many spooky texts on haunted locations in the state of Texas have been written over the years by highly dedicated and talented authors. Some consist of first hand accounts of the supernatural, while others explore the history and legend of a particular haunting. Nowadays, you can even find books appealing to the new form of paranormal tourism sweeping the nation that lists all the great haunted places to eat and sleep. In the hopes of broadening your ghostly horizons, I've included a list of books that may aid you on your journey. This is by no means a complete list, but think of it rather as a haunted primer into a world of mystery, suspense, and excitement.

Best Tales of Texas Ghosts by Docia Schultz Williams
Ghosts in the Graveyard: Texas Cemetery Tales by Olyve Hallmark Abbott
Ghosts of North Texas by Mitchel Whitington
Ghost Stories of Old Texas, Vol. 1 by Zinita Fowler
Ghost Stories of Texas by Jo-Anne Christensen
Ghost Stories of Texas by Ed Seyers
Haunted Texas: A Travel Guide by Scott Williams
Phantoms of the Plains by Docia Schultz Williams
Spirits of Texas by Vallie Fletcher Taylor
A Texas Guide to Haunted Restaurants, Taverns and Inns by Robert & Anne Wlodarski
Texas Haunted Forts by Elaine Coleman

For a more generalized study of the topic try these as well:

Apparitions by G. N. M. Tyrrell
Apparitions and Ghosts by Andrew MacKenzie
Apparitions and Survival of Death by Raymond Bayless
The Case for Ghosts: An Objective Look at the Paranormal by J. Allen Danelek
Complete Book of Ghosts and Poltergeists by Leonard R. Ashley
Complete Idiot's Guide to Ghosts and Hauntings by Tom Ogden
Encyclopedia of Ghosts and Spirits by Rosemary Ellen Guiley
Ghost: Investigating the Other Side by Katherine Ramsland
The Ghost Hunter's Guidebook by Troy Taylor
Ghost Hunting: How to Investigate the Paranormal by Loyd Auerbach
Ghost Hunting: True Stories of Unexplained Phenomena from The Atlantic Paranormal Society by Jason Hawes, Grant Wilson, and Michael Jan Friedman
Houses of Horror by Hans Holzer
How to be a Ghost Hunter: Field Guide for the Paranormal Investigator by Richard Southall, Michael Ed. Hill (Editor)
How to Hunt Ghosts: a Practical Guide by Joshua P. Warren
True Hauntings: Spirits with a Special Purpose by Hazel Denning
The World's Most Haunted Place: From the Secret Files of Ghostvillage.com by Jeff Belanger

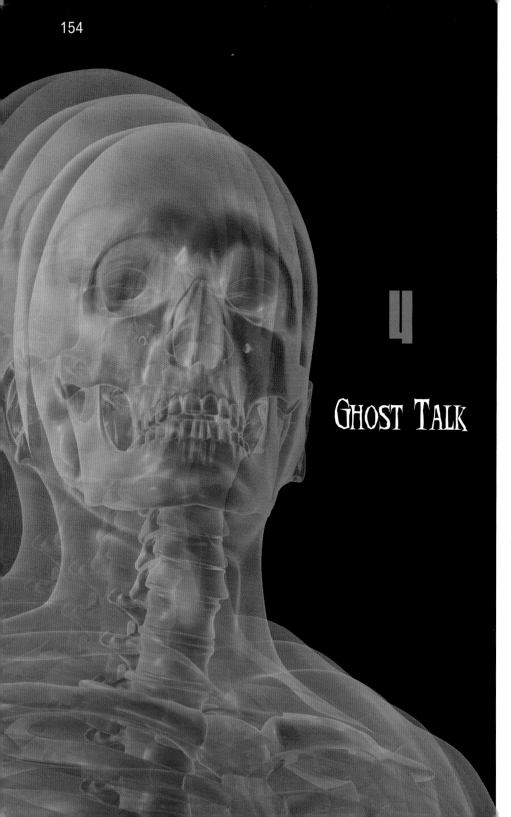

4

GHOST TALK

Just as in any specialized field of study ghost hunting has developed a lingo all its own. Whether an aspiring ghost hunter, a seasoned professional, or simply someone who loves to read about the supernatural, the following terms are essential to understanding the phenomena contained in this book. That doesn't mean this is a complete list by any stretch of the imagination and you may also find that definitions vary from one group to another, but it is a start.

anomaly. Comes from the Greek work *anomalia*, meaning something unnatural or unusual. Anomalies refer to anything strange, appearing on film, sound recordings, or any other unexplained evidence gathered on an investigation.

apparition. The unexpected appearance of a person, animal, or object in the form of a ghost, phantom, specter, or wraith. The word originated in the Middle English *apparicioun*, meaning to appear.

earthbound. Describes a spirit or soul trapped on the material plane in the form of an apparition, ghost, phantom, specter, or wraith. This usually occurs near the place of their death or some other familiar location. The reasons for a spirit becoming earthbound are varied and complicated.

ectoplasm. A phenomenon used to describe unusual mist or fog in photographs taken by researchers and is thought to be a sign of spirit activity. The term originally derived from the Greek words *ektos* and *plasma*, meaning "exteriorized substance."

EMF (electromagnetic field meter). A device used to measure disturbances in the magnetic fields, which are often associated with spirit manifestations.

EVP (electronic voice phenomena). Capturing spirit voices or ghostly sounds with audio recording devices or other electronic means.

ghost. The soul or spirit of a dead person returned to haunt a location. The word originates from the Middle English term *gost,* meaning spirit or breath.

ghost lights. Also known as will-o-the-wisp, corpse candles, and spook lights. Originally, they were called *ignes fatui*, which in Latin means "fool's fire" and described unexplained lights in the night that often receded when approached. Ghost lights are known to vary in size, color, and movement depending on the location. Although there is a great deal of folklore on the subject, science has yet to put forth a plausible explanation as to the source of the phenomenon.

haunting. To visit, appear, or inhabit in the form of an apparition or ghost. Hauntings are usually confined to a specific location and for an extended period of time that may include hundreds of years.

investigation. The process or act of research, study, or inquiry into claims of a paranormal or supernatural event.

manifestation. The attempt by a spirit or ghost to materialize itself or influence objects in the material world. This can include cold spots, disembodied voices, apparitions, or the movement of objects.

medium. A person with the ability or talent to communicate with the spirits of the dead. Also known as psychics or sensitives, the term initially meant, "one who stands in the middle ground."

orb. Is a sphere or globe of energy created by a spirit that may appear on film or digital images, but remains unseen in most cases to the naked eye. Dust, pollen, water vapor, and insects are know to produce the same effects and are designated as environmental orbs.

Ouija Board. A device used to contact the spirit world. It consists of a small board known as a planchette and a larger board marked with the words "yes" and "no," the letters of the alphabet, and the numbers 0-9. The device derives its name from the French *oui* and German *ja* words for yes.

paranormal or supernatural. Events that are beyond what is considered a normal experience or which defy scientific explanation.

phenomenon. Is an observable fact, occurrence, or circumstance.

séance. Describes the attempt by a group of individuals to contact spirits of the dead. Normally, a séance is led by one or more mediums that help channel the spirits. The term comes from the Old French, *seoir,* meaning simply – to sit.

soul or spirit. Both terms are used interchangeably in the text and describe the immaterial, life essence or personality center of each individual.

superstition. A collection of beliefs based on an irrational fear of the unknown or mysterious. The term comes from the Latin, *superstitio,* meaning to stand over.

thermometers or scanners. Any device that measures temperature fluctuations in the environment which may indicate the presence of a spirit.

urban legends. Moderns stories or myths passed on from person to person, often changing with each telling. Although the origins of most urban myths are obscure and contain little supporting evidence, many are found to have some grain of truth to them.

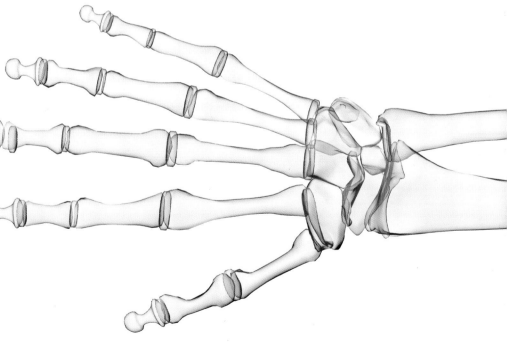

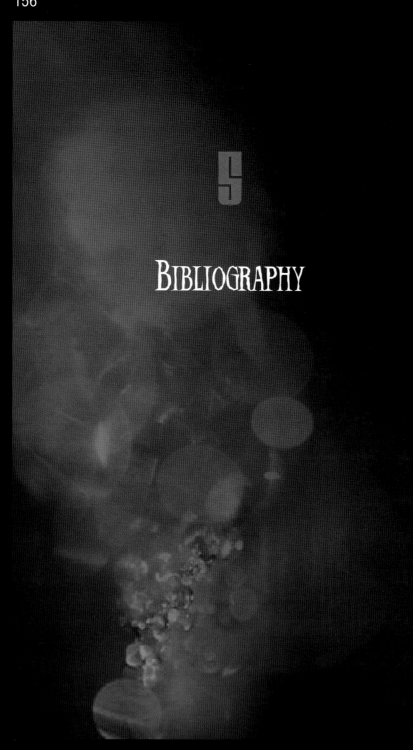

BIBLIOGRAPHY

Abbott, Olyve Hallmark. *Ghosts in the Graveyard: Texas Cemetery Tales.* Plano, Texas: Republic of Texas Press, 2002.

Austin-American Statesman, "Tales from the cellblock, eerie scenes, sounds lurk in Huntsville prison ghost lore," October 29, 1999.

Chandler, Chip, Jessica Coronado, and Marlene Feduris. "Get into the Spirit: Panhandle has history of haunts." *Get Out! Amarillo's Entertainment Guide.* http://www.getout.amarillo.com/content/getout/102904_get-intospirit.shtml (accessed August 24, 2008).

El Paso Times, "Arizona soldier hangs himself with wire at Bliss," June 12, 1919.

Garcia, Jessica. "Unsolved Mysteries," *ASU Rampage,* October 29, 2004. http://www.*asurampage.com/news/2004/10/29/Features/Unsolved.Mysteries (accessed September 19, 2008).*

Gibbs, Elaine. "A haunting tale: Old building gives workers eerie feelings," *Avalanche-Journal,* October 2004.

Hudnall, Ken and Sharon. *Spirits of the Border V: The history and mystery of the lone star state.* El Paso, Texas: Omega Press, 2005.

Lim, Marilyn. "Local haunts well know for supernatural suspicions," The Lariat Online, October 28, 2005. http://www.baylor.edu/lariat/news.php?=story7story=37562 *(accessed September 19, 2008).*

Price, Harry. *1940 The Most Haunted House in England: Ten Years' Investigation of Borely Rectory.* London: Longmans, Green and Co., 1940.

Shoemaker, John, Williams, Ben and Jean. *The Black Hope Horror: The True Story of a Haunting.* New York: W. Morrow, 1991.

Whitington, Mitchel. *Ghosts of East Texas and the Pineywoods.* 23 House Publishing, 2005.

--------------. *Ghosts of North Texas.* Plano, Texas : Republic of Texas Press, 2003.

Williams, Docia Schultz. *Ghosts Along the Texas Coast.* Plano, Texas : Republic of Texas Press, 1995.

Williams, Scott. *Haunted Texas: A Travel Guide.* Guilford, CT: The Globe Pequot Press, 2007.

Winship, George Parker, trans. The journey of Coronado, 1540-1542, from the city of Mexico to the Grand Canon of the Colorado and the buffalo plains of Texas, Kansas and Nebraska, as told by himself and his followers, New York: Allerton Book Company, 1922.

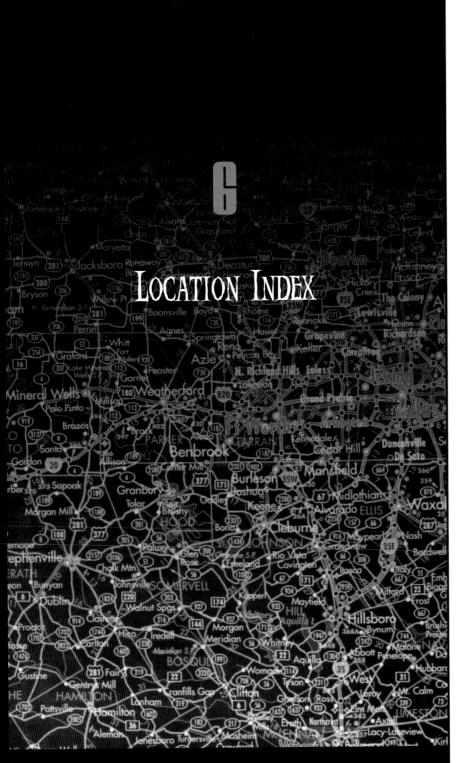

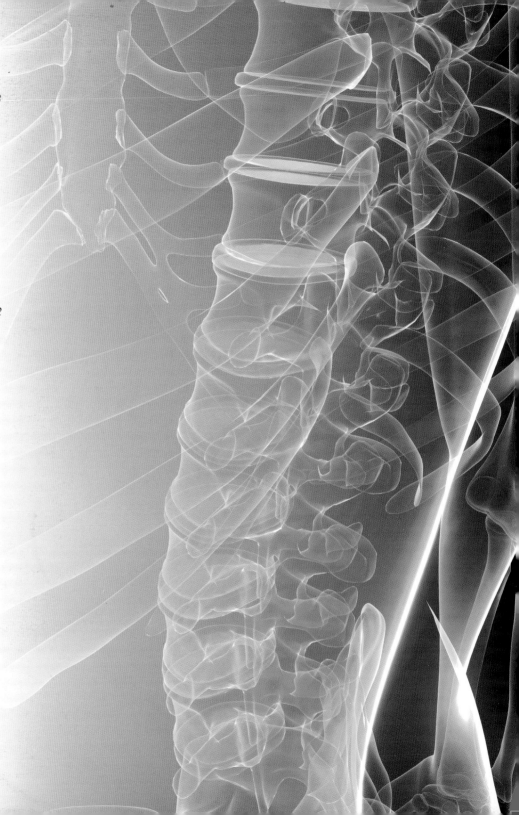